Recovering the Ancient Magic

Max Freedom Long

CONTENTS

PART ONE

PART TWO

PART THREE

LIST OF ILLUSTRATIONS

PART ONE

RECOVERING
THE ANCIENT MAGIC

CHAPTER I

AFTER an eighteen-year study of Magic in its various forms—not the spurious magic of the stage, but the genuine magic that works miracles—I come as a layman to report my findings to other laymen.

Fourteen years of my study have been spent largely in Hawaii endeavouring to penetrate beyond the externals of native magic and discover its basic secret. I have been trying to learn the very secret of secrets which is guarded so carefully by those who know it.

Nearly everyone has either heard tales of fire-walking in Polynesia or has seen moving pictures of fire-walking ceremonies. I doubt if this startling use of magic has ever been discussed, or illustrated on the screen, without arousing great curiosity. In my own case it was fire-walking which first roused my curiosity concerning the form of magic practised in the South Seas, although I must confess that I was born with a bump of inquisitiveness which always caused me to blunder in "where angels fear to tread." Once intent on the magic of fire-walking, my eighteen-year study of Polynesian magic began. From that study comes the greater part of what I now have to tell.

It will seem strange to most of you to hear an ordinary American speak so casually of magic. But consider how strange it must have been to me when I came to realize that genuine magic was being practised all about me in Hawaii. My first three years in the Islands were spent at places two and three days by steamer from Honolulu—remote and primitive districts such as Kau, Kohala and especially South Kona on the " Big Island," Hawaii.

Science teaches us that Magic is a remnant of superstition and that there is *nothing* which transcends physical matter, force and space. Our belief in this teaching is so great that it has taken the form of a complex or fixation of ideas in our subconscious minds. This complex makes it nearly impossible for us even to tolerate the suspicion that Science might be wrong in its conclusions concerning magic.

Like most laymen, I had given little or no thought to magic as a term having special meanings of its own. In my mind the word was associated, first, with the stage and, second, with the mumbo-jumbo of absurd spells and incantations. I had read of the alchemists and their search for the Philosopher's Stone and the Elixir of Life. I had smiled over the absurdities of the Egyptian *Book of the Dead* and over the infantile practices described in such books as Levy's *Transcendental Magic*. It had not occurred to me to associate magic with such things as the act of Jesus in turning water to wine or of Moses in smiting the rock. Least of all had I thought of the term in connection with hypnosis or with the mental and spiritual healing of modern times. However, I was eventually to discover that these last two things are a part and parcel of the old Magic which was once the heritage of humanity—a heritage lost in Christendom for centuries, and which we are only in recent years beginning to recover.

I had an idea that witches and sorcerers had been evil people who had rightly been burned or otherwise done away with. The churches of other days had found them deserving of such treatment, and who was I to question their findings ?

The newer and truer meaning of Magic was one which came to me only after some time spent in Hawaii. Shortly after my arrival there I began to hear of the *kahunas*. Naturally I classed them at once with witches and sorcerers. Smilingly, I listened while my white acquaintances regaled me with stories of their activities— incredible stories, they seemed to me then. Still moved by nothing but amusement, I listened while I was told that, of course, the stories were mostly exaggerations, and that if there was any truth in them, it could be accounted for by the use of suggestion, telepathy, or by simple imposition on the credulous. It was later that I heard an old man tell how he had often seen the aged Hawaiian guides scamper barefoot across the red-hot lava which overflowed from the volcanoes on one of the far islands of the group. As neither suggestion nor telepathy could explain such feats, and as I was assured that there had been no mistake about the performances, I instantly burned with curiosity. It seemed imperative that some explanation be offered. All that was forthcoming, however, was the lame statement that perhaps the fire-walkers knew of some secret preparation to use on their feet—although no one had ever found them applying it, and although the use of such trickery was hotly denied by the kahuna guides. Nevertheless, despite my complexed belief in what I may call the Scientific Attitude—a layman's interpretation of the teachings of Science—I was able to accept as full and adequate the explanations of all stories of magic except those of the fire-walking. In this last matter I came to no conclusion at the time.

In addition to my Scientific Attitude complex there were two others lodged in my subconscious. Between the three I was rendered illogical and inconsistent without being aware of my plight. From each complex I derived beliefs or convictions which were more or less openly opposed and contrary to each other. From the Scientific Attitude complex I drew the conviction that the universe was made up of matter, force and space—nothing else. This conviction left no room for anything superphysical whether it be ghost, devil, or a Supreme Intelligence who could at will act in a way to upset the laws of physics. From my religious complex I drew a firm belief that there could be, and was, some Supreme Intelligence that could, if He so chose, overthrow the laws of physics, but who, fortunately, seemed no longer to choose to do so. From what I may call my magic complex I drew the firm belief that a ghost I had once seen was real, and that there certainly were " more things in heaven and earth " than scientists dreamed of.

I had read of Freud's discovery of the complex, but quite naturally it had never occurred to me to connect his discovery with myself. Never once, in those days, did I realize how complexed I was or how absurd and illogical those complexes made me.

As time passed I automatically had days when each complex was dominant in turn. One day the Scientific Attitude would hold me and I would be all but certain that either the fire-walkers treated their feet with something, or that there was some clever trick in their performances. Perhaps the magic complex would be dominant in my consciousness the next day and I would be fully convinced that fire-walking was just as possible as my old friend continued to declare it to be. At such times I began to be able to believe to some extent that my new Hawaiian friends might be right in affirming that the kahunas were daily using genuine magic. I had by then heard solemnly told stories of how some neighbour had recently been " prayed to death," and that without ever being given a warning so that suggestion could have been responsible, or so that pure fright could have killed him. I talked with fine, honest brown men and women who told me how they had been miraculously healed when doctors had given them up for lost. I heard how financial ills had been overcome by magic and how great troubles had been cleared away in a family where husband, wife and children were at each other's throats.

My religious complex usually became dominant only on Sundays, but when dominant, it was all pervasive. From my subconscious would arise old habits of thought impressing themselves on my mind with a stubborn emotional force that swept all doubts away. Instantly I would be made to see as clearly as through crystal that the kahuna activities which I had considered beneficial, and therefore very admirable, were nothing but disguised activities of the devil. The faith of my childhood would rise up and demand of me how any " heathen " kahuna could do the slightest good when he appealed neither to the Christian God nor Jesus. I would be illogically positive that what little magic might be in use was a thing condemned repeatedly in the Bible.

I speak of these matters at length because I know that I am addressing others who have those same three complexes I had, and from which I have not completely freed myself even yet.

As my study and understanding progressed, I came, little by little, despite my complexes, to a momentous decision which could not be discounted by my complexed belief in either Science or Religion. I decided that the healing of deserving people which was constantly, though mysteriously, being done all about me, was a magnificent accomplishment in any age, regardless of the nature of the powers used. My mind wandered back to the beginnings of Christianity and I saw Jesus healing with loving tenderness and using His power to demonstrate the verity of God. I remembered the great pile of crutches and braces I had once seen at a shrine—the pile which had brought tears to my eyes as I pictured the many who had been miraculously healed—the many who had risen with wild surging joy from dark hells of suffering to find their poor crippled bodies suddenly touched by some invisible power and made whole. (I tried to shut away the picture that also rose in my mind of those poor wretches who crawled up the long steps day after day and for whom no prayers were answered.) With what pleasure I next was able to recall the unforgettable glow in a woman's brown eyes when she had risen one day in the midst of the congregation of a beautiful new church. Her testimony was: "I could not leave my bed for over four years. The doctors had given me up. I heard of the All Good and of the unreality of sickness and of error. I stand to-day, a monument to God's mercy."

I had come a long way. I had come to see that God was indeed no respecter of persons, creeds or sects. He could be in the magic used by the brown kahunas even when called upon by strange names.

Later I came to realize something far more pregnant with meaning. I realized that we proud members of a more "enlightened" race were fumbling in the dark, and that the little magic we performed was uncertain in results and insignificant when compared to the magic used by the kahunas. I was being told that when a kahuna promised a cure, he made one invariably. I thought of the few who had been able to benefit from the small part of magic we had recovered in the West: I thought of the suffering thousands who had called on God and Divine Mind in vain. I thought of the desperate thousands who had repeated so futilely the Coué formula: "Every day in every way, I am getting better and better." I was beginning to look upon the white race as a child uninstructed and trying to kindle a fire with flint and steel while across the way a master of fire had long since heated his pit of stones and was showing his mastership by walking with bare feet upon them. I saw us as children quailing before a flash of summer lightning while some kahuna paddled serenely in his frail canoe and called down an immensity of power to calm storm and wave. (I had just learned of this activity of the kahunas and had been all but convinced that they could use magic to control wind and storm. Later I was to know a white man—the only one to my knowledge ever initiated into such mysteries—who could make the winds blow light or strong, and this, strangely enough, without being aware of the nature of the power he invoked.)

Vaguely I began to wonder why magic had been lost from Christianity—the true and certain magic which Jesus had used to quell the storm, walk upon the waters, heal the blind, and raise the dead. I wondered also why the disciples had not continued to hand down the power they had received and which had enabled them to imitate the miracles of the Master. In the end I decided that the task of helping to recover the lost power—that lost Magic—was one worthy of all the best I had to give. I saw a bright vision of the darkened world made once more light by the recovery of a knowledge which would lift men from fear and suffering and enable them once more to touch the hem of the Robe. I set to work.

The task before me seemed so very simple. I imagined that all I would have to do was to go to some good brown man who worked the miracles of God on behalf of the afflicted. I imagined that I could tell him why I wished him

HAWAIIANS IN THE CHIEFTAINLY COSTUMES OF YESTERDAY

to share the secret of secrets with me, and that he would see the great need and whisper ancient revelations into my ear. I was never so much mistaken. The secret of secrets of the kahunas proved to be a secret because it was kept a secret— an unviolated secret to be handed down only from parent to child. Disappointment after disappointment followed. I failed even to find a kahuna. For years they had been outlawed in Hawaii. Those who knew where one lived would not direct me. I could find any number of people who had been healed by kahunas and who would tell of the outer practices—the practices which seemed so to savour of childish superstition—but not one could I find who knew what lay behind the age-old rituals and observances.

Months and years slipped by. I accumulated more and more data concerning the externals of kahuna magic. From that data I constructed theory after theory only to be forced to discard each in turn. I drew on psychology, psychic research, spiritualism, religions of all ages and kinds. I gathered more data, sorting and sorting, trying to match this odd bit with that, trying always to find some clue to the secret of power.

I studied history and traced painfully the dim trail of Magic as it disappeared in Christendom. I saw it degenerate into alchemy and astrology in the dark ages. I saw the last vestige of it disappear with the witch-burnings at Salem. I saw Science given birth by alchemy and astrology. I saw it grow and become all powerful. I saw that same Science put up its barriers against Magic and attack the miracles of Christ. I saw it invading textbook and commercial press with its doctrines which formed the Scientific Attitude. I watched the slow clearing away of old religious dogmas under the ruthless hands of materialistic scientists. I saw God cease to be the loving Father and become only the blind force building the electron.

For a time I became hopeless. One day I discovered the complexed nature of my beliefs ; but even in the clearer light of a less obstructed reasoning, the secret of secrets seemed more evasive than ever. Then came the idea that it was *magic and nothing less* that we had been recovering and using in our new *mental and spiritual healing* in America. It was *not* Religion or Theology, but *Magic*. Thrilled and encouraged, I set to work to trace step by step the evolution of the new theories behind such healing. I felt that if there had been even a fragment of magic recovered and put to use, there might be a chance that I could find through it the clue to what I sought.

In presenting my findings at this time, I am going back to follow through the same step-by-step study which led me to the conclusions I shall lay before you in due time. My reason for doing this, instead of coming at once to the presentation of my conclusions, is a simple one : All minds work much the same. All of us have the same set of complexes which must be met and overcome by logical reasoning acceptable to the conscious mind. And only when logic has been applied to the familiar can we come to the unfamiliar without some complexed belief promptly blinding us and making it impossible to judge with any degree of accuracy. In Part One of my report I shall hammer home to the conscious mind the logical proofs of magic and so do all I can to help drain off the Scientific Attitude complex from the subconscious mind. In Part Two I shall assemble all familiar data relating to magic, and add to it bits of data perhaps less familiar. In Part Three I shall assemble all pertinent data and bring them to bear on kahuna magic as we study typical cases of its practice.

Oddly enough, I have found that all our discoveries in psychology are things which the kahunas have used daily for centuries in the performance of magic. I have also found that every basic religious truth—whether that religion be Brahmanism or Christianity—is represented in a simple form in Kahunaism and made to serve practical purposes. Science has been right as concerns the physical, but it has gone no farther than to discover how physical matter and force react on each other. Psychology of the progressive school is right in its every step so far, but has not gone quite far enough in its discoveries to catch up with the kahunas. These magicians knew all about human personality even two thousand years ago when they still lived in a land bordering

on India. Religions are right in those sublime truths upon
which they all agree, but in the dogmas upon which they
do not agree, much useless or hindering doctrine has crept
in. Most of this dogma can be ignored, but not the part of
it that hinders us in our task of recovering and using the
powers of magic. In showing which dogmas hinder, I shall
have to speak bluntly at times, and perhaps arouse instant
and unreasoning opposition when I make statements contrary
to complexed beliefs. In this I ask indulgence and patience
even as I ask it when I point out the hindering dogmas
which have risen through certain basic misconceptions on the
part of Science.

One more word : The tendency of us all has ever been to
make a guess or theory and then advance it as a dogma or
perfect truth concerning facts. This propensity is a human
weakness found in all times and in all parts of the world.
Most " divine revelation " is nothing more than a guess
made into a dogma and preached with fanatical zeal. Moses
and his Ten Commandments, Joseph Smith and his Book of
Mormon, all the so-called divine revelations—these must be
tested by comparing them one with another. If they are
found *not* to reveal the same things, they are of *man* and *not*
of *God*. Now, knowing as I do the pit into which we all
fall, I realize that I shall inevitably become dogmatic and
begin stating my guesses as if they were ultimate and eternal
truths. Therefore, I ask that all my statements be most
carefully scrutinized and judged only on such evidence as I
can give to support them. I do not delude myself into
believing that I have discovered the final and complete key
to the full Magic of the ancient days. What conclusions I
may draw from evidence may be wrong as often as right.
Things I feel must be ultimate fact may be nothing of the
kind. Discount any of my statements. Accept only those
which seem true to fact.

It is my hope that those wiser than myself may be able to
correct my theories, add what data I have been unable to
uncover, and so help forward the full recovery of Magic
toward the day when even the humblest of God's children
will be able to share in the bright heritage so long lost.

CHAPTER II

I NOW ask that, for the sake of convenience, the reader consider himself a member of a large Round Table group—which group will comprise a court before which I can lay the proof that Magic is a *fact* and *not* the superstition which Science claims it to be.

As my proof is to be made against the opposition of the Scientific Attitude complexes severally held by Round Table members, our court may well consider itself trying *The Case for Magic versus the Scientific Attitude.*

From now on I shall present cases for examination in much the same general order as I examined them for myself in Hawaii. Before each case I will explain it in preliminary notes, and after the case proper I will offer my comments.

As everything depends on my proving at once that magic is a fact and a workable fact, I propose to use in this trial that form of magic by which heat is kept from burning human flesh. I select this form because there is nothing indefinite about it or its practice. There may be room for controversy in things which could possibly be explained as the result of coincidence rather than of the use of magic, but there is no room for such coincidence in fire-magic. Here we deal primarily with two types of purely physical material, heat and human flesh. For the present we are not concerned with the explanation of how magic can effect changes in physical matter or conditions. We are to decide on one thing and one thing only: does fire or any heated substance react on physically unprotected flesh in accordance with the laws of physics, or does it not? If it does not, the proof of magic is complete and irrefutable, and we can then safely decide that if magic is found to exist as a part of any one practice, it is possibly a part of any other similar or related practice.

In fire-magic we have something which has long been open to scientific investigation. Fire-walking has been performed regularly for centuries and is being performed in various places to-day. Many scientists and laymen have investigated and reported in writing or with still or motion pictures what they saw. As this is a fact, the present proof of the fact of magic will also be a proof that what I have said of the dogmatic presentation of misconceptions by Science is correct. I do not accuse any one scientist of being dishonest and purposely lying to laymen ; I simply wish to show that the body of Science, as represented in authoritative text and statement, has fallen into the common pit. It has made the guess that there is nothing outside the physical. From this guess it has made a dogma which, unfortunately, has been forced upon the public through school and commercial press.

CASE I

FIRE-WALKING IN FIJI

Preliminary Notes :

No scientist is justified in making the excuse that fire-walking is a thing not open to scientific investigation. Neither is he justified in saying that fire-walking can properly be ignored because its very nature makes it something outside the field called its own by Science. As I have pointed out in our investigation of fire-walking, we deal here with physical facts in the form of heat and flesh. Fire-walking cannot be ignored simply for the reason that it is contrary to the laws of physics. The accuracy of those laws is questioned by fire-walking, and the phenomenon cannot be set aside in such a way : it demands investigation before denial.

As I have also pointed out, there has been no difficulty in making complete investigations. Such investigations have been made by qualified scientists. Why have their reports not been accepted and acted upon honestly ?

In Fiji to-day there are several performances of fire-walking each year, depending upon the arrival of people in high standing who desire to see such performances. On the island of Bequa, just across from Suva, the natives are willing to oblige the curious or those bent on scientific investigation almost on demand. Any scientist is free to investigate. Scientists have investigated, but not reported.

The Case :

Two of my closest friends, George Dromgold and James B. Shackelford, of the Shackelford-Dromgold Film Expedition to the Great Barrier Reef and Papua in 1933, spent three months in Fiji *en route*. I had asked them to keep a sharp watch for fire-magic and to investigate it most carefully for any sign of faking. Upon their return to Hollywood they reported seeing the usual performance of fire-walking on two different steamer days at Suva.

They watched the great ten by twenty-foot pit being filled with logs and stones—the stones averaging from ten to twenty pounds in weight. They saw the fire burning all day and the rocks heated to redness. In the late afternoon the natives levelled off the stones on top of the deep bed of coals. Live coals glowed fiery between the stones of the platform.

My friends had kept careful watch to see if the bare feet of the fire-walkers were treated with any fluid or substance. They saw nothing of the kind used and no evidence of any insulating substance on the feet.

The fire-walking was done in the following way : chants were recited. The performers grasped green branches in their hands and covered their heads with wreaths of green leaves. They walked repeatedly across the hot stones and did short dances on them, lasting about a half minute. Their feet were in contact at every step with the nearly red-hot stones and often with the red-hot coals. After each of the seven men had performed, a layer of green leaves, about two inches deep, was spread over the shimmering bed. The performers sat down on the leaves and chanted for about three minutes.

The heat was tested by my friends by throwing wet leaves and twigs on the platform. These soon charred and burst into flame. The rocks were so hot that their faces had to be protected with hat or hands on close approach. I was assured that the rocks were almost red hot. Both Mr. Dromgold and Mr. Shackelford were convinced that there is nothing in the magic which is in any way related to the spurious magic of the stage. They tell me that it is universally conceded by the white people of Suva that the natives actually use *magic* to prevent their feet from being burned.

Comment :

If there had been any trickery used in this case it is a fair guess that the white residents of Suva would long since have discovered it. From all appearances it seems that the brown men use some form of magic to enable them to override all the laws of physics and keep fire from burning them.

.   .   .   .   .

I now refer the Round Table Court to any good dictionary for a full and complete definition of just what we mean in this test case by " magic." " Webster's International " gives a splendid exhibit of the blind adherence of our " authoritative " publications to the Scientific Attitude. I requested the editors of this estimable work to allow me to quote in full their definition of the word " magic " as well as the definitions of several other words. My request was refused, so, if the Court will bring in some dictionaries and read for themselves the definitions of " magic," as well as those for " spirit " and " God," I believe it will be found that the following definitions will be fairly close to the ones a casual reader will make for himself after a study of those dictionaries.

Magic : A system of practices mistakenly thought by uncivilized peoples to result in the production of effects contrary to the " laws " of Science. The practices are relics of superstition and rely on the use of some postulated mysterious force which does not exist ; or on the intervention by so-called supernatural beings or spirits. Magic was mistakenly believed to be practised by witches, sorcerers, witch doctors and the like.

Spirit : The part of an animal or human being which is mistakenly believed to survive after death ; *any* supernatural being mistakenly believed to exist.

God : The highest of all spirits or supernatural beings : the supreme Spirit or Supernatural Being (!)

Science : The name given true knowledge of proven facts.

Attitude : A belief in, or a leaning toward, a belief in any system as of Science, Religion, etc.

Scientific Attitude : (Not defined in dictionaries as such.) The *correct* attitude of accepting the findings of Science as the *only* set of genuine truths concerning the world and the universe. (Note : This attitude is accepted by the layman of civilized lands, whether consciously or unconsciously. It is engendered by Science, but it does not rouse the scientists to protest when the layman accepts as *facts* many things only advanced as tentative *postulations* by Science. No effective protest is made by Science when the layman uses telepathy and clairvoyance to explain away some form of magic—this, although Science *denies both* and accepts *neither* as a fact or even as a possibility.)

I will now give my own definition of magic :

Magic : That system of practices which *results* in the production of effects entirely contrary to the present-day "laws" of Science ; that body of practices using super-physical forces, or the aid of super-physical beings to accomplish physical results.

With our terms now defined, I shall next present a slightly different form of fire-magic.

CASE 2

A STAGE MAGICIAN WHO USED GENUINE MAGIC

Preliminary Notes :

Startling as it may seem, there is real magic sometimes used on the stage instead of the supposed mechanical trickery which we universally believe to be in use.

In this case we have a man travelling with a carnival and

saying nothing about the magic he uses, unless it be to those inclined and able to accept a statement of the true facts. This man and his wife performed in Honolulu and later were kind enough to try to explain their magic to me and try to tell how they had learned it. Just now we are interested only in what they did and not how they did it.

The so-called "fire-magic" usually seen on the stage or in circus and carnival is a very poor imitation of what I shall next describe. It consists mainly of such feats as holding a lighted cigarette on the tongue and inserting it into the mouth, with the coal held safely away from contact with the flesh, or of taking gasoline into the mouth and lighting its vapours as they are blown out—this being possible because the vapours burn only when well away from the lips and after mixing with air.

The Case:

The fire magician, of whom I speak, gave his performance in a small tent. A railing separated him from his audience by a distance of from three to six feet. His apparatus consisted of a pine table on which lay the few things he used The only part of his performance in which real magic was not used was the part in which his little dog leaped delightedly through a small hoop soaked with oil and set afire. Everything was done at close range and the watchers encouraged to test the heat of every article before it was brought into contact with flesh. Every move was made slowly and with no attempt to "juggle" or conceal.

The following things were done by the magician in each of the two performances which I witnessed: (1) He boiled water in a cup and drank it down rapidly while still bubbling and steaming. (2) Finger-thick pieces of soft pine wood were held in the blaze of a gas burner until they were turned at one end to glowing charcoal. He took up six of these, bit off the live ends, and chewed them. (3) He heated thick iron bars to a bright red heat in the middle and then passed his tongue along the red surface repeatedly—resulting in sizzling steam rising from his bare tongue. (4) He lighted

an ordinary welding torch; drew the flame down to a
cutting cone of blue-green; used the flame to cut through
iron bars repeatedly; gave the bars and the torch to
members of the audience for examination. Without adjusting the torch in any way, and seeming to have no protection
or method of temporarily extinguishing the flame, he introduced it repeatedly into his mouth. His mouth remained
open to its fullest extent and the flame could be seen playing
from the end of the burner, even when it had been thrust in
as far as his lips. (5) He heated an iron bar to redness and
handled it with bare hands in a way which would have
burned another severely indeed. He took a heavier flat bar
and heated it to redness in the centre. He took the heated
part between his teeth and, holding the ends of the bar in
his hands, bent it up and down twice from the centre.

Comment :

The bending of the bar. held between the performer's
teeth caused me to examine his teeth carefully. They were
strong teeth and not false. This point interested me greatly,
as the red-hot iron remained for a period of nearly ten
seconds in close contact with the upper and lower front
teeth. Although this was one of his stock " tricks " done
several times in an evening, the enamel was not cracked on
the teeth nor did they seem injured. Before the second
performance a dentist joined me. He stated that contact
with such heat would kill nerves and destroy teeth under
ordinary circumstances, as well as cause intolerable pain
while the nerves were still alive. Ulceration would result
and the teeth have to be pulled out. We scraped the biting
edges of the teeth with a penknife just before the second
performance—this to make sure no invisible insulating
substance, no matter how thin and transparent, could be
present.

The question of some solution to insulate from heat seemed
most improbable as the mouth was itself wet. Also the
edges of the teeth would hardly take such a coating—one
too thin to be detected or scraped off.

CASE 3

A JAPANESE HEALER USES FIRE-MAGIC

Preliminary Notes :

In the preceding cases we have had the two best known forms of fire-magic. For a third we must look to a less widespread, but more practical form : fire-magic used in healing certain types of disease. (Perhaps if we consider the Hebrew Children in the Fiery Furnace, the other forms may find practical uses also.)

So far as I have been able to learn, healing with fire-magic is entirely in the hands of Japanese magicians at the present time.

The Case :

In 1928–1929 there came to Honolulu a Japanese fire-healer. He advertised his powers and began his healing practice. His speciality was the treatment of arthritis. He would heat stones so hot that they would ordinarily burn flesh. By the use of magic—according to his later admissions in court—the stones could be packed around an affected joint and the trouble cured. There were several cases which he had treated successfully, notably the case of a wealthy gentleman who had been unable to walk for several months because of arthritis in the knees. After treatment with the hot stones by the Japanese healer he recovered the full use of his knees.

Comment :

This case is of importance to our study and proofs, because the records of it are preserved in court documents. After practising for some time in Honolulu, the Japanese was arrested at the instigation of medical men. He was charged with practising medicine without a licence, but, as he had administered no medicine, the charge pressed against him was that of being a kahuna.[1]

---

[1] The law of Hawaii concerning healing by the use of magic reads :
" Section 1034. Sorcery—Penalty. Any person who shall attempt the cure of another by practice of sorcery, witchcraft, *ananna, hoopiopio, hoounauna, hoomanamana* (terms describing the practice of Hawaiian kahunas), or

The court that tried him was not interested in evidence given to prove that his treatment was effective, when that of local doctors was not. The Japanese offered as his defence the fact that he was using magic and not medicine. Magic is not admitted in evidence in any civilized court. He admitted that he had used burning-hot stones to cure others. That was enough. He was fined and imprisoned as a kahuna. Later he was deported.

In the courts we have another excellent reflection of the Scientific Attitude. So much has Science imposed its dogma on our courts that Magic and Religion have at present no legal standing. What is called " an act of God " is accepted as meaning an accident. In no court could one prove that God exists. In no court would a case be accepted for trial in which a proof of the existence of God was attempted. In the face of this situation it is interesting to note that the Scientific Attitude still makes a mocking bow to the Church in demanding that an oath be taken before God and with the right hand placed on the Bible. That the real attitude of all courts is that of Science is shown by the fact that any witness may refuse to acquiesce to the demand for a religious oath and may replace such an oath by a simple assertion that he will tell the truth.

To get back to the magic of the case in hand : Had there been any trickery on the part of the Japanese healer, would it not seem that he would have acknowledged it rather than go to jail for a longer term, because he insisted that he had used real magic ? Of course, to deny his magic it would have been necessary for the healer to show how he did the " trick," and this was something impossible for him to do as there was no trick.

I claim that in this case the Scientific Attitude was not only unjustified, but that it was guilty of a great injustice both to the healer and to those awaiting their turns to be healed.

other superstitious or deceitful methods, shall, upon conviction thereof, be fined in a sum not less than one hundred dollars or be imprisoned not to exceed six months at hard labour." There is also another section of the law which classes the kahuna with bunco men and defines him as one posing as a kahuna, taking money under pretence of having magical power, or *admitting* that he is a kahuna. For this the fine goes up to a thousand dollars and a year in prison.

CASE 4

A FIRE-WALKER LENDS HIS MAGIC

Preliminary Notes :

As a final and conclusive answer to the claim that some invisible and undetectable coating is used to insulate flesh or teeth against heat, I now present a case in which there can be no doubt that the magic is accomplished by using some secret force in nature.

The Case :

I asked some friends of mine who had travelled much to tell me what they knew about fire-walking. They are Americans and I have known them for some ten years. I believe their report is entirely trustworthy.

In the year of 1917, in the courtyard of the Astor Hotel at Shanghai, a Japanese fire-walker gave a series of performances. On several occasions these friends of mine joined the crowd and watched very hot rocks walked upon with bare feet. The performance was preceded by the recital of words in Japanese and by some bits of ceremonial. For the performance itself the Japanese walked and danced on the hot stones. The stones were tested for degree of heat by the watchers and found far too hot to touch with bare hands.

On the occasion of one performance the Japanese asked his interpreter to invite any of the audience to walk on the hot stones under protection of his magic. This invitation was pressed, and at last two young white men became curious enough to wish to accept it. At his direction they removed their shoes and socks and tested the hot stones with their bare feet. To their surprise they found that, while the heat from the stones was intense on their faces, they were not burned when they cautiously touched them with their feet In the end they walked uninjured across the heated rocks three times.

Comment :

There is much evidence to show that fire-magic can be used effectively to protect anyone from being burned who may be befriended by the magician. This fact gives us iron-clad proof that magic is used, and not trickery, because those under such protection are positive that no insulating substance covered their feet.

CASE 5

TAHITI AND MORE LENDING OF MAGIC

Preliminary Notes :

This case takes us to another part of Polynesia : Tahiti. Here we find fire-walking also common. The source of this case is Hector MacQuarrie's book, *Tahiti Days* (George H. Doran Co., 1920). An entire chapter is given over to the report and there are five pictures showing the fire-walkers, crowds and pit, as well as the actual performance.

I take the liberty of condensing the chapter :

The Case :

With the help of one " Kroepelien," Mr. MacQuarrie was able to hire the fire-walkers to perform for him for a sum of two hundred francs. Six men, all clad in white, led by an older native, came to give the performance. A pit four feet deep, four feet wide and twelve feet long was used, the logs being laid over as well as under the stones and allowed to burn down to coals.

By the afternoon the fire had burned low and the rocks were white-hot. The ashes and coals were raked down and the eight- to ten-inch stones levelled. This done, the chief magician marched his six men to the beginning of the fire-walk. All wore white handkerchiefs bound about their heads, their white trousers came to their ankles, and on the fronts of their thin coats were two cloth stars, one over the right and one over the left breast. In their hands they carried long stalks of the *ti* plant, each topped with a tuft of long sword-like leaves.

The old man made a prayer in the native tongue and then led a march several times around the trench. More prayers were made, and the chief magician beat his feet with his *ti* leaves and then beat the first of the stones. The beating and prayers over, he walked quietly down " the white-hot pathway." At the other end he made another prayer, then returned to his men along the same way. Each of the men raised his feet in turn for a brushing with the leaves. Two of them were evidently nervous. All feet being brushed, the old man led the group seven times up and down the length of the stones. At times he paused to beat the feet of the two nervous men, and Mr. MacQuarrie suggests that they were burned because of their little faith, but that the burns were healed instantly by the magic accompanying the several beatings with the leaves.

After the group and the old leader had finished, the crowd was invited to walk under the protection of the magic. This invitation was promptly accepted by an old woman, and much less promptly by others assembled to witness the performance.

The old woman " muttered the most blood-curdling prayers " as she plodded down the trench. When she had finished, a queue was formed and most of the audience walked one after another across the still very hot rocks.

Mr. MacQuarrie also took his turn, but cautiously kept on his rubber-soled canvas shoes. He reports : " The stones I walked over were burning hot, but not white-hot when I walked (as they had been exposed to the air by then nearly a half-hour). This I am willing to swear by—anything : I felt the heat on my legs, on my face—fierce, intolerable. Yet the soles of my canvas shoes were unharmed. . . . I tried to discover the true significance of the ceremony, but no suitable explanation was forthcoming."

Comment :

Mr. MacQuarrie opens his account by quoting from the greatest authority on general knowledge known to him, the *Encyclopædia Britannica*. He cites several lines from the then current article on fire-walking, evidently feeling that he must cite such an authority to prove that there was such a thing.

In answer to a request that I might quote from the *Encyclopædia Britannica* the entire article on this subject, I met with a delightfully different response than that I received from the editors of *Webster's International Dictionary.*

It is very evident that this friendly editor is endeavouring to print the truth in his various editions—a tradition clearly defined in the many past editions, each of which has changed in an effort faithfully to reflect the best thought of its decade.

Each article is written by one qualified to write it. The names of the writers are made available, and the editor does nothing more than do his best to get real authorities in so far as is humanly·possible.

That the following article does not cover the matter of fire-walking very fully is no fault of the editor or proof that he has any intent or desire to misinform the public. What is made evident, however, is the fact that almost no thought in Europe or America is uncoloured and unhampered by the Scientific Attitude. As civilized people, we have unconsciously bowed to the mighty accomplishments of Science in its proper field. This is as it should be. But we have failed to keep Science in its own field. We have allowed it to encroach on fields entirely foreign to its methods of investigation. By accepting its guesses and theories, we have blundered with it—blundered most humanly, but illogically.

From the *Encyclopædia Britannica,* 14th Edition :

"FIRE-WALKING, a religious ceremony common to many races, and widespread in all ages. It still survives in Bulgaria, Trinidad, Fiji Islands and India, the Straits Settlements, Mauritius and Japan. Indian settlers in Natal performed the rite in Pietermaritzburg in the autumn of 1927, in fulfilment of a vow. The details of its ritual and its objects vary in different lands, but the essential feature of the rite, the passing by priests, fakirs, and devotees barefoot over heated stones or smouldering ashes, is always the same. Fire-walking was usually associated with the spring festivals and was believed to insure a bountiful harvest.

"The interesting part of fire-walking is the alleged immunity of the performers from burns.' On this point authorities and eye-witnesses differ greatly. In the Natal case no injuries were seen. The bulk of the reports certainly leave the impression that there is something still to be explained in the escape of the performers from shocking injuries. The preparations, perhaps physical in part, produce feelings of an intense nature associated with the phenomenon of possession. In some way anæsthesia is induced."

From the above article it will be plainly seen that its author—supervised by the anxious editor—did all that he dared do in the face of the prevailing and powerful Scientific Attitude. He stated the facts correctly, and, knowing that such facts were bound to arouse curiosity on the part of the reader, did all he could to find some explanations which would throw some light on the matter and still be in keeping with the dogmas of Science. He must have regretted that he could offer no more logical explanation than that some form of "anæsthesia" seemed to be produced. All of us know that our anæsthetics, both chemical and hypnotic, might prevent burns from being felt, but could not prevent terrible burns from resulting.

·   ·   ·   ·   ·

In these fire-walking cases it will be noted that there are slightly different methods used by the magicians. It will be well for me to state at once that, while I find methods and theories of practice differing among fire-magicians, I find nothing different in the results they accomplish, namely, the prevention of burns.

CASE 6

MORE LENDING OF MAGIC

Preliminary Notes :

On February 21, 1935, I attended a lecture at the Los Angeles Public Library. The speaker was Dr. John G. Hill, Professor of Biblical Literature at the University of Southern California. His subject was " Fire-Walking."

Dr. Hill had spent four seasons in the South Seas. He illustrated his lecture with moving pictures he had taken on his journeys.

He told of voyaging from Tahiti to a neighbouring island, and of travelling fourteen miles overland to see a fire-walking performance. The preparations were similar to those usually made. The performance itself consisted of the usual invocations—this time to " *Nahine of the Skies* " (" Woman of the Skies "), then the marching around the pit and the seven crossings back and forth. *Ti* leaves were used in the ceremony to carry, and to " dust off " the rocks.

During the ceremony Dr. Hill exposed much film. He took close-up pictures of the feet and hot rocks, and pictures of the group walking in single file over the stones. He showed one native who had been forced to walk the hot stones as an " ordeal " to prove his guilt or innocence of a certain charge. As he was badly burned, the natives decided that he was guilty, despite his denials, and so had not merited the protection of " Nahine of the Skies."

The ceremony over, Dr. Hill and his white companions tested the heat of the rocks, the following results being reported : Length of time possible to hold the hand at a distance of three feet from the rocks : eleven seconds. Time required for a bundle of wet, green branches to take fire when thrown on the rocks : thirteen minutes.

While the testing of the heat was going on, the head magician was inviting his guests to cross the rocks under the protection of his magic. One of the white men joined the natives who were accepting the invitation. He walked across the rocks. Dr. Hill stated that they were almost red-hot even at that time. The man's shoes were not burned in any way, nor were his feet, but, oddly enough, the intense heat burned his face so badly that it peeled a few days later.

After the lecture I joined a group gathered to hear Dr. Hill answer questions. He was asked for any possible explanation of the feat. His answer was that he was totally at a loss for an explanation. He could only guess that there might be some superior form of mental activity used—some form which could keep heat from burning. He was very positive in his refusal to accept his own guess as a fact.

The usual questions were raised as to the possibility of some "undetectable solution" being used. This, the Doctor explained, was impossible for the simple reason that the white man's shoes had not been so treated and would certainly have been ruined by the heat under ordinary circumstances.

In an endeavour to throw further light on the mystery, Dr. Hill told of another fire-walking performance which he had seen but not photographed. There, a young white man, described as being "quite a mystic," avowed that if the brown men's magic would protect them, his God would also protect him. He questioned the friendly magician in charge and was laughingly told to go on across the stones without fear. Disregarding the protests of other white travellers, the young man took off shoes and socks. He approached the fire-walk with set face—evidently trying to concentrate on his task and hold his faith in readiness. He followed the magician on to the rocks and was getting on perfectly when a wild dog-fight broke out close beside the pit. For a moment he glanced aside. He lifted one foot suddenly, but his face again became set and he continued his crossing. The foot lifted was found later to have a large blister on its sole. Dr. Hill vouched for this data, but made no comment on its possible significance.

Comment:

For those of this Round Table who may not have seen moving pictures of fire-walking shown in 1934 news reels at theatres, I mention the following sources of photographic or written information :

The book, *The Colony of Fiji*, edited by A. A. Wright and published by the Government of Fiji, contains several good illustrations of fire-walking.   As a commentary on the influence of the Scientific Attitude in so far as any official publication is concerned, we find in this book only one lone paragraph to describe the finest tourist attraction in Fiji. This paragraph gives a meagre statement of the facts of fire-walking, but nothing more.

Another book more easily procured in libraries is the *Seatracks of the Speejacks*.   In its log, which is written by Jeanne Gowen, will be found both pictures and full descriptions of fire-magicians and their work.

For those owning 16 mm. projectors, there is a film offered in its rental list by the National Film Library of 837 South Flower Street, Los Angeles.   Its title is *Fire-Walkers of Bequa*, and it is available (1935) to those desiring to rent it.

.   .   .   .   .

As most fire-magic seems still to be associated with some religion based on that magic and including magical practices as proof of its dogmas, we will now go to another part of the world and consider a case in which there is much magic and much religious dogma combined.

CASE 7

FIRE-WALKING AS A RELIGIOUS RITE IN BURMA

Preliminary Notes :

In Hawaii I made my living for the greater part of my stay in the Islands by keeping a Kodak and art store in Honolulu. Among my many customers there was, in the year 1929, an Englishman who had been making a trip around the world. He carried with him a 16 mm. moving picture camera and was especially anxious to photograph anything out of the ordinary.

I had known him several days when he came in one morning and asked me if there was anything in Hawaii which was very unusual and which he might " film." I certainly knew of many very unusual things in Hawaii, but it was impossible to tell him where he might go to get a picture of a kahuna at work with his magic.

In the course of our conversation he mentioned the fact that he had bribed the priests of a certain temple in Burma to let him hide on a temple balcony and photograph the mysterious and far-famed fire-walking of the devotees of the fire god, *Agni*.

I begged for the story and the opportunity to see his pictures. He went at once to his hotel and brought back the films. Let me give in detail what I saw and what I was told that day in my little projection-room.

The Case :

" You see," said my friend, with all the glow of one about to present a wonder of wonders, " I don't just tell about the things I see, I photograph them ! And it's a good thing I do ! Now take this film I'm about to show you. If I didn't have the film I'd even think I hadn't seen it myself ! Why, man ! What I saw is impossible ! It's contrary to nature ! Anyone will tell you it couldn't happen ! I'll even tell you that— and I saw it with my own eyes not three months ago ! " He paused and waited for me to look up from threading the projector. I did my best to show the proper surprise and mystification.

" Well," he said grandly," turn it on. See if you can believe what the camera got."

I pulled out a couple of chairs and threw in the switch. On the screen at the end of the projection-room lifelike shadows began to flicker and move.

" That," explained my new friend, " is the parade. It came before the service in the temple's courtyard. That bunch going past now are the candidates who had been getting ready for years to take the fire initiation of the Agni cult. Odd beggars, those brown people. See the funny looks on their faces. They all seemed to be thinking hard about

something as they marched along. Never seemed to notice
the crowd which had gone crazy with excitement just to see
them. Seems everyone hopes some day to get ready to walk
through the fire—great honour. Walk through once and
you are set for life. You become some sort of priest or holy
man. All the priests in the temple have had to walk through
fire to get their jobs."

"How do they do it ?" I asked, as I watched the long
parade move past with all its Oriental trappings.

"Wouldn't you jolly well like to know! And wouldn't
I ?"

"What do you think ?" I urged.

"How should I know ? I tried to get it out of the priests,
but they spoofed me, I think. They said theirs was the one
and only true religion and that the fire-walking proved it.
They were proud as that of themselves ! Said no other faith
could make it possible for the converts to walk through fire.
What they wanted me to believe was that their god kept the
feet of the pure and holy from being burned. Those who
weren't quite pure enough got burned." He pointed
suddenly to the screen. "See that bozo ? He's the priest I
managed to get off to one side to talk to, at about the time
the parade was done marching all over the city. Good sort.
Really rather sporting. He was smart, too."

"How do you mean ?" I asked.

"Not like most of the other beggars—suspicious and
hating white skins. And by 'smart' I mean he was smart
enough to pretend to believe me when I told him I'd studied
his religion and wanted to join up. I thought he was going
to laugh in my face at first, but I jingled money in my pocket
and he began to take me seriously."

"Perhaps he did take you seriously," I suggested as I
watched the parade continue to pass on the screen.

"He was no fool, not that one. He'd heard money. And
when I told him I would join up and pay well if I could be
allowed to see the fire-walking with my own eyes, he got my
drift. I insisted on giving him a good donation for his
church right there. He thanked me for it and told me to
meet him in a little while at a side-door of the temple. Of

course, I didn't say anything about bringing along my little movie camera."

The scene changed suddenly on the screen and the inner courtyard of the temple appeared. It was a large court surrounded by high walls. Below us and at one end was a long, high pile of burning charcoal which shimmered with intense heat. It was perhaps fifty feet long and about five feet high. Men were beginning to rake it out into a long, narrow platform of living coals as I watched.

" That's it ! " cried my English friend. " I met my priest and got in with my camera-case without his knowing what I was up to. He took me up on a balcony and hid me behind some bamboo screens. I paid some more church dues and he went off. In a minute I had a hole in the screen for the lens and one for the finder. My camera was all loaded and ready, so I had-at-it right away.

" I took the beginning and the end of the raking out of the coals," he continued as the scene changed. " See ? Now they are all done and are smoothing down the bed. About six inches deep. The charcoal had been burning for ten hours, the priest told me. Hot as Hades ! Made it so hot, even off there behind the bamboo screen, that I could hardly stand it. And see how the rakers have to keep their heads turned away and have to keep turning their bodies from side to side so they won't roast. Beastly hot !

" And now watch that gate in this scene. I began filming when I heard the noise outside. I knew the procession was about to come in. There they are ! Priests in front and the candidates next ! All men candidates—women too sinful ever to get purified. Lots of the men old ! Forty-three I counted. And see their faces ? Look like they were all going to an afternoon tea ! Got on their most polite faces ! Those big fellows in uniform are the Sikh bobbies. Find them in all British possessions. They don't belong to the temple, but the authorities send them along to keep order. You'll see them keeping it right soon."

As I watched, the procession moved into the courtyard. The candidates gathered in a silent group at one end of the long bed of shimmering coals. Behind them gathered a

mixed crowd of men, women and children, all greatly excited.
The Sikhs moved slowly through the crowd, their clubs in
hand. The priests had gone around the fire and met another
group of six priests who had come from the temple and were
taking their places at the opposite end of the bed of coals.
In the hands of each of the six was a short whip with many
lashes. Between them and the fire was a shallow water-
filled indentation in the paving. It was about six feet
wide, four inches deep and ten feet long, extending all across
the end of the glowing platform.

"What are the whips for ? " I asked. "Are they to keep
the fire-walkers out of the water ? "

"You'll see in a moment," was the hurried answer.
"Seems that when they step out of the fire into the water,
the priests have to beat them to keep their minds off their
hot feet for a second. I asked the priest, but didn't understand what he tried to tell me—something about an old
custom."

"Do neither the whips nor the fire hurt them ? " I
demanded.

"The whips do. Lay their backs open sometimes. But
keep your eye on the picture ! See ? They are all praying
now. Making a lot of funny gibberish ! Praying to Agni to
protect the pure and burn the impure. Gave me the
creeps. . . ."

The camera moved back to the silent group of candidates.
They were taking no part in the prayers, but simply waiting.
They wore only loin-cloths. Then a bent old man raised his
hand, as in greeting, to someone in the crowd behind. He
turned and walked slowly to the pathway which danced and
shimmered before him. Clasping his hands and lifting his
face as if in appeal to Heaven, he walked calmly into the
bed of living fire. I caught my breath. With a firm, steady
stride he went wading through the coals toward the priests
who waited at the far end.

I scarcely breathed as I watched. His feet were leaving
black tracks which closed over and were lost in a moment
after he had passed. On and on he went, never changing
his pace. Made slightly misty and unreal by the heat waves

rising all about him, he seemed more an apparition than a man. As I stared, my amazement was tinged with doubt. What I was seeing was an impossibility. But the end of that dreadful pacing came at last. The old man stepped from the living fire into the water and was instantly taken by the arms on either side by two priests. Their cruel whips flashed three times, cutting into the bare brown back. The old man writhed with pain. Two more priests took him and hurried him off to a bench beside the wall. They examined a foot each, nodded, and hurried back to their places.

The camera flashed around and caught another candidate just as he stepped into the coals. He was a thin, middle-aged man. His face was turned to the waiting priests and his hands were clenched and swinging at his sides. With long rapid strides he began his ordeal. His pace quickened. His head went up and his hands lifted as if away from the heat. He was half-way through and walking more and more rapidly. Suddenly his pace broke and he went on at a rapid trot. The trot increased to a run, and as he came to the end of the fiery bed he leaped frantically for the water. Hardly had he leaped before the whips fell. They fell in flashing blows that doubled the candidate as he strained in the strong grasp of the two priests.

The camera flashed back again to catch the next candidate.

"Was that second man burned?" I faltered.

"No. Only three got burned, out of the whole bunch," was the abstracted answer.

I tore my eyes away from the sight of three men striding or racing through the fire at the same time. The little Englishman was sitting chin in hand moodily watching the screen.

"Watch this one!" he commanded in a loud whisper.

I needed no urging. A very bent and feeble old man had entered the fire. His hands were stretched imploringly upward. After the first few steps he began staggering. He hesitated, leaped into the air, plunged wildly forward and fell.

Instantly attendants were at the side of the bed of coals, long drag-hooks in their hands. Frantically they laboured.

Over and over they rolled the smoking body. They dragged
it clear, coals sticking to the burned flesh. A jar of water
was dashed over the still form and it was lifted and carried
rapidly away.

"Dead before they got him out . . ." said a low voice at my
elbow. I started slightly, having momentarily forgotten my
friend. "But that didn't stop them ; they kept going right
through."

Again a splice ran through the projector and the camera
swung back from a man being lashed. It picked up another
man at the far end. He had just stepped into the fire and in
his arms he carried a boy. The child was hardly more than
six and dressed in loin-cloth only. I gasped. I was horrified.
Why should a child be endangered ! What if the big lean
man should fall ! Again I held my breath. Would the man
never start running ! Was he insane ?

"He'll make it," said an encouraging whisper. A hand
fell quietly on my arm.

Steadied by the promise, I sank back into my chair. On
and on he went, striding deliberately. The little boy became
vague and clear by turns, as the heat shimmer was stirred
or left stagnant by air currents. One small hand lay quietly
and confidingly on the bare shoulder of the man. The boy
gave no sign of fear or concern. Never quickening or slacken-
ing his pace, the man came at last to the end. He stepped
into the water. The whips fell but once on his back. He
lifted the boy high to keep him from being struck. In his
gesture was something that hinted of a love great in its
triumph. The camera followed as he set the child on his
feet and led him away toward the wall.

Suddenly the film began to change rapidly from scene to
scene. Men ran or walked a few feet through the fire before
vanishing.

"I was running short of film," explained the voice in my
ear. I just took grab shots. But now watch ! I got one of
those who got burned. . . . There he goes ! See the beggar
run ! Off at the side ! Howling his head off ! Now he's
around into the water ! No use to beat him. Priest said
he'd never walk again. Now keep an eye on this ! I just

changed films. See that Sikh! Bingo! Right on the old bean! See what happened? Crowd went crazy. Religious frenzy. Saw the others get through—wanted to try it themselves. See 'em go down. Bingo! Bingo! Women and all gone crazy! Think what would have happened if those Sikh bobbies hadn't been there to lay them out! The whole crowd would have rushed into that fire!"

Suddenly the film clicked in the projector and the screen flickered blank and white. The picture was ended.

" How do you feel? " asked the Englishman curiously.

" Rather upset," I answered truthfully.

"And wasn't I!" he exclaimed. "I'd seen it with my own eyes! For a penny I'd have joined the temple. It gets you. I was a week trying to forget it. It's like seeing a ghost or something. Can't get your mind straightened out. You go giddy. Can't strike the old balance. Keep wondering if you have *everything* wrong. . . . Can't get over the idea that there's something in it besides a trick."

" Then you really believe it is a trick? " I asked.

There was a long moment of hesitation.

" What else can it be? . . . But how could the beggars put anything on their feet that wouldn't wear off in a half-day of parading barefoot? . . . And how was it some of them got burned if they all had the same stuff on their feet to protect them? . . . "

" Perhaps they know better than we do what's behind it," I suggested.

There was a slow nod. " I almost joined the temple . . . just to find out if there was. . . . "

" Why didn't you? " I asked.

" My priest wouldn't let me. He said I didn't have it in me. Said for me to take his blessing and go out and serve my own God by showing my pictures at home and proving to the people that there was a power in religion and worship that we'd all but lost."

" And you intend to do that? " I demanded.

" I did at first," he admitted guiltily. " But the impression made on me seemed to die out. I'll show the film, but I'll let others draw their own conclusions about it. I've worn myself out trying to understand it, but I'm all right now. Science can't be very far mistaken . . . there's some trick behind it."

"Would you be entirely convinced if you did it once yourself ? " I asked.

"Funny thing," he said thoughtfully. " That priest really was a smart man. He'd been to an English university. When I asked him how long it would take to get ready to walk through fire, he laughed at me with his deep, funny eyes. And what do you think he said ? He said that even if I could learn to do what my people called a ' trick,' I would never be able to believe the truth about how I did it. He said no white man could."

I agreed that the priest was indeed a " smart " man.

Comment :

In this case it would seem that the priests did not use magic in behalf of the fire-walkers, but let them use their own powers as best they might. It is evident that some were not yet good magicians, regardless of the religious significance of the matter.

It is interesting to speculate on whether or not the feet of the fire-walkers become heated above the burning point in the coals and have to be cooled in the water. If this is correct of the affair, it would be necessary for some magic to be worked which would enable heat to raise the temperature of flesh and blood without the usual burning. In the case of the Japanese fire-healer, the flesh temperature must have been so raised in order to drive out or burn away the poisons of arthritis. This leaves us to satisfy ourselves with one of two conclusions : (1) That stones or coals or flame are rendered " cold " or, (2) that they remain hot, and the magic prevents burning when flesh (or shoes) are heated to burning temperatures. Either way we guess, we have magic—something contrary to all the " laws " of physics.

I realize that when I say that anything can be contrary to the laws of physics or Science, I run counter to the complexed beliefs of Round Table Court members. As any complexed belief lodged in the subconscious mind has a way of coming by itself quite unnoticed into the conscious mind and rousing by emotion a stubborn resistance to any statement not in accord with that belief, it now becomes necessary that we " drain off " our own Scientific Attitude complex as rapidly as possible—thus enabling us to go on considering Magic.

It takes time to make a complex, and it also takes time to drain it off. The making process begins with a conclusion accepted by the conscious mind because it seems logical or because it seems to have authority behind it. Those conditions of acceptance being fulfilled, the conscious mind repeatedly sends those thought-conclusions to the subconscious, and in about the length of time it would take to memorize a page of verse, the complex begins to form. Such beliefs once memorized, make the memorization or acceptance of a contrary page of verse or belief very slow and difficult.

As I cannot speak with *authority* against Science and the holdings of the Scientific Attitude, I must use what logic and reason I can. The proofs of fire-magic I present are unreasonable to the complex, but reasonable to the mind. Let me now tell the simple facts about the great mistake made by Science in arriving at its dogma of " nothing not physical." A logical explanation is potent against complexed and unreasoned beliefs.

Back in the days of Greece, the skeleton of Science was formed by the Philosophers. Mathematics was developed, and there was evolved the lasting method of investigating actual phenomena and writing down the results of experiments or observations such as involved matter, force, time and space—the Scientific Method. Scientific investigation was then, and still is, a process of mixing various combinations of the two elements, force and matter, within the limitations of time and space, then carefully observing the results and drawing conclusions from them. Stars, chemical combinations in a laboratory, the metabolism of the body—all such things are the sum total of the materials of Science. Observing, measuring and fabricating new and useful combinations—these are the total activities of Science. There is nothing mysterious about Science or its methods which is deserving of the present blind worship accorded them.

Now we come to the human element in Science—the scientists. All of them have always possessed both a religious and a scientific complex of beliefs which war one on the other. Thus, each scientist is compelled to leave the strict field of observation of things as they are and become a philosopher in order that he may form theories or guesses as to *what or who* has created his " materials." Philosophy and Science should be kept apart. Their very natures and fields are different. But this is never possible.

Now let us see how the dogma of " nothing not physical " was evolved with such blinding effects on later thinkers. In the very early days a conclusion was reached that, *when properly understood, nothing in the universe would any longer be mysterious or in any way supernatural.* God would even be quite *natural* and open to scientific investigation once He was understood. This was a very logical and proper conclusion—a most laudable one. But what came of that conclusion once it was spread far and wide ? This came of it : Men ceased to distinguish between " supernatural " and " superphysical," despite the world of difference. Under the first conclusion there could be tenuous matter such as creative thought emanating from God or His lesser and externalizing manifestations. Thought, consciousness—anything too tenuous to bring into the laboratory—could exist and could be changed from supernatural to natural simply by understanding it and learning how it worked.

Science, however, was fighting what it considered *groundless superstitions.* These it found in the beliefs and dogmas of both Religion and of Magic—in the theology and sorcery of the Middle Ages. In this fight, scientists slowly became unable to think clearly because of new complexes developed while attacking the most absurd and blatant superstitions. Eventually the logical dogma of " nothing really supernatural when once understood " changed to " nothing exists but the physical elements : matter, force, time and space." This dogma was a disaster to the human race, although it did much to clear away actual superstitions. In its wake came the extending of the new dogma to its logical extreme and the resulting blanket denial of any intelligence lying behind the created universe. The universe was now looked upon as a machine which had accidentally happened to *create itself as if built by a superior intelligence.* It was accepted as such and considered—logically again, once the creator had been done away with—to be a machine *running itself without an engineer or consciousness* back of it.

This unfortunate state of affairs has made the work of Science most difficult. It has complexed scientists and made them go all around Robin Hood's barn trying to explain the simplest phenomena of growth and evolution, not as God-engineered, but as the result of blind and unconscious forces reacting haphazardly on matter in the confines of time and space. That these abortive efforts have failed dismally, can be seen in the unavoidable development of the theory of *Natural Law.* This Natural Law is contrary to the blinding dogma of materialism, but nothing can be done without it. There are " laws " governing every chemical reaction. Acid invariably neutralizes alkali. A seed of wheat invariably produces more seeds of wheat. Nothing is haphazard. So we see that even the tremendous dogma of " nothing not physical " has had to substitute Natural Law for God. The holes in the dogma simply *had* to be plugged by some form of creative and supporting intelligence.

Once we are able to see with a clear vision not obstructed by a complexed belief in the mysterious and awe-inspiring infallibility of Science, the dogma of materialism becomes pitiful and absurd. But it is neither pitiful nor absurd to those blinded by this dogma-complex which even budding scientists absorb with each text read and each lecture heard while at college. The complex once established, it makes it utterly impossible for the scientist to be able to approach any problem of investigation without going to unreasonable extremes to make his observations and conclusions conform to that dogma.

Perhaps on a Sunday the same scientist will be under the influence of his Religious complex and, curiously enough, be for the moment very sure that there is a vague God-the-

Absolute behind all creation. Were the scientist less human he would see how illogical it is to carry two such contrary beliefs in the same mind ; but who is not human, and who is not complexed ?

Most complexed and human of all are we laymen. We do not understand Science to the full, and so can only rely on what we draw from the Scientific Attitude fed us through the commercial press and the school. Science is, to us, all but infallible. We do our best to accept its dogma of materialism. Many of us have given up Religion and tried to accept Philosophy in its stead, with its slightly more scientific definition of God. Magic, we have all but forgotten. Even the meaning of the word has lost its significance and become confused with stage magic and superstition. But there is hope. The " complex " is a thing at last discovered by Psychology, and Magic is on its way back to bring Religion into its own and Science into a new freedom where greater progress than ever before can be made.

Fortunately, we all have a Magic complex as well as the others I have described. This complex makes it possible for us to be good children of Science on week-days and of Religion on Sundays—while being on *all* days able to believe in *psychic phenomena*. It is a usual thing for a parlour gathering of an evening to be enlivened by having a conversation open thus : " You will all think I'm crazy, but in our family some very strange things have actually occurred." Instantly the whole group reacts to the Magic complex and becomes eager. The other complexed beliefs become dormant. Stories of premonitions, ghosts and spirit-return are eagerly discussed and apologetically related. This complex makes it possible for such a matter as fire-magic to be considered with momentary seriousness while described in this report. Quite naturally and inevitably, the other complexes will cease to be dormant very soon and will cause all Round Table Court members to say such things as : " I read of the fire-magic and was inclined to believe in it last night, but after sleeping over it, I now know that such a thing couldn't be, and that there must have been some trick. Science tells us that a belief in anything superphysical is a superstition." As we speak we may even fail to remember that we believe in the existence of God—at least on Sundays.

· · · · ·

We have examined fire-walking done as a religious rite in Burma. As we shall eventually consider a very important point concerning the nature of "purification" from sin in its relation to the ability to perform fire-magic, I will now present a short case having to do with descendants of Igorot head-hunters.

CASE 8

DESCENDANTS PROVE THAT THEIR HEAD-HUNTING ANCESTORS DID FIRE-WALKING SAFELY

Preliminary Notes :

In the Philippines the Igorotes have done fire-walking for centuries. They have also been head-hunters. To waylay the enemy and take his head is not a business which the Burma devotees would consider a help to "purification," but the Igorotes seem unaware of this. Here we see descendants of the little pink-brown people using fire-magic with the same success as did their forefathers.

The Case :

Some Igorot fire-walkers came to Los Angeles some years ago and gave several performances at the old Chutes Park on Washington Street. My friend Mr. George Dromgold saw them at work, and his description of their feats gives us the usual picture of hot rocks, green branches in hands, and bare feet treading on intensely hot stones with no resultant burns.

Comment :

This case is mainly important to show that head-hunters have done fire-walking and that the art has come down to the Igorotes of our time.

Of secondary importance is the fact that magic can be

practised in civilized countries and away from the favourite plant, *ti*, which is so largely used in the ceremonial throughout Polynesia.

.   .   .   .   .

For my final case before the Round Table Court, I will present fire-walking evidence taking us back to Hawaii.

CASE 9

A SCIENTIST DOES FIRE-WALKING AND REPORTS

Preliminary Notes :

It is with great pleasure that I now introduce before this Court my most important witness for the case of Magic, Dr. William Tufts Brigham (see *Who's Who in America*, 1922–1923), long curator of the Bishop Museum of Honolulu, and a scientist of unquestioned standing.

As, before his death, Dr. Brigham gave me the findings of his long investigation of Polynesian Magic to combine with my own, I wish at this time to tell of him in detail. Later on in my report I will draw heavily on the data made available through his years of research.

He was marvellously erudite, a master of philosophy, psychology, botany, anthropology and languages. He was skilled in medicine although never a graduate of a medical school.

In his own particular field, Dr. Brigham excelled. He was an authority on botany and on Polynesia. His museum publications reflect the dependability and accuracy of the man as well as his scholarship. It was his proud boast that those publications were the finest and most free from errors sent out by any museum in the world. In 1925 I checked on this boast at the British Museum in London. In doing so, I was surprised and delighted to learn how my old friend towered among his fellows. The very fact that I knew him personally insured me the warmest welcome on the part of the grey men of the great British institution.

Owning surprisingly few college degrees, but a fellow of

the most important societies, Dr. Brigham was an authoritative source of both earthly and unearthly information. A huge bald and white-bearded man when I knew him, he was bubbling over with humour one minute and deadly serious the next. In any mood he was intensely instructive and interesting. Being an old bachelor, he had time to spare to explore the great field of human activities.

The thing I wish to stress most is the intelligence and the innate honesty and accuracy of the man. He was honest with himself and with others. So honest was he with himself, and so well informed on how his and other minds worked, that he made me a present of a lifetime's observation along the lines of Magic. He knew full well that, as a scientist in high standing, Magic was a matter forbidden him. He also knew the ultimate value of his observations, experiences and personal experiments. Also he knew that those things could not be permitted to die with him—that they belonged to the world which he had so tirelessly served—but that Science could not yet accept them.

" When I'm gone," he said to me one evening, " you may tell what I am now telling you. I know you will tell it as nearly word for word as you are able. If I thought you would put words into my mouth which were not mine I would tell you nothing, but I trust you. You have the proper cautious approach and understanding needed in a study of the kahunas. You may say for me that I gave my word as a student and a gentleman that I would, and had, told the exact truth about what I saw and did. This is all either of us can do. Both of us will be branded unholy liars by a certain class. That class you can afford to snub, and, as I will be dead, I will have lost my childish fear of losing standing as a scientist. However, I trust that before you are as old as I am, the thing we call ' magic ' will have been taken into the laboratory, in some way, and made a part of the working equipment of the world."

As a frontispiece I have used a picture of one of the many kahuna friends of the kindly doctor. In selecting this individual as representative of a splendid school of magicians, Dr. Brigham was assisted by Mr. C. Hedeman and Dr. N. B.

Emerson. Together, these gentlemen did something un-
precedented in Hawaii—they persuaded a kahuna (of course,
one supposed to have " reformed ") to pose for his picture,
then for Allan Hutchinson of the Bishop Museum while a
wax figure in life-size was made. This wax figure now stands
in the Museum—the only visual evidence in Hawaii to
indicate that there ever was such a thing as a kahuna. On
the great glass case is a brass plate giving the simple
information that the figure was copied from life and
represents a kahuna *anaana* at his work.

The *anaana* (pronounced *ana-an-ah'*) is a kahuna of the
highest class and one who uses the full Magic. He is
primarily a healer and one who works to straighten out the
lives and affairs of his clients. However, on occasion, he does
not hesitate to kill with his famous " death prayer " when
death is deserved.

Now to give you the Doctor's account of his fire-walking
experience.

The Case :

Dr. Brigham, in his earlier days, made frequent trips to
the " Big Island," or Hawaii. There were many kahunas
working there at that time. In the course of his investigations he made friends of a number of them. He posed as a
haole, or white, kahuna, and discussed beliefs and methods
with the brown magicians on intimate terms—trying always
to get from them the secret of secrets which they guarded so
carefully.

Among his kahuna friends were three Hawaiians who
knew the fire-magic. They used it mainly to prevent lava
flows from damaging the property of clients. One of them
had been called in by Princess Ruth at the time the town of
Hilo was being approached by a slow-moving lava flow.
Everything had been done to stop the encroaching mass of
lava, which was kept hot by the burning of self-generated
gases in its substance. In a doughlike mass, and with a
wide front, it continued day after day to tumble slowly
forward, rolling and grinding, toward Hilo. Stone walls
were built in front of it and promptly torn aside and absorbed.

A SLOW FLOW OF LAVA SUCH AS NEARLY DESTROYED THE TOWN OF HILO

A large number of men spent days throwing earth and rock into the flow to thicken and stop it. Even water was ditched to a place in front of it. Nothing availed. Closer and closer it crept, destroying everything as it went. The Princess came from Honolulu by ship. She met the fire-kahuna at Hilo and went to the face of the flow. There she cut off locks of her hair at his direction and, while he recited the proper invocations, threw the locks into the slow-tumbling mass.

It is recorded in history that the flow went but two rods farther before stopping. The town was saved.

This old kahuna and two others had agreed with Dr. Brigham that they would demonstrate their fire-walking art when opportunity offered. They also had promised to let him do some fire-walking under their protection.

At a time when the volcanic mountain Mauna Loa, on the island of Hawaii, was active, Dr. Brigham happened to be close at hand. I will present the story as I reproduced it from my notes a few days after he gave it to me. As he tells the story, see him : a huge old man in the eighties, hale and hearty, although recently having suffered the loss of a leg ; mentally alert, enthusiastic, eager, humorous, and withal very earnest. It is night and he is seated in a great easy-chair beside a ponderous oak table which stands in the centre of a long low room.

" When the flow started," related Dr. Brigham, " I was in South Kona, at Napoopoo. I waited a few days to see whether it promised to be a long one. When it continued steadily, I sent a message to my three kahuna friends, asking them to meet me at Napoopoo so we could go to the flow and try the fire-walking.

" It was a week before they arrived, as they had to come around from Kau by canoe. And even when they came, we couldn't start at once. To them it was our reunion that counted and not so simple a matter as a bit of fire-walking. Nothing would do but that we get a pig and have a *luau* (native feast).

" It was a great *luau*. Half of Kona invited itself. When it was over I had to wait another day until one of the kahunas sobered up enough to travel.

" It was night when we finally got off after having to wait an entire afternoon to get rid of those who had heard what was up and wished to go along. I'd have taken them all had it not been that I was not too sure I would walk the hot lava when the time came. I had seen these three kahunas run barefooted over little overflows of lava at Kilauea, and the memory of the heat wasn't any too encouraging.

" The going was hard that night as we climbed the gentle slope and worked our way across old lava flows towards the upper rain forests. The kahunas had on sandals, but the sharp cindery particles on some of the old flows got next their feet. We were always having to wait while one or the other sat down and removed the adhesive cinders.

" When we got up among the trees and ferns it was dark as pitch. We fell over roots and into holes. We gave it up after a time and bedded down in an old lava tube for the rest of the night. In the morning we ate some of our *poi* and dried fish, then set out to find more water. This took us some time as there are no springs or streams in those parts and we had to watch for puddles of rain water gathered in hollow places in the rocks.

" Until noon we climbed upward under a smoky sky and with the smell of sulphur fumes growing stronger and stronger. Then came more *poi* and fish. At about three o'clock we arrived at the source of the flow.

" It was a grand sight. The side of the mountain had broken open just above the timber line and the lava was spouting out of several vents—shooting with a roar as high as two hundred feet, and falling to make a great bubbling pool.

" The pool drained off at the lower end into the flow. An hour before sunset we started following it down in search of a place where we could try our experiment.

" As usual, the flow had followed the ridges instead of the valleys and had built itself up enclosing walls of clinker. These walls were up to a thousand yards in width and the hot lava ran between them in a channel it had cut to bedrock.

" We climbed up these walls several times and crossed

them to have a look at the flow. The clinkery surface was
cool enough by then for us to walk on it, but here and there
we could look down into cracks and see the red glow below.
Now and again we had to dodge places where colourless
flames were spouting up like gas jets in the red light filtering
through the smoke.

"Coming down to the rain forest without finding a place
where the flow blocked up and overflowed periodically, we
bedded down again for the night. In the morning we went
on, and in a few hours found what we wanted. The flow
crossed a more level strip perhaps a half-mile wide. Here
the enclosing walls ran in flat terraces, with sharp drops from
one level to the next. Now and again a floating boulder or
mass of clinker would plug the flow just where a drop commenced, and then the lava would back up and spread out
into a large pool. Soon the plug would be forced out and the
lava would drain away, leaving behind a fine flat surface to
walk on when sufficiently hardened.

"Stopping beside the largest of three overflows, we
watched it fill and empty. The heat was intense, of course,
even up on the clinkery wall. Down below us the lava was
red and flowing like water, the only difference being that
water couldn't get that hot and that the lava never made
a sound even when going twenty miles an hour down a sharp
grade. That silence always interests me when I see a flow.
Where water has to run over rocky bottoms and rough
projections, lava burns off everything and makes itself a
channel as smooth as the inside of a crock.

"As we wanted to get back down to the coast that day,
the kahunas wasted no time. They had brought *ti* leaves
with them and were all ready for action as soon as the lava
would bear our weight. (The leaves of the *ti* plant are
universally used by fire-walkers where available in Polynesia.
They are a foot or two long and fairly narrow, with cutting
edges like saw-grass. They grow in a tuft on the top of a
stalk resembling in shape and size a broomstick.)

"When the rocks we threw on the lava surface showed
that it had hardened enough to bear our weight, the kahunas
arose and clambered down the side of the wall. It was far

worse than a bake oven when we got to the bottom. The lava was blackening on the surface, but all across it ran heat discolourations that came and went as they do on cooling iron before a blacksmith plunges it into his tub for tempering. I heartily wished that I had not been so curious. The very thought of running over that flat inferno to the other side made me tremble—and remember that I had seen all three of the kahunas scamper over hot lava at Kilauea.

" The kahunas took off their sandals and tied *ti* leaves around their feet, about three leaves to the foot. I sat down and began tying my *ti* leaves on outside my big hob-nailed boots. I wasn't taking any chances. But that wouldn't do at all—I must take off my boots and my two pairs of socks. The goddess Pele hadn't agreed to keep boots from burning and it might be an insult to her if I wore them.

" I argued hotly—and I say ' hotly ' because we were all but roasted. I knew that Pele wasn't the one who made fire-magic possible, and I did my best to find out what or who was. As usual they grinned and said that of course the ' white ' kahuna knew the trick of getting mana (power of some kind known to kahunas) out of air and water to use in kahuna work, and that we were wasting time talking about the thing no kahuna ever put into words—the secret handed down only from father to son.

" The upshot of the matter was that I sat tight and refused to take off my boots. In the back of my mind I figured that if the Hawaiians could walk over hot lava with bare calloused feet, I could do it with my heavy leather soles to protect me. Remember that this happened at a time when I still had an idea that there was some physical explanation for the thing.

" The kahunas got to considering my boots a great joke. If I wanted to offer them as a sacrifice to the gods, it might be a good idea. They grinned at each other and left me to tie on my leaves while they began their chants.

" The chants were in an archaic Hawaiian which I could not follow. It was the usual ' god-talk ' handed down word for word for countless generations. All I could make of it was that it consisted of simple little mentions of legendary history and was peppered with praise of some god or gods.

"I almost roasted alive before the kahunas had finished their chanting, although it could not have taken more than a few minutes. Suddenly the time was at hand. One of the kahunas beat at the shimmering surface of the lava with a bunch of *ti* leaves and then offered me the honour of crossing first. Instantly I remembered my manners ; I was all for age before beauty.

"The matter was settled at once by deciding that the oldest kahuna should go first, I second and the others side by side. Without a moment of hesitation the oldest man trotted out on that terrifically hot surface. I was watching him with my mouth open and he was nearly across—a distance of about a hundred and fifty feet—when someone gave me a shove that resulted in my having my choice of falling on my face on the lava or catching a running stride.

"I still do not know what madness seized me, but I ran. The heat was unbelievable. I held my breath and my mind seemed to stop functioning. I was young then and could do my hundred-yard dash with the best. Did I run ! I flew ! I would have broken all records, but with my first few steps the soles of my boots began to burn. They curled and shrank, clamping down on my feet like a vice. The seams gave way and I found myself with one sole gone and the other flapping behind me from the leather strap at the heel.

"That flapping sole was almost the death of me. It tripped me repeatedly and slowed me down. Finally, after what seemed minutes, but could not have been more than a few seconds, I leaped off to safety.

"I looked down at my feet and found my socks burning at the edges of the curled leather uppers of my boots. I beat out the smouldering fire in the cotton fabric and looked up to find my three kahunas rocking with laughter as they pointed to the heel and sole of my left boot which lay smoking and burned to a crisp on the lava.

"I laughed too. I was never so relieved in my life as I was to find that I was safe and that there was not a blister on my feet—not even where I had beaten out the fire in the socks.

"There is little more that I can tell of this experience. I had a sensation of intense heat on my face and body, but almost no sensation in my feet. When I touched them with my hands they were hot on the bottoms, but they did not feel so except to my hands. None of the kahunas had a blister, although the *ti* leaves had burned off their soles.

"My return trip to the coast was a nightmare. Trying to make it in improvised sandals whittled from green wood has left with me an impression almost more vivid than my fire-walking."

Comment :

There you have Dr. Brigham's story. You will now doubtless be interested to know how a scientist tried to figure out the reason for his being able to do what he had done.

"It's magic," he assured me. "It's a part of the bulk of magic done by the kahunas and by other primitive peoples. It took me years to come to that understanding, but it is my final decision after long study and observation."

"But," I objected, "didn't you try to explain it some other way ? "

The doctor smiled at me. "Certainly I did. It has been no easy task for me to come to believe magic possible. And even after I was dead-sure it was magic I still had a deep-seated doubt concerning my own conclusions. Even after doing the fire-walking I came back to the theory that lava might form a porous and insulating surface as it cooled. Twice I tested that theory at Kilauea when there were little overflows. I waited in one case until a small overflow had cooled quite black, then touched it with the tips of my fingers. But although the lava was much cooler than that I ran across, I burned my fingers badly—and I'd only just dabbed at the hot surface."

" And the other time ? " I asked.

He shook his head and smiled guiltily. " I should have known better after that first set of blisters, but the old ideas

A LAVA FLOW SUCH AS DR. BRIGHAM FOLLOWED TO FIND A
BLOCKING UP AND OVERFLOWING WHICH WOULD PROVIDE
A SURFACE FOR FIRE-WALKING

Flow from Mauna Loa in 1918.

were hard to down. I knew I had walked over hot lava, but still I couldn't always believe it possible that I could have done so. The second time I got excited about my insulating surface theory, I took up some hot lava on a stick as one would take up taffy. And I had to burn a finger again before I was satisfied. No, there is no mistake. The kahunas use magic in their fire-walking as well as in many other things. There is one set of natural laws for the physical world and another for the other world. And—try to believe this if you can : The laws of the other side are so much the stronger that they can be used to neutralize and reverse the laws of the physical."

In this case we have an instance in which the magical control of heat was of such a nature that it did not protect the leather in Dr. Brigham's heavy boots, but did protect his feet.

This feature of the case is interesting when we remember that the soles of the author MacQuarrie's shoes were undamaged in his fire-walk. All in all, it would appear that fire-magic works in strange ways which are little related to the "laws" of Science.

.   .   .   .   .

I have now laid before the Round Table Court representative cases of fire-magic. I ask that they be accepted in evidence, either in whole or in part.

I affirm again that I have proved that the case for Magic is properly grounded on such facts as anyone so desiring may investigate.

Instead of investigating Magic, Science has chosen to scoff at it, and either try to explain it away or deny its existence. I further affirm that the child of Science—the Scientific Attitude—is guilty of a grave offence against the layman.

This offence is grave in that it is utterly unjustified and in that it has fostered a misconception so deep-seated that it is now all but impossible for the average layman to bring his conscious mind to bear on Magic because of the prejudicing complex in his subconscious mind.

I claim that I have given proof that Magic is a fact and not

a superstition. To make clear this claim I will now proceed
to argue the case :

1. I claim that the evidence introduced in this trial is of
such a nature as to demand proof of faulty observation in
each and every case. Lacking such proof of entirely faulty
observation, the verity of the evidence is not to be questioned.

2. I further claim that if Magic is proved to exist, even in
the slightest degree, in any of the cases cited, it is then proved
that Magic is *possible* in *any* unexplained practice frowned
upon or denied verity of data by either Science or the
Scientific Attitude. I do not claim that because fire-magic
is proven, the carrying of a rabbit's foot is a further proof of
Magic. What I claim is that well-authenticated practice,
the observable results of which are of such a nature that they
cannot be explained in terms of the physical, must *necessarily*
be considered material for investigation rather than something to be condemned as superstition because it happens to
be contrary to any theory offered by Science.

· · · · ·

To sum up : I argue that not *all* the cases presented as
evidence can be considered instances of erroneous observation or report on the part of those witnessing or taking part
in fire-magic performances ; that, as the evidence is not to
be denied, this Court must pass judgment on it and determine whether or not Magic is a fact as falling under the
definitions used in this trial.

I now challenge :

1. Did or did not men with bare feet walk over stones
heated almost to redness in any of the cases cited ?

2. Did or did not any of these men walk over heated stones
without the customary burns resulting ?

3. Did or did not the moving-picture cameras make
correct records of fire-walking as reported in the case of the
Burma fire-walkers, the fire-walkers observed by Dr. Hill,
or in other cases cited ?

4. Did or did not the fire-eater do things contrary to all
the " Natural Laws " known to Science ?

5. Did or did not all cases cited show conditions present

which would ordinarily cause burns as a result of activities described ?

6. Did or did not white men, with no protective coating on their feet, duplicate the performances of fire-magicians in such a way as to prove that there was no trickery used ?

7. Could or could not any one of the instances of fire-handling cited in these cases be duplicated without the use of Magic as defined for use in this trial ?

.   .   .   .   .

I will now argue the case for the Opposition, using such arguments as are given by the Scientific Attitude to explain away fire-magic at such times as the denial of observed and photographed facts is not possible.

1. As Science assures us that there is *nothing* not of a physical nature and not to be accounted for in terms of the physical, Magic is manifestly impossible, whether it be fire-magic or any other form of magic.

2. Science is of sufficient authority that its statement alone is all the proof necessary. Science has proved its absolute authority by its great accomplishments. Scientists know more than any other class of men. Because of their amazing wisdom, their statements of fact must be accepted by all men less wise.

3. Common sense tells us that a high degree of heat will *always* burn human flesh. This common knowledge in itself is enough to prove that there must have been some trick used in the above-cited cases—this, despite the fact that the physical means used are still unknown to layman or scientist.

4. The laws of Science have been established through repeatedly testing given reactions under identical conditions. Such tests have established *beyond question of doubt* that such heated substances as mentioned in the cases cited *must* give off, radiate, or otherwise transfer heat to other objects contacting them. All human experience shows this law to be correct ; therefore it is impossible that there could be any force existent which would change this law for a moment, no matter what might be done under pretence of using magic.

5. Thousands of other superstitious beliefs have seemed in the past to be fully as well authenticated as these cases of fire-walking. Perhaps cameras were not used in the old days, but no one doubted the general beliefs. Science came and proved these beliefs to be superstitions. As history always repeats itself, Science will some day dispel the superstitious belief in fire-magic.

6. Those of us accepting the Scientific Attitude as the one correct attitude toward life and the world of phenomena have, however, not been left by Science without means of giving a full and complete explanation of the methods used in fire-magic. These methods are purely physical. They are : The use of some physical means of insulating human flesh against heat ; the use of hypnosis by so-called magicians to make investigators imagine they were seeing or doing something they did not see or do.

7. In these cases the photographs offer no conclusive proof. The native witch-doctors very probably used hypnosis to make the investigators think the objects touched or walked upon were hot when they were only warm. A camera might show the difference between lighted or unlighted charcoal, as in the Burma case, but marvels of trick photography have been seen in the movies, and it is known that even if the cameras did not show heat, the photographs could have been " faked " to show heat.

.   .   .   .   .

To sum up : In the face of the fact that fire burns and that everyone knows that it burns, no explanation of this supposed magic is necessary. No matter what argument or evidence may be cited, it is impossible to throw doubt on so well established a fact as that fire or very hot substances will burn human flesh.

The Scientific Attitude is entirely justifiable in its reflection in commercial literature and through the layman. It has made no mistake in denying the existence of magic in any form.

Rebuttal from the Defence :

In the popular mind, fireproofing is mistaken for insulating.

Cloth and other materials can be made to resist heat to a small degree by treating with mineral salts such as alum. The only insulating materials we know and use are *anything* but invisible. It would take a very thick coating of asbestos, for instance, to protect feet from intense heat. In the cases given in evidence, the white men treated their feet in no way. In the performances of the fire-eater, his teeth were scraped on the edges before he bit down on the red-hot iron bar and began bending it.

In the matter of hypnosis, the theory advanced by the Scientific Attitude is wholly untenable. It is impossible to hypnotize more than about two-thirds of any average group. Your own Science found this in its tests. Moreover, it is impossible that all individuals ever witnessing fire-magic or taking part in it could have been hypnotized or that the magicians seen and photographed in action could so have hypnotized themselves. All men cannot be hypnotized. Cameras do not lie.

In order to " fake " moving-picture films, the amateur photographers would have had to be prepared to use elaborate settings such as are used in a studio. All of the thousands of tiny individual pictures taken on a film *cannot be changed* by any " faking " process and each " frame " left exactly like the next. Furthermore, the companies developing such films for amateurs are the only ones touching them as they are so developed. As the cost of such faking—even if it were possible on the film—would run into hundreds of thousands of dollars and require thousands of hours of labour, such secret " faking " in each and every film is out of the question.

All three of the explanations so blindly accepted by the layman from the Scientific Attitude are absurd and preposterous.

Rebuttal by the Opposition :

Words can be made to seem to prove that black is white, or any other foolish proposition. The Scientific Attitude does not stoop to bandying words with anyone. It rests on the past achievements of Science and on simple statements of physical facts.

No matter what evidence is offered or what is said about it, the *fact* remains that fire burns and that we all *know* it burns. Any effort to prove that fire does not burn under any and all proper conditions is a mark of ignorance and superstition, and anyone making such an effort deserves all the opprobrium heaped on him by sane and civilized people who have come to realize that the Scientific Attitude is entirely logical and entirely correct.

·   ·   ·   ·   ·

Our trial is now finished and it remains only for the decision to be given by the Court. I have done my best to present all the evidence and to give a true reflection of the Scientific Attitude in the "rebuttals." I have many times encountered just such arguments as I have given for the opposition. That they are rather startling in their display of inconsistency and lack of logic can only be explained as I have explained them, by pointing to the Scientific Attitude complex which seems to have become an all but universal affliction.

I now suggest that if any of the Round Table members be rash enough to decide in favour of Magic after this trial, he should at once write down his decision in black and white. From long experience I have learned that anything the conscious mind may decide, which is contrary to a complexed belief, very soon is no decision at all. The subconscious has an insidious way of refusing to help us get back complete memories of the important points which have caused a decision contrary to its complexed beliefs. Automatically we find that *we turn back to old habits of thought and belief even after having decided to change them for new and better ones.*

I once read the conclusions of a learned man who was trying to explain why savages were so slow to see that their heathen beliefs concerning magic and religion were nothing but rank superstitions. He wrote : " This belief is helped by the general inability of the human mind to consider *negative* evidence when strong forces of belief are entrenched on the side of *established institutions.*"

Now, amusing as it may seem, the argument cuts *both* ways. The savage can use it against us and our sacrosanct materialistic dogma of Science. In trying to realize that magic is *not* a superstition we find the shoe on the other foot, and soon it will be pinching unmercifully. It is as hard for us to believe that the brown man can walk barefooted over red-hot stones without being burned as it is for the brown man, who has just done it, to believe it impossible—impossible because someone who cannot do it or understand how *he* can do it, has said it is impossible.

We would say to the savage—or in this case to the mysteriously wise brown man :

" But there *must* have been some invisible solution used to coat your feet so that they wouldn't be burned ! It is simply *impossible* that it could be otherwise, unless you have hypnotized me and my camera ! Why, if it isn't a trick, *all the laws of Science are threatened !* "

The brown man would probably reply :

" White man crazy like anything ! How could find something to put on foots that no can see and still can stop fire from burning ! What you mean by that ' hypnotize ' word ? You think I smart fellow like you ? How could do that kind ? How could find stuff to put on foots when white man not could find in *all his medicine ?* What-a-matter you, anyhow ! You ask me do fire-walking so you can see. I do. Then you get mad like anything because you not know secret my father teach to me. 'Cause *you* no can do fire-walking, you want make *me* think I no can do ! What-a-matter ? You crazy some kind ? *More than thousand year my people do fire-walk.* Just because *you* no can do, you trying make *me* think I no can ? You sick in head ? More better you take camera and go back to hotel where sun not so hot on you ! "

PART TWO

CHAPTER I

BEFORE the Round Table became a Court and tried the Case for Magic *versus* the Scientific Attitude, I explained that I would incorporate in Part Two of my report the step by step progress toward Magic which I made over a period of eighteen years. This, I explained, was to help those ambitious to understand—to say nothing of those ambitious to practise Magic—to drain off their complexes as they went along.

At the present time I will not take time to go into my theory as to how fire-magic is made possible. If I did I should fail. No one would understand what I was talking about. But if Round Table members will forget our Court and settle themselves at their ease, I will get on at once to my task of teaching the common language of Magic, so that when the time comes to go back to the fire-walkers I can make myself very clearly understood.

Remember that you are being subjected to a process of having your complexed beliefs in dogma drained off. Also remember that you are to remain alert and suspicious, challenging my every statement and forming your own opinions as to the meaning of all data presented. I have told you that I may be wrong as often as right. No good magician was ever made who did not first learn to make up his own mind about anything which confronted him. I am about to present each Round Table member with an aeroplane of which they know nothing. When in the air it will be too late to examine the engine and the struts. From familiar skies you will plunge into those unfamiliar. I will soon be taking you into the unknown where clear and uncomplexed thinking and eternal vigilance will be the only chart to guide. Science will be left behind immediately.

The charts of Psychical Research, Spiritualism and Psychology will serve for a time ; but after that we leave the old landmarks behind and fly out over uncharted seas to find the far and tiny island of the Ancient Magic. Look well to your controls and wings as I prepare you in Part Two to take off into the unknown.

Science has found no Magic in the field of the physical, so we leave at once for the superphysical, and arrive at spiritualistic phenomena. I will draw both from my own experiences and from those well authenticated by the Society for Psychical Research.

Continuing with our case numbers, we have :

CASE 10

IS THERE MAGIC IN TABLE-TIPPING ?

Preliminary Notes :

As the force which moves tables in spiritualistic séances is not recognized by Science, we can be sure that it comes under our definition of Magic : " Effects produced by any superphysical force or by ' spirits.' " Here we have a type of phenomenon known to all laymen. Our Magic complex is partly founded on it. That tables do tip, despite the angry denials of Science, shows how ungrounded is our belief in materialistic dogma. In fact, so well known is table-tipping and kindred phenomena that Science has been in a dither about it for some time. Its denials are fruitless. Even the stage magician Houdini's denials were not taken seriously after his book had been read and put on the shelf. We have our complexed beliefs in Magic and most of us have helped tip tables. We even know that a group of leading scientists belong to the Society for Psychical Research and are busily engaged trying to discover what force it is that makes tables and other objects move as of their own accord.

In order that we may have the data listed and ready to scrutinize, I will now present a typical case of table-tipping from my own investigations.

The Case :

Desiring to test the genuineness of table-tipping, I went repeatedly to two mediums. One was a professional, long retired. The other an amateur. Both were women. Under test conditions, in a lighted room where I could watch hands and feet and knees, I saw tables of many sizes tap and tip and dance. As a specific instance (working with the amateur medium) : a small stool, weight four pounds, height two feet. Hands, only, laid on it—my hands and the medium's. Our feet and knees were kept well back

The stool tipped and tapped and circled on one leg   It moved across the bare floor to the full extent of our ability to follow it with our arms. It pulled from under our hands and fell to the floor. This was repeated at six different sittings, some in broad daylight. Location : a room over a garage which housed the family cars. No possible mechanism to move the wooden stool from below.

Comment :

To get the truth about table-tipping and similar matters, we must first gather all data, consider all possible explanations, and eliminate one by one those which are not logical or which do not match the data.

The Scientific Attitude says that no physical object can move unless some physical and measurable force is applied to move it. All superphysical force is denied.

In texts on physics one never sees such a thing mentioned as the force used in table-tipping. Science remains silent on the subject.

Scientists honest enough to investigate spiritualistic phenomena of this type have been many, but their conclusions are not officially recognized. The explanations given by these scientists vary greatly. Some think that an invisible force of an electric nature comes from the medium and is guided by her conscious or subconscious mind in moving physical objects. Others, when such an explanation will not fit, go so far as to say that there are unseen superphysical entities using some superphysical force to cause the phenomena. These even admit that these entities sometimes resemble the conscious human being as it might be if it could operate on a superphysical plane and without a physical body. A few accept the beliefs of Spiritualism.

As there may be some of the members of the Round Table group who may not be acquainted with the phenomena here described, I refer them to the many volumes of reports of the Society for Psychical Research for additional cases and evidences relative to the matter. For a condensed report covering the investigations of some two hundred careful workers of the S.P.R. over a period of years, I suggest a most convenient and valuable reference book, Richet's *Thirty Years of Psychical Research.* (MacMillan, 1923.) I shall refer to this source at frequent intervals.

Some mediums can work in bright light and others only in subdued light. Many charlatans have been discovered, but there are thousands of cases where no trickeries were possible. The phenomena are as well authenticated as any sane person could ask. For those unable to find proper reference books available, I will make a short list of some of the most famous and dependable reported investigations :

1. Sir William Crooks tells in his writings how a chair turned around with him while he held his feet up from the floor. Also a chair moved by itself from a corner and slid across the floor to push against his extended hands—this in bright light and under the eyes of several other investigators. On five different occasions Crooks reports that a heavy dining-table rose from the floor as high as half a foot, hands being laid on its top and all feet checked for trickery as they rested on the floor beneath the table. Working with the noted medium, D. D. Home, and in a room brilliantly lighted by two " alcohol-soda flames," a water-bottle and tumbler rose into the air with no visible hands touching them. They remained floating above the table for about five minutes. Upon examining them, no wires or other physical means were found lifting and manipulating them.

2. The female medium, Eusapia, was first reported on by Lombroso in 1891 at Naples. Later the phenomena produced by her were investigated and reported on by such men of science as : J. Maxwell, Camille Flammarion, Ochorowicz

(hypnotist of great ability), P. Curie, Mme. Curie, d'Arsonval, Courtier, Sabatier, F. Meyers, Sir Oliver Lodge, Mr. and Mrs. Sidgwick, Carrington and many others. Morselli has written her story in detail.

Eusapia preferred to work in the dark. With investigators holding her hands tightly to make sure she could not be tricking them, she demonstrated down the years that objects could move without the aid of physical touch or mechanism. In a darkened room and tightly held by hand and foot, her presence caused a bedlam of knocks and sounds to be heard. Objects flew about the room. Bells rose from tables and rang themselves ; pianos played tunes ; various objects sailed in from other rooms. Matches were often struck and objects seen floating in the air. In full light there was less movement of objects, but the sounds continued to come, some raps on chairs being so violent that they moved both chair and occupant. Sir Oliver Lodge reported that under rigid test conditions some notes were played on an accordion placed not far from the medium and investigators. A music-box floated over their heads playing. The door locked itself and the key floated to them ; it returned and replaced itself in the lock. Eusapia stood up and placed her hands on the corner of a forty-eight-pound table ; it rose straight into the air some eight inches.

3. When the human body is moved instead of some object, the phenomenon is called levitation. Reports of such instances are not so common as of the moving of inanimate objects, but the authenticity of the reports is just as well established. From Bible times on we read of different individuals being lifted into the air.

In the presence of the Emperor and Empress of Russia some years ago, and with the Grand Duke of Oldenburg, Grand Duke Valdimir and others of the Imperial household having their curiosity satisfied, the medium Eglinton was levitated until his feet dangled in the air level with the shoulders of the men.

Dr. Nicholas Santangelo, of Venosa, in experiments with the mediums Ruggieri and Cecchini, had the following experience while holding to the hands of the pair : Ruggieri began to rise into the air. The doctor was raised with him until his feet struck the chandelier. It was dark in the room. When he was let down and a light struck, he found himself, not on the floor as he had supposed, but on the top of the table.

Stainton Moses, an American medium, was often levitated, but he did not like it and "discouraged it as much as possible." On August 30, 1872, he was sitting in his chair when the chair lifted with him until his chest was six feet from the floor. He checked the height by making a pencil-mark on the wall and later measured its height from the floor.

Morselli writes in detail of how Eusapia rose in her chair at a séance to a distance of thirty-two inches from the floor. This happened in total darkness, but while she remained so suspended the distance from the floor was measured and arms passed in all directions about her to make certain that she was not being lifted by wires or other means.

The medium D. D. Home was levitated in the most extraordinary ways so far reported. Many have described his levitations as eye witnesses. James Watson, an investigator living in London, once saw Home being lifted over the heads of the sitters and hurriedly gave him a pencil. Upon reaching the ceiling of the high room the medium obliged by marking the paper there to prove that he had actually been levitated. The editor of the *Cornhill Magazine* reported that at a séance which he attended, Home floated out of his chair and levelled off so that he sailed horizontally through a window open only some eighteen inches. Continuing to float on his back in the air, he moved quietly through the night from that third-floor window to another which was open in an adjoining room. Having entered in the same way he went out, but by a different window, he was returned unharmed to the dimly lighted room and continued to float about it for "several" minutes, his feet or parts of his body often touching the sitters. High and low he floated and at last returned to his chair none the worse for his experience.

·   ·   ·   ·   ·

The question before us is a simple one : Is there something outside the medium which causes objects to move and which moves small animals, and sometimes the medium with or without his chair ?

S.P.R. members such as Richet, being as loyal as possible to the materialistic dogma of Science, make a fair show of explaining the movements of objects other than the medium, and this in semi-physical terms. They tell us that, under control of the subconscious mind of the medium, some force goes out from him and acts to move objects. Ectoplasm is the name given to this force when it can be seen and photographed.   It is guessed that an *invisible* form of ectoplasm moves objects and plays musical instruments—all under control of the subconscious mind of the medium, who is often in a trance.

When it comes to the medium lifting himself by the boot-straps, so to speak, and taking along the chair—that seems hard to admit as a power latent in any ectoplasm, visible or otherwise. However, in ectoplasm we have something very definite to study, and especially where it is formed by some mysterious force into tangible objects—this being its principal activity except at times when it is simply moving physical objects or operating instruments. Let me present collected data concerning ectoplasm.

CASE II

PHENOMENA THOUGHT TO BE DUE TO ECTOPLASM

Preliminary Notes :

Before including in one case several to be found in Richet's book, I wish to mention the fact that in the séance room there has often been observed the phenomenon of some object suddenly growing out of thin air and falling on the table. This is commonly called materialization. The reverse of the process is the dissolving into thin air of some object and later its being slowly built up as it is returned. Flowers, metal objects, and even small animals are included in the list of things so affected.

In studying this type of phenomenon I endeavoured to draw a sharp line between things done by visible and photographable ectoplasm and things possibly done by something else—things at least done with no visible ectoplasm present. My end was to learn whether or not there were two things involved, or only the same ectoplasm in visible and invisible form.

So far as I have been able to learn, ectoplasm of the visible type usually comes from the medium's body only in dim light and during a condition of trance, although I have run across a few accounts of instances where the trance condition was not necessary.

For pictures taken of ectoplasm, our reference book, Richet's *Thirty Years of Psychic Research*, may be seen.

The Case :

The mediums are gathered together in this composite case, each has been searched for concealed objects or trick mechanisms. The room is one in a home to which no medium has access and one which has been carefully guarded to exclude mechanisms of fraud.

Eusapia is taken by Sir Oliver Lodge, Fredrick Myers and J. Ochorowicz for the first experiment. They hold her tightly and the lights are turned out. Someone objects and a single candle is lighted. Dim hands materialize and come out of the air to touch the investigators on heads and shoulders.

Sir William Crooks joins the group. A hand touches him and he grasps it firmly. He can feel it dissolve in his grasp.

Morselli tries the same experiment and finds that the hand he has grasped is warm and mobile like any hand, until it also dissolves.

Mr. Oxley and his group take the medium Mrs. Firmin. A light is turned on to give better illumination. The medium's " guide," whose name is " Betty," is seen to form out of thin air : first the feet, then the body, and at last the head. It fades again.

Dr. Richet's group sets to work with another medium. Holding her hands, they order out all lights except the candle.

Soon a glowing spot is seen in the air near her. It becomes nebulous and wavers ; it takes vague form ; a thread from it is seen connecting with the medium's body ; the form gradually takes the shape of a hand wearing a fingerless black glove and protruding from a sleeve not attached to a body. A flashlight picture is made which later shows the same thing. The experiment continues. Another outline forms and from it grow the legs, body and face of a guide called " Bien Boa." Another picture is taken. (See pictures reproduced in Richet's book.)

A group brings in sets of floor scales. Mr. W. J. Crawford is in charge. Later he will publish his report in his book, *Experiments in Psychical Science.* The medium, Miss Kathleen Golighter, is asked to cause tables to lift without being touched. She does this repeatedly while the scales are being placed here and there on the floor, under her and under the table legs. No ectoplasm is visible, but the scales register decreased weight of the medium as the table lifts. A scale placed on the floor between medium and table registers weight as the table lifts and the medium grows lighter. It is concluded that the ectoplasm has formed a lever or fulcrum and has rested on the empty set of scales while the table was being lifted by its fulcrum. The distance is measured from scale to table and medium to scale. The weights registered are found the same as if the medium had used an ordinary lever to pry the table into the air.

Comment :

Ectoplasm, visible or invisible, has been given as the mechanism by which all things can be materialized or dematerialized. It is also said to come from the medium and play musical instruments which have been enclosed in wire mesh cages to keep human hands from touching them.

Speculations are still rife as to what the composition of ectoplasm may or may not be. When considered as a physical " fluid " coming from the medium's body, it is hard to account for the solid hands that are grasped. Surely nothing *solid* can come from a human body for materialization purposes. More than that, mediums have been locked in cages and the ectoplasm has come outside and formed itself into graspable hands.

In the cases of "doubles" the ectoplasm has often been seen to form a more or less complete replica of the medium right at her side, although the "double" usually seems an attempt to change the exuding ectoplasm from the shape of the medium into the shape of some deceased person, this seemingly in an attempt of the ectoplasm to show how a former earth-body appeared.

Where it is claimed that invisible ectoplasm reaches out into a garden and brings in a flower, the imagination is not strained unduly; but in cases such as Madam H. P. Blavatsky continually demonstrated and taught her colleagues to demonstrate, it would seem necessary for this type of ectoplasm to have reached from some "mahatma" in India across to America to write messages on blank paper sealed in envelopes for that purpose.

To help complicate matters, the objects materialized or dematerialized at a séance are not simply moved. They fade away or build up out of nothing. Of passing interest, but of no great value as an explanation unless to the investigator himself, Mr. William Danmar, who reports of it in his book *Modern Nirvanism*, is a fact first mentioned by Zoellner and later verified by Danmar. This fact is that metallic objects such as coins and knives which have been dematerialized or "spiritualized" in the séance, invariably are found, upon their being again materialized, to be hot or at least warm. Some articles show signs of having been slightly scorched—papers especially. Non-metallic objects such as flowers come back wet, as if they had been sprinkled to keep them from overheating. Danmar tells of one medium who was asked by her "spirit guide" to provide a basin of water for sprinkling purposes. Danmar also reports that where ectoplasm passes through the cage enclosing a medium, and into the outer room, the wire or bars of the cage are heated by its passage. During such materialization and dematerialization, this investigator satisfied himself that matter could be dematerialized and passed through solid objects. Wooden and metal rings brought linked together into the séance room (to prevent fraud) were made to separate from their form as a chain and become separate links without being broken. Glass alone seemed impenetrable.

The Scientific Attitude has been so instructed by the propaganda of Science as to declare flatly that all such materializations and dematerializations are sleight of hand performances. It is declared that the celebrated stage " magician " Houdini duplicated every spiritualistic phenomenon, and proved that all resulted from trickery. This is refuted by Houdini himself. His signature is affixed to many written certifications of what to him was the genuineness of phenomena not performed by trickery. Moreover, there are many things done by mediums that Houdini never did.

In Lewis Spence's *An Encyclopedia of Occultism* (Dodd, Mead and Co., 1920), may be found, on page 161, an account of a phenomenon often demonstrated by the medium D. D. Home, who floated out through the windows and back. He could lift a glowing coal from a fire and hold it in his cupped hands while blowing it to its greatest heat. Also he could bury his face in a hearth full of coals without being harmed. Mr. S. C. Hall reported that he had watched Home do his fire feats and that the medium had then laid a bright coal on a handkerchief and left it there for several seconds without the linen being so much as scorched. Following this demonstration, he laid another glowing coal on Mr. Hall's head without burning his hair. Miss Homewood and Lord Lindsay write that they saw him also put a very hot lamp-chimney into his mouth.

Psychic Research investigators are rather baffled at this handling of fire. Oddly enough, I can find no record of any one of them postulating the use of invisible ectoplasm as an insulator for either the coal or the thing it touched.

Considering fire-magic in the light of the use of ectoplasm of the invisible type, it would be necessary to conclude that the flesh itself was surrounded and protected by the " fluid." In the source mentioned above, and on page 19, is given Brinton's report as well as Washington Mathews' report embodied in Bulletin 30 of the Bureau of American Ethnology

—both reports relating to fire-handling by American Indians.

Brinton saw Indians plunge their arms into kettles of boiling water or syrup without being burned. They also picked up large coals and heated stones with bare hands. They fire-walked over hot coals and ashes.

I will quote a paragraph from Washington Mathews :

" It is said that the Chippewa sorcerers could handle with impunity red-hot stones and burning brands, and could bathe the hands in boiling water or syrup ; such magicians were called ' fire-dealers ' and ' fire-handlers.' . . . The Arikara in what is now North Dakota in the autumn of 1865 walked and danced on the glowing embers and threw them around with bare hands so that spectators fled."

Next in our study of ectoplasm we will come to ghosts of two kinds. One shows itself either in or out of the séance room and the other does not show itself, but makes its presence known by moving things and making noises.

To have ghosts running about at a distance and quite independent of a medium's presence to supply ectoplasm, has given scientifically inclined investigators much to worry about. The lame explanation advanced at present is that the ghosts steal ectoplasm and store it up in old houses against their need to materialize and do some haunting. This entails stealing and storing ectoplasm on a large scale and suggests a splendid keeping power of the stored substance. Furthermore, it entails something still more worrisome which is a commentary on ectoplasm as a possible explanation of fire-magic. Mediums suffer acutely if their visible ectoplasm is *cut*, *burned* or *injured* in any way while it is outside their bodies. This was discovered very early by investigators bent on taking a piece of ectoplasm home to their laboratories to test its chemical composition. Some claim that a cut in ectoplasm produces a similar cut in the body of the medium. Be that as it may, we still have ectoplasmic ghosts, visible and invisible, given over to us for examination by the S.P.R. records.

CASE 12

GHOSTS.   ECTOPLASMIC OR WHAT?

Preliminary Notes :

Ghosts doing haunting are said by Bozzano to haunt, on the whole, either objectively or subjectively.   By this is meant that sometimes they are seen and sometimes they make their presence known without being visible to human eyes.   This last type of haunting is done by what the Germans call the *poltergeist*, or noisy ghost.   Let us study this type first.

The Case :

1.   In *An Encyclopedia of Occultism* may be found a famous case of a poltergeist in America.   I give this in preference to the many cases originating in Europe.

The " Ashtabula Poltergeist " appeared first in the home of a young widow living in Ashtabula County, Ohio—this, in about 1860.   The young woman had heard of the spiritualistic phenomena produced by the Fox Sisters in Rochester a short time before.   Desiring greatly to get in touch with her lately deceased husband, she endeavoured to contact his spirit.   No success followed upon her efforts, but one day objects began flying about the room in which she sat.   Noises broke out on all sides.   Terrified, she ran from room to room.   The disturbance followed her.   From that day on there came times when the poltergeist became active.   Friends and investigators came, but they found nothing to see or touch.

Hoping to lose the invisible ghost, the young widow moved to Marlborough and matriculated in a medical school.   Very soon after settling down in new quarters with a room-mate, both were terrified by fresh activities of the poltergeist.   Doctors from the school investigated at length.   One even wrote in his record that the stair rods tore loose and followed her.   Many less alarming things occurred.   Nothing could be done about the poltergeist, but the doctors solemnly undertook to explain what it was.   According to them it was a

" magneto-odylic force " coming from the young woman herself and causing the phenomena.

2. In Santa Barbara, California, a friend of mine obtained the use of a haunted house rent free, upon promising to clear it of a ghost. He moved in. At midnight the unseen ghost made its presence known to man, wife and tiny baby. A great depression settled over the spirits of the adults, and the baby began to scream. The depression was followed by hair-raising fear and horror. (A barber had murdered his wife in the same room some months earlier.)

With prayer and will and the use of the Hindu form of intonation of the sacred word *aum*, the ghostly presence was made to leave. This haunting continued for several nights and was met in the same way—eventually resulting in the haunting coming to an end.

3. While in London in 1925, I called on Bishop James, who was noted as a ghost expeller. As a side line and a means of getting funds to carry on his work with the downfallen, he made frequent trips over Europe to rid houses and castles of ghosts which had defied all others and had driven out the rightful owners. From him I had a straightforward account of ghosts which he had seen and ghosts which he had only heard or sensed by the fear and depressive atmosphere they engendered. In no instance, so he assured me, had he failed to find the ghosts and sent them away. The method he followed was to address the ghosts in English and explain the trouble they were making and the injustice they were perpetrating. If a request did not remove the ghosts after a lengthy argument had been made to them, he resorted to commands given in the name of God. At the time of my visit with him he showed me a letter he had just received. In it he was asked to come at once to Austria where a modernized castle had been invaded by a visible ghost as well as an invisible one who clanked chains and groaned in the traditional manner. I was much intrigued and begged the Bishop to write me in Hawaii and tell me what he actually found, upon going to Austria to investigate.

Two months later, upon my return home, I found his letter awaiting me. In it I was told that the information

given concerning the two ghosts and their activities had been
correct. I was also told that the visible ghost took a blessing
and departed on request, but that it took four nights of hard
work to expel the poltergeist.

Comment :

When I made my own study of ghosts I drew data from
my own personal experiences as well as from those of others.
I will now give that data.

CASE 13

A VISIBLE GHOST IS SEEN

Preliminary Notes :
None.

The Case :

At the age of fifteen I lived in Evanston, Wyoming. One
night, after a visit with a friend, I saw a ghost while on my
way home.

It was ten o'clock and there was a brilliant moon. Leading
my bicycle, I trudged along the cinder sidewalk past an old
log house which faced the old Blythe and Fargo barns. The
house had been empty for some months. Its fenced-in
yard was bare and the ground packed hard by rain and
wind. Often I had played marbles there with my companions.

As I passed the house I was startled to see a strange little
old lady picking up sticks from a wood pile, which I had
never seen there before. With spine acreep, I stopped and
stared, open-mouthed. Some intuition had told me at once
that I was watching a ghost pick up ghostly sticks from a
ghostly wood pile.

Having been taught at school that there were no ghosts,
I was confronted by a great problem. Also, my habitual
bump of curiosity began to function. Holding my ground
as a valiant and scientifically inclined young man should, I
called out a loud but wavering " Good evening ! " The
ghost paid not the slightest heed to my salutation. She

picked up one more stick of cedar wood, then walked feebly
to the old house. Arriving at the door, she did not go
through the motions of opening it, but walked directly
through its panels.

That was enough for me. With one leap I was on my
bicycle and away.

When I told my story the next day I was quietly hushed
by my family and loudly ridiculed at school. Indignant at
having my word doubted, I went to an elderly lady living in
the neighbourhood and described my ghost. To my delight
I was told that my description fitted an old lady who had
lived in the house years before, and that at that time there
had been a wood pile in the yard.

As a check on my ghost, to make doubly sure that she was
not a living human being, I had looked for footprints on the
floor of the old house the morning after I had seen her. The
door had been locked, but through the windows I had seen
the dust lying deep and undisturbed on the rough flooring.
It was marked only by the tracks of rats and mice.

Comment :

Despite its efforts, Science has never succeeded in convincing the layman that such things as ghosts and spirit visita-
tions are ungrounded superstitions. It has succeeded only
in making us ready to doubt the reality of the other fellow's
ghost, while remaining ready to defend our own most stoutly.
In any parlour gathering at least a few reports of " real "
ghosts can be heard. Ghosts die hard. People have
occasionally seen or felt them all down the centuries.
What is seen with the eyes is usually considered a verity—a
thing hard to dismiss with denials not accompanied by very
acceptable explanations. The theory of " hallucinations "
does not impress a normal human being who has had no
other form of hallucination, but who is very sure he has
seen a ghost.

.   .   .   .   .

During the twelfth and thirteenth years of my stay in
Hawaii I had an opportunity to study an invisible ghost at
first-hand. This is the data :

CASE 14

AN INVISIBLE GHOST IS FELT

Preliminary Notes :
Place : Honolulu.

The Case :

One night I was awakened from sound sleep by feeling my bed violently shaken. I thought an earthquake had occurred, and soon dozed off again. Once more I was awakened by the same shaking. Gradually it dawned on me that there could be no earthquake as nothing was rattling. I turned on a light to look about my room and observed that the light hanging from the ceiling was not swinging even slightly. Much interested, I lay awake waiting for another shake. None came. During the remainder of the night I slept undisturbed.

The third night following I was awakened just as I dozed off. Several times I dozed and each time I was awakened with a start by the bed shaking and continuing to shake for a moment after I had sat bolt upright and began feeling for the light switch.

For a time I suspected that I was imagining or dreaming that the bed was being shaken by some invisible hand. But later the shaking would continue a full twenty seconds after I was wide awake—providing I did not turn on the light. I decided that I was indeed favoured by a real ghost.

I experimented for some nights, trying to talk to the ghost —trying to instruct it to meet me at my medium friend's house so that it could tell me through table-tipping what it wanted. Failing to establish communication in any way, I at last became annoyed at being awakened so rudely from one to six times during the night. Having observed that light stopped the shaking at once, I burned a night-light. All went well after that unless I forgot to burn the light, in which case my ghost invariably returned.

After some months of trying intermittently to get back to sleeping in the dark, as I preferred to do, I moved to an empty room in a large old house I had rented to use as a photographic dark-room. Here the shakings were so violent, when I left no light burning, that the whole bed creaked and the floor shook. I began to wonder if my photographic abuse of the rear rooms of the old house had annoyed some former resident.

One night I drove out and picked up a mediumistic friend who was able to see ghosts. We parked the car before the house and watched. Light came only from a distant street lamp. After about two hours the medium saw something which I could not see at all. It was the ghost of an old man in cut-away coat who entered the house carrying a medicine bag.

Subsequent questioning of old residents in the neighbourhood brought out the fact that a doctor answering the description of the ghost had built the house and lived in it for thirty years, dying there finally.

The shakings forced me to burn my night-light no matter where I went to live. The annoyance finally ceased at the time the old house was torn down.

Comment :

I believe myself to be in no way mediumistic or capable of producing ectoplasm unconsciously for the use of a ghost. I may be wrong in this, but at séances I am useless without a good medium to join me when I lay my hands on a table. Never, except in the two cases mentioned, have ghosts or " spirits " made themselves known to me.

CHAPTER II

MY next step after studying table-tipping and learning that it was genuine, was to proceed to the study of the types of intelligences which were seemingly involved in the phenomenon.

I will now give the results of my further investigations.

CASE 15

TABLE-TIPPING TEST FOR EVIDENCE OF INTELLIGENCE IN THE GHOSTLY FORCES

Preliminary Notes :

The conditions in this test are the same as those in Case 10. The same amateur medium and stool were used. This medium was of the Scientific Attitude despite her work with simple magic. I know positively that she was not using trickery.

The Case :

1. In answer to spoken questions, the stool tapped a leg on the floor either two or three times for " Yes " or " No." The questions asked were ones to which I alone knew the answers.

Questions and answers : 1. Have I a letter in my inside coat pocket ? (Yes.) 2. Is it from a woman ? (No.) 3. Is it from Henry ? (No.) 4. Is it from J. B. W. ? (No.) 5. Is it from a relative ? (Circling of indecision.) 6. Is it from someone signing only initials ? (Yes.) 7. Are those initials J. H. ? (No.) 8. Are they R. L. ? (Hesitation, then Yes.) 9. You are wrong. (Yes.) 10. Are they B. L. ? (No.) 11. Are they L. B. ? (Yes.) The last answer was correct.

2. The same medium, while working alone with the stool one day, was told in answer to a question concerning the health of her husband who was spending his vacation at sea, that he had died.

The ship on which the husband had sailed was not equipped with radio, it being a small schooner. I sat with the lady, and together we questioned the force using the stool. It stuck to its statement that the husband had died. Not once did it deny it during the course of three sittings.

When the schooner arrived at Seattle the husband cabled back to his wife in Honolulu that he had had a perfect voyage and had never felt better in his life.

Comment :

From the psychic activities so far examined, three conclusions are to be drawn. 1. That some superphysical force exists which can and does affect physical objects. 2. That this force can show an intelligence resembling that of human beings. 3. That information given by it cannot always be relied upon.

Turning to official Science for an explanation of the intelligence in the force, we get little more than denial of all phenomena.

Turning to Psychology we get the following explanations from its several schools : 1. The Behaviourist stands with Science and also denies the phenomena. 2. The realist school of Psychology explains that all phenomena is due to the action of the subconscious mind of the medium or sitters —the latter supposedly influencing the medium because their subconscious is in telepathic touch with the medium's subconscious. 3. The idealist school (for want of a better name) of Psychology is not quite so sure that all the phenomena can be assigned to the subconscious, but makes no effort to describe any other source from which it might come.

The subconscious mind is described by Psychology as differing from the conscious mind in that it lies below our level of consciousness and beyond conscious control. It has been assigned the ability to accept " suggestions " from the conscious mind of the individual or from the conscious mind of an operator using hypnosis. It has been found to retain memories long beyond the power of the conscious mind to recall. It is supposed to control the physical processes of the body.

. . . . .

The above explanations do not in any way explain by what mechanism the subconscious could generate an invisible force and use it to move physical objects. For an explanation of this we must turn again to the Psychical Research groups.

From Psychical Research, as I have said, we have ectoplasm as the explanation of the movement of objects— telekinesis. Ectoplasm is thought to be latent in the body of the medium and to flow out from her and become active. The intelligence behind ectoplasm is usually said to be the subconscious mind of the medium or of the sitters.

The only other set of explanations we have are those offered by the intelligent force itself, and accepted by Spiritualism. In giving messages by' writing them in a closed box in which pencil and pad have been placed, the force has often identified itself as the spirit of some dead person. Mediumistic persons are often " taken possession of " by this force at times when it speaks through them. Often the force speaks in a voice and language not known to the medium. The force always claims to be a " departed " spirit, frequently of a relative of the medium or sitter, or even the spirit of some famous person long dead. In automatic handwriting done through the hand of a medium, varieties of penmanship are displayed and the same claims repeated. Books which have been produced in this manner claim to relate the experiences of the spirits after their " passing over."

If it were not for the fact that these communications received through mediums, supposedly from spirits of the deceased, seldom give the same description of the state after death, modern Spiritualism would have prospered more greatly. As it is, investigators incline to believe that the differing views of heaven or the hereafter may be accounted

for by the differences of opinion in the subconscious minds of
medium or sitters. Upon this discrepancy in the descriptions given by the force itself of its state, investigators
base their theory that the subconscious and some form of
ectoplasm is at work—and *not* a spirit.

However, there are other activities of this intelligent force
which, when taken together with the hauntings and poltergeists, upset the theories which have been advanced. These
other activities are displayed as abilities not normally native
to human beings—the ability to see events occurring at a
distance, and even events before they occur.

      .   .   .   .   .

Note.—Let me pause for a moment at this time to define
a word which I shall use constantly from now on, but not
with the meaning given in the dictionaries. All through my
report I shall need a word for the act of " seeing psychically
into the distance " and so becoming aware of what is going
on there at the moment. The word MONITION is the one I
have selected to use. This changes or adds to its dictionary
meaning : " a warning or advice." The words *premonition*
or *precognition* will continue to serve to convey the idea of
any " seeing into the future " *regardless* of distance. I will
use this fuller meaning of *monition* for the sake of clarity and
brevity. In looking over the writings of Psychical Research
investigators I find that special words have been invented,
such as " cryptesthesia," but that none of these fit exactly
into the idea of " distant seeing."

      .   .   .   .   .

Monition is not quite so black a heresy against the dogma
of " nothing not physical " as is premonition (precognition).
Science can explain away monition only by the use of the
theories of mind reading and telepathy—both of which it
vehemently condemns. But premonition ? Science throws
up its hands in holy horror ! By no pretended acceptance of
condemned theories can such a thing be made to fit the
sacrosanct dogma. If there is anything *real* in the physical
universe it is the *past :* if there is anything utterly *unreal*

and beyond physical power to apprehend, it is the *future*. Future events *cannot* be *physical* realities by any stretch of the imagination—so argues Science. *Therefore*, all premonitions are happy guesses confirmed later by coincidence.

Most of the psychologists stand firmly with Science and deny the genuineness of premonitory phenomena. Those psychologists who do not deny its genuineness still hesitate to admit that precognition is an ability latent in the subconscious or conscious parts of mind. They leave the matter up in the air.

Psychical Research groups split on the matter, some deciding with the psychologists of various schools, and not a few agreeing with the doctrines of Spiritualism. The Spiritualists assign all premonition to spirit communication with the living. They affirm that spirits have an ability greater than have the living. Many theories are offered to explain how a man can show a greater ability after death than while physically alive.

Let us now push aside the dogmas of Science and Spiritualism. Our only hope of getting to the truth of the matter lines in unbiased and unhindered examination of the phenomena.

CASE 16

PRECOGNITIVE ABILITY OF THE INTELLIGENT FORCE

Preliminary Notes :

While a very small part of the predictions made by this intelligent force are accurate, coincidence cannot explain the many genuine premonitions. I give one for which I can vouch, as it comes from my own experience.

The Case :

At a sitting with the retired professional medium mentioned in Case 11, the table tipped and moved with nervous trembling over to me. The medium sensed that a warning was being given. I began asking if this or that was about to happen to me. Soon I asked : " Is there danger to me from automobiles ? " The table tapped an emphatic " Yes."

I continued to ask questions, but could get no definite idea of when or where any accident might occur.

Two days later I had the only real automobile accident in my fourteen years of driving in Hawaii. A drunken truck-driver came toward me and, being mindful of the warning, I took no chance, but did my best to get out of his way instead of waiting for him to stop. I escaped with only the loss of a front fender. Had I not been forewarned I might have been killed.

Aside from communications through tables or, more directly, through automatic handwriting, there is a better method, though less dependable because it is more suscep-tible to trickery on the part of the medium. By this method the medium gets the messages from the intelligent force through her mind. However, the mediums prove beyond a doubt the genuineness of their communications in cases where the message received correctly forecasts the future or tells of a distant happening. Let us examine another of my tests of the activities of this mysterious force. .

CASE 17

THE INTELLIGENT FORCE COMMUNICATES AS IF BY THOUGHT TRANSFERENCE

Preliminary Notes :

Working with the same amateur medium as in Case 11, this test was carried out in bright light in the evening.

The Case :

For four months I had been endeavouring to find the original of a photograph. It was one from a negative in the possession of the Williams Studio in Honolulu, but it had been purchased with other negatives and no one could say who had made it. The picture had been reproduced twice in the *Mid-Pacific Magazine*, but the editor was unable to say from what original book-plate, drawing or what, the copy had been made. I had gone through many books in the three available libraries—Carter Library, Library of Hawaii, and

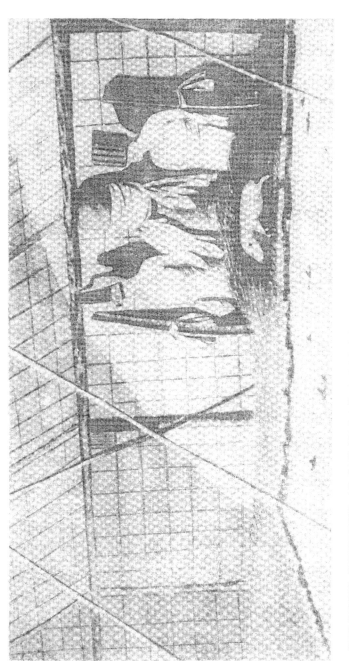

THE PHOTO IDENTIFIED AS ONE MADE FROM THE PLATE IN *VANCOUVER'S VOYAGES*, SHOWING THE MAT AND PIG WHICH WERE ADDED WITH INK TO THE PHOTOGRAPH

The central stone is the symbol of creative force. The male and female figures are the sex-dualities of the *Aumakua* figuratively represented. The half of the woman's headpiece matches the reversed half worn by the man—signifying the "over-head" or superphysical nature of the union. The lines on the insides of the palm trunks represent the rising *manas* ascending to the *Aumakua* when the flow is reversed.

the library of the Bishop Museum. No one had been able to aid me, although it was generally thought that it must have been a plate in some book of early travel. The photograph showed the interior of a crude temple which I hoped might be Hawaiian. (This because of the symbolic nature of the altar piece and its close similarity to those of pre-Vedic India.)

At last I went to my medium friend to see what could be done. The photograph was laid on top of the stool and a vocal request was made that a spirit attend the sitting. When the table began tipping under our hands, the spirit was addressed in words and asked to find some other spirit who could tell us where the original of the photograph might be found. The table became motionless and so remained for about five minutes. It began tipping again and with a more rapid movement than before.

Procedure :

" Do you know about this picture ? "

(Tapping.) Yes.

" Do you know where to find the drawing from which this was taken ? "

Yes.

" Can you tell us where ? "

The stool circled.

" Can you spell it out with taps at the right letter as I recite the alphabet ? "

No.

" Are you Hawaiian ? "

Yes.

" Can't you spell in English ? "

No.

" How can you tell me, then ? "

The stool tipped on two legs and leaned its top against the medium's knees. I pulled it away. The stool tapped meaninglessly and tipped toward the medium again.

" Could you tell the medium ? "

Yes.

Medium : " I'm listening. . . ."

Medium : " Strange, but I see as in a dream two very old

Hawaiians. And they seem to be telling me that they were once keepers of the original temple—at the time the drawing was made by the artist."

" Is that right ? " (to the stool).

(Stool tapping.) Yes.

" Where was the temple ? In Hawaii ? "

Medium : " They say it was on the Island of Kauai . . . at a village called Elele. They saw the artist draw the picture of the inside of the temple."

" Where is the drawing from which this picture was made ? "

Medium : " They say it is in a book in the Bishop Museum."

" But I've looked there time and time again."

Medium : " But they say it is there."

" Just where ? "

Medium : " They say in a big book in the library."

" How could I find that book ? I have searched so often and failed."

Medium : " They say they will go and see what they can find out about it."

(A wait of several minutes. Again the stool tapped.)

" Did you learn anything ? "

(Tapping excitedly.) Yes.

Medium : " They are showing me a young man up on the top floor of the Museum . . . in a back room. . . . He wears only trousers and Japanese sandals . . . he is hot . . . he has boxes before him. . . . The boxes are filled with square cards . . . they say he can tell you where the book is."

I thanked the spirits and we closed the sitting. Early the next day I went to the Museum. I inquired for a young man such as the medium had described. There was such a person and I was directed to him. He was checking the card-index system for the library. I showed him the photograph. He took up a card upon which a similar photograph had been pasted.

This card had never come into my hands although I had been through the files repeatedly. It was under the wrong heading and the young man was planning to correct it and file it in its proper place. However, the card told that the original plate was to be found in *only one* of forty-odd volumes of *Vancouver's Voyages*, all of which I had run through in turn in my search, and which had seemed to me to be duplicates. A note said that the plate had been scratched and replaced by a different one before the edition was completely run off.

I went downstairs and found the book. The original of the photograph was the first illustration in it. I found, when I looked at the plate in the book, that the one who had made the photograph had carefully drawn on it with black ink a pig on a platter and a fringed tapa mat to go under the platter —these placed before the phallic stone in the original drawing of the altar.

That evening I went again to the medium, but I did not tell her of the alterations I had found. After the same Hawaiian spirits had reported their presence by tapping with the stool, I asked :

" Do you know in what way this photograph is different from the original drawing ? "

(Tapping.) Yes.

" Can you tell me in what way ? "

Medium : " They show me the picture as it was in the book. They point to the floor. There is no pig or dish . . . no mat under them."

" Can you tell me who made that change ? "

Medium : " They show me a white man—I never saw him before—he is drawing the pig and things on the photograph. It is a clearer photograph than yours."

" Can you tell me why he made that change ? "

Medium : " I see him talking to a very old Hawaiian. The old man is looking at the picture. He is explaining that the pig and the mat were very important as offerings. He explains that they were usually there and tells the white man just how to draw them in."

As to this last bit of information covering the way in which the original drawing had been changed in the photograph, I was never able to verify or to disprove the assertions made.

Comment :

Some Psychical Research workers advance a peculiar theory to explain how the subconscious mind can obtain knowledge which is not possessed by either medium or sitter—knowledge not even forgotten by them. This theory will be found mentioned in encyclopedias. Because of this mention, the Scientific Attitude has accepted this as a theory advanced by Science.

The theory is this : There is an unconscious " leakage " of thought and memory from all minds, and this leakage is transferred unconsciously by telepathy to the subconscious mind of the medium. When this occurs, the medium gets the information and thinks a spirit has given it to her.

Science, through its official writings, denies that there is either " leakage " or telepathy.

Let us now examine data which is said to prove the existence of spirits.

CASE 18

SPIRITS PROVING THEIR EXISTENCE

Preliminary Notes :

I draw now from the reports of the Society for Psychical Research and other sources to get, not so much a case, as authentic data drawn from many experiments.

The Case :

Spirits, when pressed hard by the scepticism of Science, have resorted to amazing feats to prove their existence. The most convincing of these feats are called " cross-correspondences " or " complementary correspondences."

Mr. Gerald Balfour wrote a report for his group of S.P.R. investigators on the case known as " The Ear of Dionysius." Here there seems to have been the spirit of a very learned professor at work. There is no denying that he gave to various mediums, through automatic handwriting, quotations from a book so rare that only a few scholars knew of it. This book (from which the case takes its name) was written in Greek by the almost unknown Hellenic poet, Philoxemus.

Having given quotations from this book to several mediums, the spirit then revealed his identity and told where the book could be found—in the library he had left behind him. A check was made and the rare book located.

Another and very famous spirit has worked for years with a S.P.R. group, but has never identified himself by name. In the early days of the society he took to giving mediums parts of paragraphs which had no place at all in what they might be writing at the time. Later it was discovered that these parts, when collected from various automatic hand-writing messages given different mediums, fitted together and made complete messages. This has been going on steadily for some twenty-five years. The investigating group has changed membership gradually, but the same spirit still continues his elaborate effort to give proof that he is what he claims to be.

Comment :

Hundreds of almost as convincing cases are on record. Most of them are of a type which cannot be explained by the leakage-telepathic theory. The evidence of spirit existence may be based on the spirit's ability to imitate the handwriting or voices of the dead ; upon ability to mould ectoplasm and reproduce their former faces so that they can be recognized—sometimes even garments once worn ; or, in their communications, the mention of things unknown to medium or sitters—little events in their past lives—these mentions of events often having been checked and found to be facts.

From such evidence, Sir Oliver Lodge and many other thinkers have been convinced that the dead live as spirits.

Another proof which is less positive is the display of premonitory ability by mediums who assert that they can show that ability only because of spirit aid.

Sir Oliver Lodge writes of the medium, Mrs. Piper, that even when strangers were introduced to her under a false name she was able to tell them accurately of the dead members of their families and what had caused their deaths, although many had died before her birth. She was able to take a collection of objects and describe the dead or distant owner of each. Often she gave the names of long-dead relatives.

Working with the same Mrs. Piper, R. Hodgson brought before her a Mr. Hart, who had been a close friend of the spirit " George Pelham," who purported to speak through the medium at times, and who was accepted as one of her " guides." " Pelham " (pseudonym for Robertson) spoke through the entranced medium. The voice and inflection were entirely familiar to his old friend Hart. The spirit called attention to the fact that Hart was wearing a pair of cuff-links which had once belonged to him in life. He also mentioned the Howards, who had been his friends before his death, and gave a message to be transmitted to the Howards' daughter.

I will not ask the members of the Round Table to take time to go through more cases of this kind, but will simply outline my own findings and take it for granted that they will be checked by each for himself if my word is doubted.

There are not only spirits, but there are different classes of them. These can be classified and identified in the following way :

1. Those spirits showing little or no intelligence resembling that of human beings—the poltergeists, on the whole, are, in part, sub-human.

2. There are spirits who are able to tell correctly of their past lives, or of thoughts passing through the minds (or lodged in the memories) of medium or sitters. These belong to the class identified largely through their lack of ability to *reason*.

3. There are spirits who reason well indeed, but who cannot give correct information as to their past lives—who lack memory. This lack of memory makes it possible to identify them.

4. There are spirits who can tell correctly of distant events and of future events, this ability being their identification.

5. There are spirits who have a combination of the abilities

of any two or any three classes. These may be a class identified because of their perfect memory and ability to reason, or they may belong to the class which remembers, reasons and has monitory and premonitory ability—a class small in numbers compared to the others, but in which are found spirit individuals who can materialize and dematerialize physical objects.

The poltergeist seems only able to use the invisible ectoplasm. The reasonless spirits seldom use any form of ectoplasm other than the invisible. The memoryless but reasoning spirits, as well as those who can reason and also remember, seem always able to manipulate both visible and invisible forms of ectoplasm. The remembering-reasoning-monitory-premonitory spirits can use any form of ectoplasm and can manipulate it in such a way as to materialize, dematerialize, bring objects from a distance, " precipitate " writing upon paper in sealed envelopes, cause levitation, etc.

With this tentative classification presented, our next step—following in the order of those I took in my personal study and investigations—is to examine data which may give a clue to the nature of the force we have called " invisible ectoplasm."

CHAPTER III

WE shall eventually come to kahuna practices in which we can see those magicians employing spirits of the classes I have outlined. As we examine these practices we shall discover full proofs that the classification is correct.

The kahunas are master handlers of all the spirits of the less able classes, and work very effectively at times with the aid of the last and most able class—although the kahuna has the same monitory and premonitory ability himself and seldom needs to ask a spirit for aid.

The thing the investigators of the West have guessed to be ectoplasm of an invisible kind is looked upon by the kahunas as a force to be found in any material substance, whether it be mineral, vegetable or animal; water, air or fire.

This force the kahunas collect in excess quantities and use as they see fit in performing magic. They also believe that a spirit may collect enough of this force to enable it to move physical objects, or to do other work. In cases where the kahuna has "captured" a number of low-class spirits and has kept them to send out to do his bidding, the spirits are usually given a surplus of *mana* to increase their strength. This is done by "feeding."

The word *mana*, as used by the kahunas, has no proper counterpart in English. It indicates a vital force which may be likened to electricity. This force can, like the voltage of an electric current, be "stepped up" or "stepped down," thus getting the kahunas' three grades of *mana*. The *life* of all things from crystal to man is *mana* of the lowest voltage. The mental or reasoning (not the remembering, for that belongs to the part of man enlivened by the low *mana*) part of man has for its life force the next higher voltage of *mana*. The part of man which is a unit still higher than the reasoning mind (identified by an ability to see into the future and to materialize or dematerialize objects) is enlivened by the third and highest voltage of *mana*.

Let us now look to the West to see if we can find anything which may be compared to any of the three grades of *mana* which the kahunas claim to use for various purposes.

In the West we come at once to hypnotic force. This force is supposed to include that which was formerly thought to be a force in itself : animal magnetism.

Now both of these forces are real and both are different grades of force. One—animal magnetism—is purely physical ; the other is purely mental. As I have stated before, hypnosis belongs to Magic. It is a force which cannot be generated by physical means. Animal magnetism is a force generated automatically in all physical bodies, although an excess of it may be accumulated with the help of the mind. Some people have an excess of this force resident in their bodies at most times. They are the " magnetic " people who are " filled with electricity." Scientists are already measuring this force, and may one day be able to generate it mechanically. Perhaps they have already done so, but have not recognized its nature.

All the world over, aboriginal magicians have known of this force and made good use of it. The American Indians had several names for it, varying with the tribes. It was called everything from *orenda* to *manitu*.

As Science gives us no data on animal magnetism other than that of an historical kind, and as Psychical Research has little to offer. I suggest that we now plunge for a moment into an uncharted region of the sky through which we are flying our imaginary aeroplanes. For our guide let us take one of the many cults which are sold by the dollars' worth in the West.

CASE 19

ANIMAL MAGNETISM DEMONSTRATED

Preliminary Notes :

It was almost by accident that Animal Magnetism was discovered in the Dark Ages. For centuries the common lodestone had been known to attract iron. This power was something which could be transferred to steel to make of it a magnet in turn.

Early in the Christian Era, Paracelsus was endeavouring to perform magic with perhaps some success. Whether he originated the idea of Animal Magnetism or not is unimportant, but at least he exploited it. It was his belief that a steel magnet could magnetize the human body and heal illness.

Now the only test of magnetism was its power to attract. The natural thing for a magnetized physical body to attract was another body. Experiments were made. From a tangle of misconceptions there at last emerged, through the years, a knowledge that the human body could be made to attract other human bodies. Many were the ways of gathering this " animal magnetism." First, so it was taught, a magnet had to be carried on the person ; and second, some ritual or formula had to be used to help along the transfer of its magnetism to the body.

Of course, the magnet type of magnetism is not transferable, but there was that other type normally found in the body and which can be generated in excess quantities. It was this type that had really been discovered. A few people were found to have it naturally as a gift. Others learned to acquire it by holding a magnet and using the will to force a transfer from it to themselves—or so they supposed they were doing.

The common feature of animal magnetism and hypnosis is that they are developed by a *mental process* accompanied by a *period of practice*. They are forces not fully understood even to-day, except as they are seen to work in certain ways. Here we have something easily seen to be similar to the invisible force used at séances, the difference being that the medium generates this force and allows it to be controlled by spirits, while outside the séance-room there is more or less conscious control of the forces by the operator.

For a proof that there is such a thing as animal magnetism I present the following data :

The Case :

In the year 1927 a Russian teacher of occultism visited Honolulu. He held classes, claiming to be able to teach his pupils to use a new and marvellous set of occult forces. I joined the first class, and now draw the material for this case from his demonstrations and my own experiments.

In his first lessons, Baron Ferson—the teacher—told us that it was possible to collect what he called the " life force " from the atmosphere about us. To do this he instructed us to practise standing with feet wide apart and arms extended horizontally at the sides. While in this position it was necessary to use the will and to make the affirmation, " The universal life force is flowing through me now. I feel it."

I at once guessed that the Baron's " life force " was the old animal magnetism under a new name.

Before setting the class to gain proficiency by practising the art of collecting the " life force," the Baron demonstrated his own proficiency. He took the prescribed position and made the affirmation. This done, he announced that he had an extra charge of the " life force " in his body. He stated that its presence could be detected by its magnetic power to pull. To demonstrate this pull he placed his hands on the shoulders of a subject who was asked to stand with her back toward him. When the Baron's hands were removed from her shoulders and slowly drawn away, she was seen to be pulled by his hands as by a magnet.

Several subjects were tested and, as is the case with hypnotic subjects, some were found far more sensitive to the " pull " than others. One of the most sensitive subjects was then placed on the far side of a concrete wall while the Baron took his position on the inner side. The class gathered in the arched doorway, watching both of them. When the Baron raised his hands, the subject was pulled toward him violently. She would have been jerked off her feet had not two men been stationed beside her to hold her by the arms. The Baron raised his hands several times and the young lady was invariably jerked toward him.

A part of the Baron's teaching was that this " life force " could be transferred to human beings to heal them, or to physical objects when such a transference might be desired. He told of a man who had transferred the " life force " to tanks of fuel oil and made them give much greater heat in a furnace, this resulting in a great saving of oil. (I in no way vouch for this or other similar statements, but only mention them in passing.)

To demonstrate the transfer of the " life force " to *objects*, the Baron placed his hands on three chairs in a row of twenty which the class had just vacated. Prior to this he had sent out of the room three of the most sensitive subjects. When they came back into the room they were instructed to walk down the row of chairs and sit down in any chair that pulled them. All three chairs were filled, the first by having the young lady of the wall test almost precipitated into it as she came near.

As a class member I found the matter interesting, but suspected the use of " suggestion." I took time to practise and soon could accumulate some of the force. Working with a friend, we removed the possibility of suggestion by trying the " pull " on a brindle bull pup. The dog was a good subject. Soon both of us could put our hands on his back and remove them, causing him to take several steps backward, although he whimpered and showed every sign of puzzled indignation. In a very short time we could pull him back, although he dug in his claws and resisted—this, strangely enough, without our feeling the slightest pulling weight on our hands. In the end, an amusing thing happened : the dog got tired of the tests and bit my friend. Thereafter, when we tried to experiment with him, he promptly fled into hiding.

Comment :

While this is the only part of Baron Ferson's teaching that belongs to this case, it may be of interest to Round Table members to hear that the class was taught that the " life force " operated on three planes : the physical, mental and spiritual. Taking the same position, the mental " life force " was gathered by changing the affirmation to fit a mental accumulation. The change was in turn made to fit the spiritual nature of man, and in this accumulation there was a ritual of devotion attached. The accumulation in the physical was splendidly demonstrated by the class. As to the mental and spiritual forms of the " life forces "—from which we had been led to expect so much—the demonstrations given by the Baron were disappointing. When we have finished with the kahunas and their comparable *manas*, we shall be in a position to learn just why the Baron's demonstrations and those of his pupils were unsatisfactory.

While on the subject of animal magnetism, I will offer a bit of supplementary data concerning something perhaps related to animal magnetism in part, and also to hypnosis in part.

In India the snake charmers seem to exert a strange influence over snakes. Snakes in turn are said to exert a hypnotic influence over birds, although this is often thought only to be the effect of the birds' own fright. Relative to this point, I once caught a young wild rabbit. I handled it most gently and placed it on a stump so that I could make a photograph of it. The chase to catch the little fellow had been less than ten feet, but, to my distress, it lay down on the stump and died of pure fright—this despite its being hastily put back in the grass and left alone as soon as I realized what was happening.

No conclusive data can come from the things just mentioned, but there is something reported by Lewis Spence in his *An Encyclopedia of Occultism* which is very definite. Under the heading " Horse-Whispering," he gives information which I now condense :

Horse-whispering is a strange method of taming incorrigible horses by whispering to them. It is an art long practised by gipsies who trade for bad horses, tame them, and sell them at a fine profit. The American Indians also were reported to have learned the art. The most reliable source of information concerning this ability comes from reports on the activities of horse-whisperers in Ireland. The most famous of these was Con Sullivan. This Irishman could tame the most vicious horse in a matter of minutes or hours. Once tamed, the horse remained tamed. One of the Earl of Rosmore's fine racing horses pulled his jockeys off his back with his teeth. No one could handle or race him successfully. Sullivan was called and allowed to remain in the box stall with the horse for about an hour At the end of that time he called in the Earl. The horse was on its back, playing with Sullivan like a kitten. Both were badly exhausted. The horse gave his trainers no trouble after that, and was raced with great success.

As no horse-whisperer seems ever to have told the secret of his power, all that is known is that some old formula was whispered into the ear of the recalcitrant animal and he was tamed.

Perhaps some form of animal magnetism was involved in this practice, or perhaps some projection of hypnotic force. For the present the matter can rest while we get back into charted regions again and consider hypnosis in detail.

The magnetizers of the Middle Ages anticipated Baron Ferson in their belief in the curative power of animal magnetism. For many years they used it to heal, and often with success. Following the Bible practices, hands were laid on ; but God was not usually appealed to for aid—the magnetism being depended upon to act of itself. Naturally there was much religious dogma mixed in the matter from time to time. An Irishman named Valentine Graterakes dreamed one night that he had been instructed to heal magnetically by the laying on of hands. He began his practice and became famous. All kings were supposed to have the healing " magnetic touch " as a divine gift. Part of their duties was to heal, and the healing was reported to be effective in a small way.

Little by little the names of the most successful healers

were listed in history. At last, in about the year 1800, came
Mesmer, practising the " magnetic cure " on a large scale.
He wore a silk-lined leather coat to prevent the escape of his
magnetism, and he treated many at one time by placing them
in metallic contact with a vat of water which he had endeavoured to fill with magnetism from his own body. As
his patients stood holding iron rods protruding from the
" magnetic bath," Mesmer went among them touching this
one or that to give him an extra charge.

As Science was by that time a brawling infant already
preaching its dogma of " nothing not physical," the early
scientists tried to discredit Mesmer. This doughty individual, however, had become famous and was in high standing
with the nobility. The scientists grumblingly acceded to the
general demand that they stop denying the cures and make
an investigation.

Several bodies of learned doctors investigated. Their
reports were at first filled with denials and attempts to
explain away the phenomenon. The story is too long to
tell here, so let it suffice to say that after three hundred years
of animal magnetism, Science discovered hypnosis and
accepted it into its holy of holies. It is the one bit of magic
it *has ever* accepted.

In the evolution of hypnosis, animal magnetism was lost
in the shuffle. In a short time the doctors were using
hypnosis to help discover the subconscious mind. This
part of mind they grudgingly added to the accepted " facts "
of Science ; but later, upon discovering its heresy against the
dogma, they did their best to get rid of it. With the
discovery of hypnosis, Psychology was evolved and proudly
called " The Science of Mind." Still later, Science found
Psychology threatening the dogma and turned to attack it.
One of the noted warriors of Science, Loeb, issued the famous
statement not too long ago : " The story of the subconscious
mind can be told in three words : there is none."

As psychologists worked with the physical body as do
physiologists, Science could disown only the schools of
Psychology which refused to conform to the great " nothing
not physical." At present, the *newest* of the psychologists,

calling themselves the Behaviourists, are the only ones fully accepted by Science. They loudly deny the possibility of there being *anything* other than a chemical set of physical reactions resulting in the formation and use of " thought habits." They deny the conscious as well as the subconscious mind as things in themselves. Next in order come the Schools of Psychology which endeavour to retain the subconscious mind at least, but who are semi-outcasts because of that daring. Last in the list come the nearly total outcasts of the William James School who stoutly affirm the conscious mind and the subconscious, as well as " monads," or individual conscious entities inhabiting the body.

Let us now look into hypnosis for ourselves.

CASE 20

HYPNOSIS

Preliminary Notes :
   None.

The Case :

As Science has accepted, tested and proved hypnosis, there is no necessity for us to do more than review its findings. Anyone of normal ability can learn to hypnotize in about a month of daily practice, and this without having the slightest idea of the real nature of the force he is using. Like the physical pull of animal magnetism, the compulsive force of hypnosis cannot be sensed as a thing present in the body.

Before I begin listing the effects which hypnotic force has on a subject, I wish to correct a mistaken idea held quite universally by the layman. Science has proved conclusively that hypnosis *does not* " weaken the will " or otherwise injure anyone. Nor is the popular idea that once hypnotized one falls under the eternal control of the operator correct, or that once hypnotized a person can then never become a hypnotist. I once learned the gentle art. I studied with a friend. We took turns practising on each other. I have been hypnotized nearly as often as I have hypnotized.

I once heard an amusing tale told of a hypnotist travelling about giving public performances. In his audience one night was a powerful hypnotist of a waggish turn of mind. When the call was made for subjects and the showman began using his force to draw those subjects to him from the audience, the waggish hypnotist came forward, pretending that he had been caught. Once on the stage he silently began working to put the showman to sleep. The effect of his endeavour was very amusing. While the showman made his ridiculous and unnecessary passes, and laboured to put to sleep the row of victims he had placed in chairs, he. himself began to grow sleepy. He blinked stupidly and suddenly lay down on the stage and began to snore. After the applause from the audience had died away, the local man bowed, awakened the showman and permitted the performance to go on. I cannot vouch for the truth of this story as it is usually supposed that the mind must be made receptive in order to accept hypnotic commands given mentally or orally.

To get down to listing facts concerning hypnosis :

1. Hypnotic force is gathered in a way not fully understood.

2. It can be sent out to a subject by the simple method of willing or purposing to send it.

3. The hypnotic force, when resident in the operator or transferred to the subject, does not make its presence known by any bodily sensation.

4. To hypnotize a subject, the subject must usually be mentally receptive, although powerful operators are able to work when such a receptive state is not present.

So far as we know, the attention of the subject must first be attracted to the operator. That being accomplished, the hypnotic force, in some mysterious way, cuts off the conscious mind of the subject from its subconscious—either wholly as in resulting deep sleep or in part as in states of light suggestability. The process has been found to be one of paralysing the *inhibitory* power normally used by the conscious to control the subconscious. In this matter of inhibition the conscious acts as a filter for all external impressions, including worded commands or suggestions. So long as the filter is not paralysed, it keeps worded suggestions from reaching the subconscious mind in an effective way. It also has another function : The subconscious often generates strong impulses to act and tries to force them on the body. At times when the conscious does not wish the body to act— as, for instance, a yawn in company—the filter acts as an inhibiting barrier against the generated impulse of the subconscious, so keeping the act from being performed.

With the conscious mind gone, the subconscious has memory left it and a very elementary ability to reason. The reasoning conscious mind being cut off, and the inhibitory filter removed by hypnotic impact, the subconscious reacts to the conscious mind of the operator as if it were its own.

The subconscious thus placed in contact with the conscious mind of the operator, accepts without question every suggestion made it *unless* such a suggestion is contrary to a *complexed* belief lodged in the subconscious. Because of complexes which act as barriers, immoral suggestions are refused.

5. Suggestion can be sent from the operator's conscious mind to the subconscious of the subject, either by spoken words or by a *silent* mental command. A picture or image visualized strongly by the operator becomes to the subject's subconscious an *external reality*. If the operator visualizes a hot iron touching the hand of the subject, a blister rises. If he visualizes the blister gone, it quickly disappears. If a lion is visualized, the subject at once behaves as if a real lion were present.

In this silent transfer of mental commands and images, we have the *definite proof of telepathy*. Also we have definite proof that a telepathic thought can *only* be sent by a conscious mind and can *only* be received by a subconscious mind. The "leakage" theory is here discredited because the thoughts of the operator are not transferred to the subject *unless* he wills so to transfer them.

6. The conscious mind of the subject can observe all that is being done unless it is forced into a condition resembling sleep. As an observer, it is helpless to interfere with (inhibit),

or take over, control of the subconscious until allowed to do so by the operator. It is cut off from contact with the subconscious by progressive degrees as hypnosis deepens, but it can reason and recall some types of memories from the subconscious at will. In light states of hypnosis the conscious mind is aware that there is no lion present, but finds itself unable to resist the wild fear and impulse to flee forced upon it by the subconscious.

When the conscious mind has been put into a deep sleep by the use of hypnosis, and again awakened, it is unable to recall memories of what was done by the subconscious while it was asleep. This may be accounted for by the fact that it takes an "associated thought" to draw up from the subconscious the memories which *must* have been left there as a record of what had transpired during the hypnotic period.

7. The subconscious often refuses to heal bodily injuries or disorders because of some complex it holds. Suggestion can force it to knit broken bones, conquer disease germs and do many other things ; but once away from the operator for a period of days or weeks, the original complex may cause the subconscious to duplicate the old conditions of illness. The subconscious mind cannot heal its body miraculously, but healing within the normal ability of the subconscious can be demonstrated. There are certain tissues in the body which cannot be replaced if once destroyed. Certain kidney, heart and nerve tissues come under this classification.

I have had the pleasure of observing the late Dr. Richard Frissell's use of hypnosis to force the subconscious to heal a broken bone which it had refused to knit for four months. Many nervous disorders, swellings, pains, circulatory derangements, etc., were successfully treated by Dr. Frissell through hypnosis, although no permanent cure of epilepsy was possible. In the case of a patient suffering intensely from a hardening liver, nothing could be done to save him, but he was kept entirely free from pain for the several months before death occurred.

An outstanding fact which is soon to be of vital interest to our study is that, because of complexes, many illnesses seemingly cured by hypnosis do not remain cured. Were it not for this, hypnosis would stand well to the fore in medical practice to-day.

8. The complexes of the subconscious cannot always be *discovered* by the use of hypnosis although those which *can* be discovered can be broken or drained off by counter-suggestion. (Also by autosuggestion.)

Freud attempted to make hypnotic cures permanent by discovering and draining off the complexes which undid the cures made by the use of suggestion. He found that unless the normal conscious mind co-operated after each treatment, the complex was likely to return. His greatest difficulty, however—and the one that caused him to give up the hypnotic method of discovering and draining off complexes—was this : The complex doing the most damage was seldom left in its original form by the subconscious. This was because the conscious mind had inhibited it from acting in response to the dictates of the complex. An example of this change in the form of a complex may clear the point : A complex is formed at an early age by the forcing of a child, against its will, to attend church. The child loves its parents and wishes to obey them, but hates church. The complexed dislike for church is changed from that dislike—and its accompanying revolt against loved parents—to a complex of an entirely different type which accomplishes its original purpose of keeping the child out of church—this, by round-about means. The parents are still loved in the second phase, and the church is accepted for their sake. But the modified complex makes itself known by a strange new malady. Every time the individual smells incense the odour sickens him and causes fainting. Under the influence of hypnosis the child is asked why incense sickens him and causes fainting. The answer is not the complete tale of the rebelling against church attendance and parental command : it is, " Incense has always made me become so sick that I faint and have to be taken home."

To get around this subterfuge of the subconscious, Freud was forced to change his methods and question his *unhypnotized* patients at great length to bring out by an

" association of ideas " the " forgotten " memory of the incident causing the complex. This method he supplemented by the study of dreams in which the complex appeared in symbolic form.

9. The subconscious mind under hypnotic influence can take a suggestion and carry it out even after the normal condition has been regained. It does this by means of the mechanism it uses to force its complexed beliefs on the conscious. If a suggestion is given that in one hundred hours after hypnotic treatment the patient will sneeze violently six times and then start to sing, the suggested activities will occur. The conscious mind will not know why the sneezing occurred or why there came an overpowering impulse to sing.

In this connection we see that the subconscious alone is aware of the passage of time. It needs no clock and is accurate almost to the minute. The conscious mind has taught it this measure of time in hours and minutes, but the conscious mind has to depend upon the subconscious, very largely, to keep track of passing time and send up reminders to do certain things at certain hours. In states of preoccupation, the conscious has little sense of passing time.

10. Under deep hypnosis, major operations can be successfully performed. Data proves that the conscious mind is almost entirely responsible for the observation of all reports coming in through the five senses. The subconscious feels hardly any sensation that does not come to it relayed by the conscious mind. The subconscious, then, is seen to have among its particular tasks : (A) that of keeping the bodily processes active ; (B) that of retaining memories ; and (C) that of serving the conscious mind. However, it has the uncanny ability to *force* its desires upon the conscious through *emotions* which it generates, and which it uses as inhibitions to keep the conscious from evolving or accepting ideas which are contrary to those of a complex.

The memory displayed by the subconscious in hypnosis is surprisingly perfect and includes things long " forgotten " by the conscious mind. To " forget " is to be unable to recall memories by the mechanism of " association of ideas."

11. Here are some odd bits of data which must not be overlooked : The conscious belief of an operator that a certain condition prevents him from using hypnotic force will prevent that use. As an illustration : In the early days it was thought that the presence of *any* iron object near the operator would prevent him from "magnetizing" his subject. The presence of such an object invariably *did* prevent the use of hypnotic force. But the inhibition was in the *mind* of the operator and not in the *iron*. This last fact was discovered when an operator found that he had been working successfully on a subject and that, quite unknown to himself, he had forgotten to remove his penknife from his pocket. Thereafter he was no longer hampered by the presence of iron.

12. Hypnosis has given us definite proof that there is a subconscious or subliminal part of mind. The use of self-hypnosis or autosuggestion gives positive proof of this. A mind cannot hypnotize itself any more than one can lift oneself by the bootstraps. If it can hypnotize some part of itself, this proves that it has two parts, one of which can effect the other.

Comments :

This brief outline of hypnosis covers most of the points which will aid us in our approach to the kahunas and Magic. But before we go on we must pause to come to exact conclusions as to the abilities of the subconscious and conscious minds respectively—these to be normal abilities only, and those which can be demonstrated *at will* under test conditions.

I list those conclusions, but ask that they be accepted only if the proof has been sufficient. As I proceed I will give fresh proofs in the form of argument or illustration.

1. The subconscious holds nearly all memories. These it sends up to the conscious when they are fished for with a line baited by an "associated" memory, idea or sensation.

2. The subconscious holds all memories except the one or two which may be held for a moment at a time by the conscious. The conscious is constantly sending down for

fresh memories with great speed, as well as sending down fresh memories to be held for it while it turns its attention to a single idea and the few memories with which it is comparing that idea.

Under hypnotic influence the subject often answers questions and talks, but it will always be observed that it only gives our memorized ideas or related memories and that it *never uses reason*. It will accept the most absurd suggestions, and act on them without the slightest evidence of applying an iota of reason or logic to the situation. In this it greatly resembles many of the " spirits " who visit séances and exhibit memory but not reason.

3. The subconscious has no ability to sense the external world except through the conscious mind. Nearly all reports of the five senses are registered only by the conscious mind and filtered down to the subconscious after being identified, and after reason has been applied to those reports to determine what they are and what outside conditions they represent.

To illustrate and prove this point : Even though Science's newest and most loyal child, Behaviourism, denies that any of us can really think, reason or be conscious, I feel all those at the Round Table will find it easy to agree that we *do* think and reason, and that we *are* conscious.

The " thought habits " which Behaviourism sets in place of all conscious activity, are related only to memory, and memory is almost the sole function of the subconscious mind. The truth of this last statement is self-evident if we examine our own consciousness to see how many memories are held in it from moment to moment. True, we can usually recall from the subconscious the memory of what we did three hours ago, but that memory is not present in the conscious mind unless we happen to have called it up and are thinking about it.

We have a good example of this truth in one of the most common experiences of daily life. Husband and wife arise in the morning. The wife puts the bread in the oven to toast. The husband throws coal in the stove and opens all the drafts. They firmly intend to remember to take out the toast and to

turn off the drafts. Now we shall see how long the conscious
mind can retain a memory. As long as the thing to be
remembered is constantly kept in mind, and thought about,
it remains there. If it is not thought about for a single
moment, it falls into the dark void of the subconscious. To
continue our story—but that is not necessary. We all
know the end. Man and wife get to talking about the
startling news in the morning paper. The subconscious
minds are unable to make their reminders heard because
of the excited occupation of the conscious minds. The
toast burns to a crisp and the stove nearly sets fire to the
house.

I think we may safely say that the conscious mind has
almost no ability to remember. Now for more proof that the
subconscious mind has almost no ability to reason   Take
the case of a certain type of insane person : The subconscious mind is *there*, otherwise the bodily functions and
processes would stop. The conscious mind is *not there*
because this type of insane patient has proved not to
be susceptible to hypnosis. It is not susceptible because
the preliminary and necessary state of *attention* cannot be
forced. Here we have a fine opportunity to see what the
real abilities of an isolated subconscious may be. Does the
completely insane person know what is said to him or does
he recognize objects placed before him ? He does not. He
may fumble aimlessly for food, but if there is not some
vestige of the conscious mind left in him, he has to be fed
by hand like a baby. He goes through motions of a reflex
nature—such motions as have, during periods of sanity,
been learned by the conscious mind and given over to the
memory of the subconscious. The patient can walk and can
babble meaningless sentences and verses, but the power of
reason is gone. When confronted by people or by any set of
objects, he does not know what they are. He may finally
become vaguely aware of one and touch it, but without the
conscious mind being present to call from the subconscious
the proper memories to be used to reason out what the object
may be, the subconscious has no way of finding out.

From this data on what the subconscious mind *cannot* do

when left alone I draw the conclusion that everything else done by the normal mental man is done by the conscious mind. All impressions of the five senses have to be noted by the conscious mind alone and given meaning by the lightning-like reasoning process which says in a trice: "I see something round and red. Subconscious mind, give me all the round red memories which fit this object." In a flash the subconscious responds valiantly with round red memories. "Ball?" reasons the conscious. "Too irregular for a ball. Apple? Doesn't smell right or look just right. Ah! Now I have it! It fits this memory of touch, smell and sight perfectly! Listen, Subconscious! I know what it is! It's a tomato! Please remember that we picked up a tomato to-day at about ten o'clock!"

At times we find a derangement in which the contact between certain classes of subconscious memories and the conscious mind has been cut off. A blow on some part of the head may be responsible for this *amnesia*, or some complex in the subconscious may have caused it to refuse to send up certain painful memories which the conscious mind has *only too well* instructed the subconscious to "forget." The conscious mind of the sufferer is still reasonable and fine. The difficulty is that, try as the sufferer may, he cannot remember who he is or where he has come from. His own name is gone and the past is a blank. The poor conscious mind is in terrible difficulties. Then at last the barrier may be broken and memory can come flooding back.

4. The subconscious controls bodily processes such as growth, repair, circulation, etc. It has ability to receive telepathic messages and to read the thoughts and memories of others to some extent—possibly only the thoughts held as memories in the subconscious minds of others. It measures passing time. It receives and acts upon suggestions not contrary to any of its major complexes.

5. The conscious mind *sends out* telepathic messages, but cannot *receive* them except through the subconscious. It *reasons*, but has almost *no* ability to *remember* a thought after it has been put aside for a new one. It constantly draws on the subconscious for memories with which to

enable itself to make comparisons and arrive at reasoned conclusions.

6. The conscious mind registers nearly all reports made through the five senses and passes them on to the subconscious to be acted upon with resultant bodily activity, or to be stored as a memory.

.   .   .   .   .

This data having been gathered and examined, we now pass completely out from under the ægis of Science and into forbidden territory. It is mandatory that we go further in our investigation because none of the normal abilities of the human mind throws the slightest light on such things as fire-magic—to mention but one practice in Magic.

So far we have investigated the reactions of the conscious and subconscious minds which may be produced at will. We now come to the reactions and abilities which cannot be commanded, but which are exhibited now and again as if by accident : I speak of monition and premonition.

If the ability to see at a distance or into the past or future were an ability of the conscious mind, we could use that ability at will. As it is, we have no sensation which tells us from what source these things come. Very naturally the subconscious mind is suspected of sending them up. Under laboratory or test conditions the subconscious cannot display these abilities at the will of the hypnotic operator. It displays them only at rare moments and not when commanded to do so. Therefore we lack all proof that it has such an ability of itself.

Now if premonitions do not come solely from the subconscious and as a display of its abilities, we can only guess that they come from some outside source and *through* the subconscious to the conscious.

If there *is* some outside source, as it certainly seems there must be, our next task is to study the abnormal phenomena of premonition and try to find data to enlighten us as to the identity of this outside source. Whatever it is, it shows greater ability along some lines than does either the conscious or the subconscious.

CASE 21

MONITIONS AND PREMONITIONS

Preliminary Notes :

Science says there are no things such as premonitions and monitions. However, we need little argument here to prove that Science is again wrong. Perhaps no other part of psychic phenomena is so well known to us all. Hardly an individual has missed having a number of monitions or premonitions.

A hypnotized subject sometimes shows a flash of premonition and describes a future event. Monitions are less rare. Monitions and premonitions also come as dreams, or in waking moments. In waking moments this superphysical information arrives in a way that has all the earmarks of the subconscious sending up something which it has received by telepathic means. It could have no other way of getting this type of information ; this *because*, as we have seen, all it knows of the outside world is what it learns through the conscious mind or through telepathy, or through reading the memories in another subconscious mind.

In order that we may have data to examine, I turn again to Richet.

The Case :

From the very many well-authenticated cases given in *Thirty Years of Psychic Research*, I select the following one which was reported to Richet by Dr. Tardieu of the Mont Dore Hospital, France, in 1913.

In 1868 Tardieu left a medical school as a young doctor. At 5 p.m. on a day in the following July he was visiting in the Luxembourg Gardens with a young mathematician named Sonrel. Suddenly Sonrel stopped conversing and began excitedly describing something which was coming to him as an elaborate premonition. He described seeing them both in military uniform ; next, he saw himself mortally ill and due to die in three days ; he saw himself asking Dr. Tardieu to look after his wife and children ; he saw a vast and cruel war ; he saw France victorious.

In August, 1870, two years later, the predicted war broke
out. Both took part in it—their rank and uniforms being
the same as seen in the premonition. Sonrel had married,
and when Dr. Tardieu attended him before his death from
smallpox, he asked him to look after his wife and children.

Comment :

There we have our case. Once more we ask ourselves—
even as I did in the course of my investigations : If the
subconscious mind has to depend entirely on a conscious mind
for all information concerning anything outside the body,
then *where* did this premonition come from ? Could there
possibly be a latent premonitory ability in the conscious
mind ?

The answer to the last question is : Information of this
kind could not come from the conscious mind. If I, who *am*
the conscious mind, and therefore am aware of its every
thought, cannot see at a distance and into the future at
will, then that is not an ability I possess as a conscious
mind.

Now we come to ordinary " mind-reading." This is
primarily an ability we have assigned to the subconscious
and to it alone. It is an ability displayed in hypnosis at
command of the operator. If we find ourselves reading the
thoughts of someone else, as who has not, we can be quite sure
the subconscious is at work and has chosen to send its reading
up to us. But let us have a case to examine lest we overlook
something.

CASE 22

MIND-READING

Preliminary Notes :

In the mind-reading demonstrations of the stage there have
been many genuine and some not genuine. A complicated
set of code words is sometimes used to imitate mind-reading
between the actor on the stage and the one in the audience.
The Scientific Attitude would have us believe that all mind-
reading is justly condemned by Science.

I once undertook to test the possibility of reading the thoughts of others. I chose a study-hall for my laboratory. My method was to fix my eyes on the back of a student's head, quiet my own thoughts, and wait for impressions. I practised thus for ten-minute intervals for several days before I began getting results.

Moments would come when a thought or impression would float into my mind as if I had remembered something. Knowing that these memories had nothing to do with my own past, I accepted them as things coming from the mind I was trying to read. To a few of my closest friends I dared to confess my activities, that I might ask them whether I had read aright. I picked up trifling things for the most part—things being thought of aimlessly when the conscious mind was not actively engaged. I received memory-like impressions of a new dress which was being planned ; of a desire to go skating ; of a young man's bashful love for a girl.

Soon I exhausted my friends, or rather made them wary of my glance and so of no use to my experiment. I concentrated my attention next on a youth who seemed much given to reverie.

At first I read from his thoughts the picture of a strange room, small and dimly lighted and close—but desirable, despite its crude furnishings and bunk beds. Later I got an impression of a little old Chinese who had prominent teeth, but almost no chin. He seemed to be talking with my subject about something I could not get clearly. Later I got the name of the Chinese as " Squirrel." This amused me and made me think I had supplied that descriptive name myself because of the teeth and chin.

Finally came a reading which told me that my subject longed almost continually for that room and the Chinese—longed for something to be had and *tasted*, because of the room and the man " Squirrel."

Having accumulated sufficient data and a sufficient picture of what was heavy on my subject's mind, I took him aside one day, introduced myself and began to question him. I got nothing but the stoutest and most angry denials.

My next step in the rather long experiment happened to
be related to this one of the room and the Chinese, but I did
not realize that it was related when I began it.

In setting myself to read the thoughts of another young
man, I was amazed one day to read in his thoughts the same
longing and the same picture of the room and the Chinese.
However, I read more fear than longing. The fear was at
war with the longing for the peculiar " deep taste " I had
sensed or felt as in my own body. What surprised me most
was the recurrence of the name " Squirrel " in connection
with the same Chinese.

I approached the second student and questioned him. I
told him I had a feeling he was afraid of something, and asked
if this could be so. He paled and said that in a way I was
right. I next began to tell him of the room and the Chinese.
He began to tremble and asked who had " squealed." I
then assured him that I had no information directly. I
explained my mind-reading test and told him how I had
found a startling similarity between his thoughts and those
of one who seemed to be his friend. My subject considered
the matter—still white and shaken—then laughed nervously
and denied everything, even that he was afraid. Also, he
asked me to mind my own business.

It was some months before I got to the bottom of the
matter and learned that what I was convinced I had " read "
was correct. A group of young men had taken to smoking
opium out of curiosity. The Chinese to whose rooms they
were in the habit of going was indeed called " Squirrel."
I had seen his face correctly. The opium-smoking group
had, one by one, contracted the opium habit. The two young
men whose minds I had read so successfully in the study-
room were a part of the group. The first was not afraid ;
he was only desirous of his " smoke." The second was not
only desirous of his " smoke," but was afraid that he had
formed the habit and could not break it.

Comment :

In this case we see that both the conscious mind of the
reader and that of the individual whose mind was being read

had to be in an idle state in which the memories coming up from the subconscious mind came as of their own accord. Unquestionably there was no part played by the conscious mind in the display of this ability, except in so far as it may have directed a slight hypnotic influence to my subconscious and so set it to its task. Years later, while assembling data leading toward Magic, I came to realize what part must have been played by my eyes when I held them on my subjects. Those master magicians, the kahunas, seem to find some aid necessary to help them to establish contact between their consciousness and that of the individual worked on. I have never heard of them using the " evil eye " method which I must have unconsciously imitated, but there is no doubt in my mind that the eyes of the kahunas are penetrating. What they use, however, when at a distance, is the well-known *maunu*, translated " bait." This is a finger-nail, hair or a garment touched with the perspiration of the subject, or in fact anything once a part of the body. With this the kahuna seems to make a contact perhaps analogous to that made by a dog given a scent and set on the trail of a fugitive. Later on we will see what powers or entities the kahunas send along this invisible connecting link, and for what purposes. At present we have much more ground to cover before an approach to the kahunas would result in anything but confusion.

CASE 23

TELEPATHY

Preliminary Notes :

Telepathy is a power we have also assigned to the subconscious mind and seen demonstrated in hypnosis when an operator passes his silent suggestions or visual pictures on to his subject.

As telepathy is an ability of the subconscious and not of the conscious mind, it is easy to see why telepathic experiments get such uncertain and accidental results. Unless one is well trained in handling his subconscious, it is only by

chance that it will exert itself to pick up a telepathic message
and hand it up to the conscious mind.

Telepathic interchance from mind to mind is so common to
human experience that its frequent and unheralded manifestations demand little proof. There is even an old, old
custom among us of locking little fingers and making a wish
when two people start uttering the same words at the same
moment.

Psychologists in universities throughout the world have
investigated this phenomenon. The " willing game " of the
parlour is telepathy, when a good subject is present and his
subconscious will react to thoughts sent him by the waiting
group. Beginning with such things as these, the work of
scientific investigation has continued year after year. In
Leland Stanford Junior University much has been attempted
in the past, but no definite results reported. Similar experiments are being carried on at Duke University and with
slightly more hopeful results. However, until it is fully
realized that the subconscious alone has this ability, nothing
very conclusive can be decided upon.

The Case :

Richet reports many well-conducted experiments in which
telepathy and mind-reading are not clearly differentiated.
People in one room are set to receive thoughts and images
projected to others who are out of their line of vision. Anything received is noted down on paper. Often the experiment
suddenly begins to work fairly well, but the results are
scattered and uncertain as to time.

Many aboriginal peoples have long been experts at
telepathic transfer of thoughts. The Apache Indians in
Arizona have not only had this ability but the ability to see
at a distance. They were made most dangerous enemies in
the early days because troop movements of their adversaries
were instantly known to them.

In Tahiti there is a lesser kahuna class similar to the
kelo-kelo in Hawaii. The duty of these lesser magicians is to
operate what is called by whites, " the coco-nut radio." All
around the island on which Papeete is located, there live

individuals (many of them wise old women) belonging to this radio chain. Let me state in passing that women make as expert kahunas as men.

Many have been the tests made of this " coco-nut radio." A person leaves Papeete for a trip around the island. No physical means is used to send messages—no smoke signals or drummings ; but the traveller's arrival is always anticipated and preparations made to receive him. Any important news is also made known immediately by the same mysterious use of telepathic powers.

My own experiments in trying out telepathy have been none too successful and the results very uncertain. My one really good demonstration was made when working with a Californian friend while I was first in Duluth and later in Denver. One day, while in Denver, I was idly day-dreaming when I caught a flash which informed me that my friend— a mining engineer—had wired me to join him. I rushed out and wired at once that I was beginning to pack. Our messages crossed in transit. His told me that he had decided to open a mine and that he wanted me to come to him at once. He offered to teach me assaying and give me pleasanter employment than I had at the moment. As I had never been connected with mines in any way, the invitation was of such a nature as to preclude guessing or coincidence.

Comment :

Again we see the relaxed state of the conscious mind in which the subconscious is able to send up the message it has received. We can still safely say that the *conscious mind* of itself has *no* ability as a mind-reader or as a telepathic receiver. On the other hand, it would seem that the conscious mind is the sender of telepathic messages.

This is of considerable importance to our study. We are looking for some outside source of monition and premonition. We see that these things come in the form of thought-pictures. This demands that they be sent out by some form of consciousness similar to that of a human mind. The subconscious is best studied while under hypnotic influence.

In this state it has never demonstrated an ability to send thought-pictures which could be picked up telepathically. In mind-reading by professionals the " reader " always has to *speak* to the operator on the stage to tell what he reads from minds in the audience. The possibility that in telepathy one subconscious mind is reading the memories of another at a distance, is discounted by the fact that in hypnosis memories in the operator's subconscious are not " read " or received, but only the mental command or visualized object sent out by an effort of will by the conscious mind. The conscious mind alone is able to project hypnotic force to a subject, and with it images and silent commands. This gives us definite proof that the conscious mind is best suited to project any telepathic message.

Now, if these arguments are properly *grounded on facts* we can come to only one conclusion concerning the source of monitory and premonitory information. There is some *outside* source superior to the conscious mind in *ability to observe*—one which can project its messages to our subconscious minds. As the conscious mind is *aware* of all its activities and knows that it does not receive those messages in a way that makes it possible to know their source, we must conclude that the *subconscious mind* acts as the receiver and sends up the messages to the conscious. As this can be done only when the conscious mind is in a *receptive or relaxed state*, and only when it is allowing a play of uncontrolled memories to enter it, we must also conclude that we have here the reason why the reception of telepathic communications is so uncertain. In other words, the more the *attention* of the conscious mind is fixed on getting such messages, the less it is relaxed and thus capable of receiving them as they are relayed from the subconscious.

Let us use a mathematical symbol to represent, for the present, the unidentified consciousness sending monitory or premonitory messages to us at rare intervals. Let us call it " X " in our equation.

Our next material for inspection comes from premonitory information which seems to be received by the conscious mind with the aid of a gazing crystal. Let us examine data to get further proof of monition and premonition and at the same time to see if the facts fit with our conclusions.

CASE 24

CRYSTAL GAZING

Preliminary Notes :

In crystal gazing we find nothing more nor less than a mechanical device which helps an individual to relax his conscious mind so that it may receive messages. As a rule, a sphere of crystal or glass is the mechanical aid used.

The Case :

I once came upon a book on crystal gazing while in Lovelock, Nevada. Improvising a crystal from a glass paperweight which had a round, magnifying top, I set to work. The book instructed one to become " receptive and expectant " as one gazed steadily into the shining surface of the crystal. With practice one was supposed to be able to observe a clouding in the crystal, followed by a clearing, which would reveal a small moving picture of distant places or future events.

My practice yielded me no results, and after a few weeks I gave up. A little later I became acquainted with a lady reputed to be " naturally psychic." Urging her to try the crystal, I gave her the book and the paper-weight with its backing of black velvet. In a few days she had become proficient in the art.

Among dozens of demonstrations of her ability, the following will serve our present purposes :

Monitions.—She described distant friends of mine and told what they were doing at certain hours. Checking by letter I found she had seen correctly at distances up to a thousand miles. The times tallied with the activities. A strange feature of the experiment was that when anyone went underground she could no longer see them in the crystal. On one occasion she described perfectly a photographer friend of mine in Utah. He sat outside a mine reading a small book. His camera-case was at his feet. He rose and went into the mine, thus being lost to sight. Later on, after I had gone to Virginia City, Nevada, I received daily letters from this psychic telling me what I had done at certain hours in preceding days. At one time I went down into a mine. She saw me up to the moment when I descended in the cage.

Premonitions.—She described seeing me enter the town of Mason, Nevada, although neither of us had been there. She also described my entrance into the hotel in which I was afterward to live. In this town she saw me photographing Indians who were arriving in droves and encamping outside the town. She also described me as I photographed a baby and conversed with a comely matron with red hair. All these premonitions " came true " before the month was out. She also described the next town I visited after leaving Mason. This was Yerrington, Nevada, and she saw accurately the one long street and the lodging house in which I was to live. The keeper of the lodging house was described exactly as I later found her to be, even to a slight defect in vision. As a matter of fact, the first thing I did when, some weeks later, I recognized Yerrington as fitting former descriptions was to look for the lodging house sign which had been described in detail as " a globe painted on a square glass box." I found the sign and was met by the woman as soon as I entered the office.

Comment :

The data derived from this case fits perfectly into the conclusions we have reached. The lady sat down and relaxed her attention—gazing dreamily into the crystal and holding a mental command over her mind to pick up the sight of things at a distance, or in past or future. She picked up very little of the past, and had no control over the time of seeing or of the type of things she saw—they came when they would and their coming could not be forced. It seemed that she was being shown scenes by some external intelligence which chose the time of showing, and also the scene, as it saw fit.

·   ·   ·   ·   ·

MAX FREEDOM LONG
Sketched in Honolulu in 1930 by Samuel Levin.

In my study in Hawaii I examined with the greatest care all data I could find concerning the crystal gazings of the kahunas. Not all of these fascinating individuals use a crystal, but only certain weaker classes of them. The crystal of the kahuna is a smooth black stone picked up at some time on a beach and placed in a calabash bowl. Water is poured into the bowl and swished from time to time over the stone to give it a shining surface in which to gaze. The results of crystal gazing among the kahunas are not so uncertain as they are in the West. Usually the kahuna sees immediately what he desires to see. The more powerful kahunas do not depend on "crystals." They see as mediums sometimes see —directly or clairvoyantly. There is one of the lower classes of magicians called the kahuna *kanaka* or "man" kahuna. He works the simpler magic, seemingly with little knowledge of just how he gets his results. He does as his father taught him to do, and that is all. Now this type of kahuna, as well as some similar types has, in common with all kahunas, a frequent need of knowing what is not visible to the eye. When a lesser kahuna cannot "see" for himself, he hires from a third class of near-kahunas one called a *makaula*, or "eyes." The work of a *makaula* is to exercise a rather uncertain monitory or premonitory ability, as well as to read for the kahuna what is in the "inside" of a patient.

There are two other ways in which information is sometimes obtained by some classes of kahunas. One is through dreams—a matter we will take up very soon—and the other through the help of seemingly superhuman denizens of the spirit world.

I say "superhuman" denizens only to get my thought across to Round Table members. What I mean is some type of spirit showing a degree of ability above that of either the subconscious or conscious mind—a monitory and premonitory ability. This spirit type is similar to the one found giving like superphysical information at séances. It checks at this time with the "X" of our equation in that it has abilities not resident in conscious or subconscious parts of mind. We will search for more and more proof that this source of monitory and premonitory information *is* our

" X " and is a part of the secret of secrets of the kahunas. At present we will gather data concerning its activities in the West and in Polynesia. Later this data will help us when we have gathered much more data—the total of which will give us the answer to our " X."

.   .   .   .   .

I have spoken of spirits bringing premonitory information. This is a thing which occurs in the West very frequently. In our source book given us by Richet, many cases of this type are recorded and authenticated to the point of proving the phenomenon. I will draw on Richet and then on Polynesia to give us a new case.

CASE 25

MONITORY AND PREMONITORY INFORMATION GIVEN THROUGH GHOSTS

Preliminary Notes :

The ghosts of this case will be of both the visible and invisible kinds. They will also be human, above human and hardly human.

The Case :

1. Richet as a source :

On page 254 we find a report telling of a man who had just been visiting a friend who was only slightly indisposed. The visitor was at home with his wife when suddenly he saw an " apparition " of his friend. Jumping to the conclusion that this indicated his sudden and unexpected death, the man noted the time. Later checking proved that the friend had died at that minute.

C. Flammarion is quoted as saying that the chance of coincidence or guessing in this case is reduced to one chance in eight million. Others calculate the chance as one in seven hundred thousand.

2. Richet finds that nearly all such " cryptesthesia " is subjective. His proof is that while one person may see a

" ghost " and know of a distant accident or death, others in the same group may see nothing. This conclusion agrees with ours that the subconscious mind is involved in all such matters unless the ghost is actually one visible to human eyes and so to a camera—perhaps an ectoplasmic ghost.

On page 258, Myers is quoted as giving the opinion that a subconsciously received message of a monitory nature may be kept in the subconscious and not sent up until such time as the conscious mind is momentarily relaxed and unengaged.

On page 273 is the report of a Mrs. Paget who saw the ghost of a brother who was a sailor. He appeared as if entirely real in his wet oilskin and cap. She said : " Miles, where have you come from ? " She recognized the familiar voice as he exclaimed : " For the love of God do not say that I am *here !* " Instantly he vanished. A later check disclosed the following facts : The brother had nearly drowned in Melbourne. He had been revived after being unconscious for some time. His appearance in his sister's kitchen in Europe came some ten hours after his unconsciousness.

In this case we see a visual as well as an auditory message, received by the subconscious and kept for ten hours before it was sent up to the conscious.

3. Leaving Richet and turning to Polynesia, we come to a permanent but invisible ghost living in Samoa and giving both monitory and premonitory information through a period of years.

Most of the Polynesians are naturally better able to see ghosts and spirits than are we of the West. It is no uncommon thing for them to note that the ghost of a dead relative has come into the house. Often these hold conversations with the living members of the family, and nothing is thought at all odd or unusual in the procedure. " Grandma came to call," and that is all there is to it. That the whites scoff at this matter is no proof to those who see her that " Grandma " could not or did not call. The wiser ghosts often come to give warning of some coming event, and seem to have the mysterious premonitory ability at times. The less wise ghosts are often notably unreliable in their predictions.

Often the ghosts are not related to the family at all. One very interesting ghost was described to me by an old friend of many years' standing. She was a Samoan princess residing in Honolulu. From her I gathered much data concerning kahunas in that land. The particular ghost to which I allude was one called "Tivitivi." He was not a human ghost in the eyes of the natives, but a ghost of a higher order. He could talk and whistle, but was never visible.

As a small girl, this lady had loved to wait in the dusk at the edge of the village with other youngsters. They would almost hold their breaths as the sun dropped from sight, and invariably they would hear a merry whistling coming nearer and nearer, although the whistling Tivitivi could not be seen. He would often pass right through the group of waiting children as he made his way toward a special house which was set aside for his use and in which food, drink and flowers of the best were always waiting.

In return for the worshipful favours of the people, the kindly Tivitivi often spoke to the little girl's father as he waited respectfully in the dusk by the door of the house. Warnings came echoing out from the room—warnings of coming storms or attacks from other tribes. Sage counsel was frequently given touching on the various affairs of the people.

The food seemed never touched by the ghost, but it was considered unfit for human use after he had supposedly drawn from it the ghostly essence of nourishment, and so was never eaten by those who carried it away each morning to make room for fresh food and drink.

4. I now offer data concerning a happening which I have checked and found reliable.

In this case we have a ghost appearing, and brown people deriving monitory information from the bare fact of such an appearance.

A few years ago, in Tahiti, a number of native women were sitting outside a house enjoying the coolness of early twilight. They were chatting merrily when one of them gave a cry of surprised delight and pointed to the side gate of the big garden.

There, coming toward them and dressed as he always dressed when at his home in the islands, was a white man whom they all loved, but who was known to be in California. Excited greetings were shouted as the women rose. " How did you come home when there was no ship ? " they called.

But the old friend deported himself strangely. He did not appear to hear or notice the women. A hush fell over the group as he veered off along a side path and went striding past them without so much as turning his head.

When he had disappeared around the house a wail went up. " It is not our friend ! It is his ghost ! He is dead ! "

A moment later, as checked for time, a beloved servant of the white man saw him come toward his house on an island some twelve miles distant. With a cry of welcome the servant rushed through the garden toward his master, only to have him turn aside and walk rapidly to the water's edge and away across the waves into the gathering dusk.

Early the next day came a cablegram announcing the death of the man in California. A check on the time of death proved that the ghost had appeared across those many miles only a few moments after the death of the body.

5. Back to America now : A friend of mine reported only recently an experience shared by a mother and daughter. The sweetheart of the daughter was arriving by plane and was expected for dinner. At the time set for his arrival the doorbell was rung. The daughter ran to greet her lover, but found no one in sight. She went to tell her mother of the odd experience. The bell rang a second time. Both women rushed to the door. Again there was no one to be seen. They waited just inside the closed door to catch the culprit the next time the bell was rung. It rang long and loud after another moment. They flung the door open and still no one was to be seen. Soon after that there came a telephone message saying the plane had crashed in landing and that the young man had been killed.

The sequel to this story came in the form of an automatic handwriting message which told how the victim of the accident had failed to realize that he was dead and had hurried on to fulfil his engagement. He had rung the bell and had been surprised when he could not make his presence felt. Only after all his endeavours had proved futile did he begin to suspect that death had overtaken him. It became harder each time for him to make the bell ring. At last a dead relative had come to take him in charge.

Comment :

Here we have both visible and invisible ghosts which we can account for as entities perhaps clothed in something of an ectoplasmic nature. That the bell was rung seems to indicate that the ghostly young lover had brought ectoplasm with him from his own body, but that this ectoplasm was not visible to the two women. It was late evening and the porch was lighted.

In spiritualistic séances the " spirits " often materialize only a hand, but they play instruments and do other things with seemingly no materialization at all. Turning to the kahunas for an explanation of this matter we run into their *cult of secrecy* at once and are unable to get much definite information. However, going over the heads of the kahunas and to India—which borders on their old homeland—we come at once upon a possible explanation. We hear that each of us has seven bodies ranging in denseness and visibility from the physical to the very tenuous " etheric." Even here we run into some confusion, as not all of the bodies seem to be bodies ; some are called " bodies " and some " vehicles." Madam Blavatsky is our source for this theory from India. In instructing the Theosophical Society, which she was instrumental in founding, she does not make the matter of bodies and vehicles very clear. Fortunately, our study will begin to bear first fruit very shortly, and when I have laid some further data before the Round Table I will be able to make myself understood as I draw from data a clearer explanation of ghostly bodies and vehicles.

Having referred so often to automatic handwriting messages, it seems well to examine this mechanical aid to monition and premonition before going on to dreams.

CASE 26

AUTOMATIC HANDWRITING

Preliminary Notes :

Here we again find the subconscious active in its own field, and the " X " also active at uncertain intervals in giving monitory and premonitory information.

The "Ouija Board" is an instrument with which we are all familiar. We are also familiar with the type of misinformation usually obtained through its use.

Automatic handwriting resembles the Ouija board in the results obtained through it, although there is the advantage that the handwriting itself may be compared with that of the dead person signing the message.

In doing automatic handwriting, the operator usually finds the gift one which takes a little practice to develop. The conscious mind simply assumes a negative and expectant attitude. The expectation may be of the nature of a hypnotic command to the subconscious.

Where messages cannot be traced to the subconscious and its memories, the logical conclusion must be either " spirit " intervention or the intervention of the quality "X," or both. As spirits have very satisfactorily proven their existence in the West, and as the kahunas handle them like trained animals, it would seem safe to credit them with at least some of the messages they claim to give.

Now for the case.

The Case :

1. Amusingly enough, the two best automatic handwriting experts I happen to know are perhaps the two most sceptical women in my list of acquaintances. Nevertheless, these ladies can sit down before a tablet of paper, one holding the pencil while the other touches the actual writing hand with her fingers, and begin almost at once to write automatically with great rapidity—the handwriting not resembling that of either lady. The messages appear to come from a very prudent and reasoning spirit who signs himself " Rusty."

I can certify that neither of these ladies consciously directs or causes the writing.

Often this Rusty will attempt to tell what is going on at a distance, but never will he make more than a logical guess as to the future, saying that he is no more able now to look into the future than he was in his life upon the earth. He tells who he is and where he formerly lived, but the names and addresses of people given in answer to a request that he make checking possible, seem not to be real names and addresses. All letters sent out come back.

Very naturally, I have endeavoured in the past to get aid through this Rusty in my task of learning the kahuna secret of secrets. Very obligingly he consented to find a kahuna spirit. One came one night and gave his message in the handwriting of one hardly able to write, and who used broken English, typical of the old-time Hawaiian (quite unfamiliar to both of the ladies but entirely familiar to me). He claimed to have been a friend of Dr. Brigham, and wrote that he had been a kahuna of the *anaana* class—the class dreaded because its members not only heal, but kill with Magic.

In answer to a question as to how this Magic is performed, the old kahuna spirit explained that one got to be a magician by thinking " good, good, good," until such time as a very strong light seemed to appear " inside." Thereafter one became a most powerful kahuna. I asked how one could remain " good " and still use magic to kill. The hurt reply was that killing was not at all bad if it was deserved, or if the victim would be better off and happier as a spirit.

When questioned concerning the mechanism of magic, a reply was given which seemed to be considered entirely complete by the spirit-writer. It was that one got *mana* of various sorts out of water, air, fire and the like, and used it to " help people or to make them be good."

He informed us complacently that he had a " very good place " where he now lived, and ventured the information that he was soon to return to Hawaii because he would be needed there to teach.

In answer to questions about Dr. Brigham's state after death, he said that the kindly doctor had gone "into the long sleep."

As any of the statements made in the kahuna spirit's message could possibly have come from the reading of memories held at that time in my own subconscious mind, and as we have seen the ordinary results of automatic handwriting, I will now come to a case in which monition was displayed as well as premonition.

2. As I have said : The world over, friends gathering for an evening's visit will turn often to the discussion of things not accepted by Science. How often do we all hear someone afflicted with the Scientific Attitude complex speak reluctantly and begin with : "Now, you may think I am crazy, but such and such a thing actually happened right in my own family."

On one such occasion one of my closest friends, upon whose word I can rely completely, began a recital in just the words given above. His story had been written by him and published in article form in a metaphysical magazine some years earlier. It had to do with messages received through automatic handwriting—some of which he still has in his possession.

A playmate of my friend had died when they were both quite young. The bereaved mother had moved away. Soon a letter came from her saying she had felt impelled to write one day while in her kitchen and had found, when she took a pencil in her hand, that something seemed to seize her whole arm and write with it. The message—it was on a piece of wrapping paper—was a letter written through her by her dead son and addressed to the playmate he had left behind. In this message he told of the surprising change called "death" which had come to him ; how his grandparents were now taking care of him ; and how the pet rabbit, whose death the two boys had mourned, had not really died, but was in his new home with him. The childish handwriting was unmistakably that of the dead playmate.

The mother, a very religious woman, was frightened by what was happening, but continued to allow her arm to be used. Many similar messages were received and mailed on. Some of them were addressed to the mother of the living boy instead of her son. These letters came from various ones of her dead relatives, these being entirely unknown to the woman who took down the messages. The handwriting in in all these letters compared exactly with letters written in life and preserved. Those from the grandfather were written in the same odd hand he had used in his diary, and worded in the same fine style which that educated gentleman had used—this, notwithstanding the fact that the woman whose arm was used was poorly educated.

At last a letter came from the boy saying it was becoming " harder and harder " to get the letters through—but that anyway, " mother will soon be here." The prediction later proved to be correct.

Comment :

The subconscious has been taught to write by the conscious mind and has a memory filled with things to write and also a set of muscular reflexes. But it never shows ability to write when not directed by the conscious mind. Therefore, we must conclude that the conscious mind of the medium is replaced by something similar to it which takes over the subconscious mind and the arm in order to write through them. Any of these writing spirits may be placed by applying our classification test to their abilities, memory or reason.

Our data in past cases gives no indication that a spirit subconscious may replace a living subconscious in a body, but this possibility will later have to be considered if all data is to match the facts. At present, however, we have still to investigate the activities of the subconscious mind during " sleep "—a normal state in which the conscious mind ceases to register external impressions.

·   ·   ·   ·   ·

We have data on mediums using clairvoyant ability to get messages from spirits. (Case of the medium and the kahuna spirits who located the original of the photograph.) In this case there is no indication that the subconscious was involved, but other cases have led us to conclude that it must have received the message and passed it up visually and audibly to the conscious mind of the medium.

Where no spirits seem to be present to give this monitory or other premonitory information, we postulate our " X." Psychology answers that the subconscious is the " X " and that it has an ability greater than the conscious mind working with its tools, the five senses, to contact external conditions.

The usual basis of proof of this claim made by Psychology is found in dreams and what is seen in them. As Psychology is none too safe a guide because of its tendency to conform to the dogma of " nothing not physical," we will do well to examine dreams for ourselves and see what additional data we can find.

CASE 27

WHAT PART OF THE CONSCIOUSNESS IS INVOLVED IN DREAMS?

Preliminary Notes :

A glance at *Webster's International Dictionary* will show the source from which I draw the psychologist's definition of dreams in order that we may have the proper reflection of the Scientific Attitude where this phenomenon is concerned.

A dream is defined as a train of thoughts coming during sleep, and which may be accompanied by emotions or the seeing of apparently real scenes or events. It is pointed out that dreams may be garbled reproductions of memories— often old and new combined. They are said to be sometimes logical in their sequence of events, and sometimes illogical. No mention is made of premonitory dreams—as might be expected—but there is mention made of the fact that some dreams show a definite process of reasoning.

To this definition, which I have reconstructed to avoid copyright infringement, we have but to add our " X " and we then have evidence of the activities of the subconscious, the conscious and the " X " working either together or separately in dreams.

The seeming reality of dreams gives us the hint that the subconscious is accepting its own or other memories or thoughts as realities, even as it does in hypnosis when pictures are projected to it by the operator and mistaken for realities.

Where reason occurs in dreams we are forced to conclude that the *conscious mind* has had the *tables turned* on it by the subconscious and that it is *forced* to " see " what the subconscious draws up from its memories and itself sees *as realities*. As the conscious mind is thus seen to be involved in the seeing, *its reason* controls the action in the dream.

Another possibility is that the conscious and subconscious do not go to sleep, but only the body and the five sense organs. If the thinking and remembering parts of mind are awake and at work, logical conclusions can be reached in dreams and held as memories to be examined when the whole body awakens. This would explain how problems are solved in sleep—a thing all of us have experienced for ourselves.

Everything is clear to us and to psychologists until we come to monitory and premonitory dreams. Here we must go on alone because we have decided that *neither* the conscious nor subconscious has monitory or premonitory ability.

Visiting and informative spirits who come to us in dreams might serve always as an explanation were it not for the fact that our data seem to prove that the subconscious has a considerable ability to sense or see spirits. This is made evident by the fact that one person sees a ghost while his companion does not. Both individuals have eyes. Must we follow the argument farther? If a spirit came to give premonitory information in a dream, we should have frequent reports that such a spirit had been *seen* in dreams. The fact is, that most of our premonitory dreams seem to come of their own accord and without a spirit in attendance.

Another very significant fact is that the standard premonitory dream seems always to come in the form of a complete moving picture of the future event—this in all cases except those in which we dream that we are reading of the event or that someone is telling us of it.

Now, as remembering into the future is impossible, and as the conscious mind has no way to sense anything except through the five senses, or by drawing up memories and reasoning forward in order to guess the future, we have two possible conclusions open to us. The first of these is that the conscious mind can *imagine* some future event (after a *guess*) and that the subconscious takes this imagination and uses memories to make it seem a living reality in a dream. This theory does not hold water, however, when we consider the *people* in many premonitory dreams—the people we have not yet met and of whom we can have no memory. Our second conclusion is : " X " again in some form—an " X " that *does not show the use of logic or reason,* but which presents all premonitory information *in the form of a picture* brought to life and containing unknown places and people.

The only premonitory information *not* coming as a complete picture is the type received when wide awake. This type falls into a class in which there seems to be a " spirit " acting as intermediary between " X " and the medium, or other clairvoyant individual. In Richet we find a mass of data which, on close inspection, seems to show that where the dream premonition was not received as a *picture,* it was always received in a way suggesting that someone or something had seen the original picture and had described it in words or by a telepathic transference of thought images to the subconscious of the " seer."

I have had many premonitory dreams, and I have never had one which was not in complete picture form and unaccompanied by any evidence of reason. My ordinary dreams are of but two kinds : I dream that I am seeing a real scene, or I dream that I am *thinking.* I never feel that I am getting outside and unpictured thoughts from some unseen source.

After these many preliminary notes we are now ready for the case proper. I have offered my conclusions here instead of saving them for the " comment "—this to enable members of the Round Table to know beforehand the direction in which the investigation moves.

The Case :

As it would take much time to give a detailed account of my many experiments with my own dreams—made over a period of months—I will simply list my findings and the data to be derived from them.

During my long study of the kahunas I took time to carry on extensive experiments with my own dreams in an effort to get more enlightening data on the " X " of the kahuna secret or secrets. I will tell in this case only of those dreams which were not of the premonitory type.

Like many others, I had observed that there were times when I could hold the *waking* consciousness to some extent even in sleep and so *know that a dream was only a dream.* Deciding that I could watch my subconscious at work if I could develop this ability to hold the dual consciousness for long periods, I set to work.

With practice and the aid of a small electrical device which would awaken me many times at irregular intervals during the night, I soon was able to make extensive observations of my dreams. I acquired the following data :

1. I was never awakened at any time that I was not in the midst of a dream. I concluded that I dreamed continually when asleep and that I was unaware of my continual dreaming only because I could not remember *all* my dreams upon waking.

2. I learned that it was possible to keep awake, *as a conscious entity*, and observe dreams in all their apparent reality *without* mistaking scenes and people for physical realities.

3. I learned that I could take a *conscious* part in my dreams. I could imagine a scene and have it accepted as *real* by the subconscious ; this resulting in the imaginary scene appearing as if *real* before me in the dream I was observing. In this way I could force my subconscious to dream to order. I would give it the scene and the characters, and it would instantly make them real before me and carry

the characters through a series of scenes. This series was often, in a short time, mixed with old memories or made absurd by want of reasoning judgment. My subconscious was utterly unaware of the absurdity of the acts it caused my characters to perform. Never once did I find any dream which was going forward as if guided by reasoning judgment unless I was so guiding it.

4. I learned that I could force myself to walk through what seemed to me to be solid walls. I could do this by assuring myself that the wall was only a dream wall and that I would not bump my nose as I walked into it. I also learned to take chairs and similar objects—even people and animals and houses—and lift them into the dream air, making them remain there suspended.

5. I found that the subconscious was directable in exactly the same way as in hypnosis. I could give it the pictured image of a great symphony orchestra, and it would furnish from its perfect memory every phase and stanza of almost any piece of music I had ever heard played. Of course I had always to be on the watch for the many illogical changes which the subconscious continually tried to make in such dreams. Any event or occurrence might react on the subconscious as an " association of ideas " and so switch it automatically from one train of images to another—from symphony music to thunder and storm. Then I would have to stop the change by sending out the original picture once more.

.   .   .   .   .

Later on, I accidentally made still another discovery about dreams. One day while practising meditation and while my mind was unoccupied and receptive, I noticed what I soon identified as a dream coming up from my subconscious. Following this discovery with more experiments, I learned that my subconscious dreamed by day as well as by night.

This new series of experiments gave me the following data :

1. I dream by day as well as by night, but cannot know to a certainty whether I dream during the times when my conscious mind is busily engaged or not. I could observe my

dreams by day only when I relaxed and became receptive. At such times I held the dual consciousness and the dreams were a little less real than at night ; this, because more of the conscious element was present.

2. I found that a dream could be broken into by an activity of my conscious mind, *but* that dream invariably had progressed or had changed entirely when I relaxed and looked for it again. In such progressions I often found that a minute or so of waking time was sufficient for an hour of dream progression. One instance : I found that I was dreaming in the day-time of constructing a cabinet for a phonograph. I roused from the relaxed state several times in the course of a half-hour, and each time I relaxed and observed my dream I found that I had made remarkable dream progress. I planed, sanded and cut many boards. By the end of the half-hour I had finished and varnished, not a phonograph cabinet, but, illogically enough, a very fine studio camera and stand which sprayed water to make a pretty fountain, and at the same time played some unfamiliar music which I could hear but faintly.

Comment :

While I may be wrong, I have concluded that, because I found that I dreamed night and day, possibly without a break, all other people must do likewise.

Thus I discovered that it is possible for anyone to get a premonitory dream, day or night, and it follows that such a dream might be sent up into the conscious mind as a vivid picture or in the form of the dream itself, and so give the monitions or premonitions which come in waking hours.

I wish now to mention something which I consider very important. In the records of hypnotic experiments can be found cases in which the subject was hypnotized (and so cut off from his conscious mind), then set to work observing his dreams and describing them as they came. No effort of the operator was made to send a thought or image to the subject. In such experiments many premonitory dreams have been described by the subjects.

On page 356 of his book, Richet notes three classes of

premonitions : those coming to a hypnotized individual and seen as a dream ; those supposed to come through the aid (or meditation as we have postulated) of a spirit ; and those coming to individuals in the normal waking state.

Hypnotized subjects have furnished Richet with a large number of cases to record and study. Here is but one. It will serve as a typical example of the many. A subject dreamed of a woman she had never seen before, but who came to her weeping and who carried a dead child in her arms. Six weeks later the subject was confined and lost her child. I take it that the strange woman must have been the nurse seen in the premonitory dream. And so the cases run—page after page.

. . . . .

Having consulted Richet, we can now feel that we have overlooked no class of monition or premonition, and so can go on to their most usual source : dreams of the normal kind.

In passing I may say that I am inclined to think the reason my experiment in the dual consciousness state gave me no premonitory dreams was that I was constantly in control of my subconscious mind and so prevented it from getting a premonitory dream from our " X."

CASE 28

THE PREMONITORY DREAM IN NORMAL SLEEP

Preliminary Notes :
    None.

The Case :
    My father had the natural " gift " of being able to see, in his dreams, many things which were yet to come. At one period in his life these dreams came with great frequency and regularity. As a child I often heard him tell my mother of his dreams over the breakfast table. I also heard the excited comments they made when the dreams " came

true." One night my father fell into a light sleep and saw in a dream our village hotel crowded with people who had been brought in after a disastrous train wreck. An engineer, notably sober, had become intoxicated and run a " helper-engine " down the hill, off schedule, crashing into a passenger train. Many were killed. Father awoke from his dream, dressed hurriedly and went to the station-master. The station-master was sceptical. While they were discussing the dream, the news of the wreck was flashed in by telegraph.

At another time my father saw, in a dream, an old man, dead and frozen stiff, lying in a strange room. He went the next day to the village store and related his dream. His description of the old man fitted a pioneer by the name of Regan. The son became worried and begged my father to drive ten snowy miles with him to a ranch to see if the old man had really died. Upon their arrival at the ranch, the frozen body of the man was found, just as my father had seen it in his dream.

In another dream he saw a barren set of sage-covered hills turn into a busy railroad town. He saw a coal mine and then an oil derrick. The town faded, leaving only foundations and a railroad station. The oil derricks increased on the hills about the neighbourhood. They also faded, and the hills became bare and covered again only with sage brush. Two years later he recognized the scene of his dream in the new town of Spring Valley, Wyoming. The coal mine was opened and operated. About a year later, oil was struck near the town ; but the oil sands became clogged with paraffin and the wells were abandoned, the derricks being removed. Soon the mine was found too dangerous to work ; it was closed and the houses torn down and taken away, leaving only the station. Still later, another attempt was made to get the oil. Many wells were bored and again given up as useless after a short period of production. Sage brush again covered the hills.

Comment :

In recent years, many investigators have attempted to solve the problem of premonitory dreams. As most of them

were partly hampered by a complexed belief in the materialistic dogmas of Science, they arrived at quaint conclusions.
Such investigators were faced by but two possible courses :
(1) To admit the existence of a supernatural (or superphysical) mechanism which enables one to dream of events
not yet transpired ; (2) To conclude that our idea of *time*
is wrong.

A famous example of an investigator who accepted the
second course is found in the Englishman, Dr. Dunn. He
must have been quite complexed in his belief in the dogma,
"nothing not physical." At any rate, he assembled many
data by keeping a record of his dreams for fifteen years.
Some of those dreams came true years after he had written
them down, while others came true in a few days or weeks.

Having assembled proof of monition and premonition in
dreams, Dr. Dunn then evolved a theory which, like most
theories, was based on a false premise, and so could be made
to sound logical only by a play on words. His dream data
seemed to him proof positive that the *past, present* and
future of *time were all one* and that they are *here with us* at
every moment of the *present.* (This may possibly be a
superphysical fact, but never a physical fact.) As he knew
that he could not eat yesterday's or to-morrow's meal
to-day, he turned to mathematical graphs for assistance.
Drawing a cube on paper, he indicated the three dimensions
known to Science. This done, he moved the entire cube in
several directions and proclaimed that he had moved it in
several *new dimensions* similar to the fabled "fourth
dimension."

Naturally these "mathematical" demonstrations were
not acceptable to Science or to logical reason ; but they
looked well and went into his book, *An Experiment with
Time.* To back up his graphs, he drew comparisons which
sound quite plausible to most laymen, but which were not at
all logical. He compared time to a river and the individual
to a man floating on that river in a canoe. The upper part
of the river he compared to the *future* and the lower part to
the *past.* He said that because there are bends in the river,
the man in the canoe cannot see the upper and lower reaches

of it—the *past* and *future ;* he can only see the little section of the river upon which he floats—the *present.*

The argument was then given that *all* of the river—the past, present and future—exists ; that all of it can be seen by a man in an aeroplane, even if the man in the canoe cannot see it. Here the analogy is made to become proof (an impossible feat) of the theory that time and distance are *identical.* The reader is given the suggestion that, as the river is always there in its full length at any moment of time, the past, present and future of time itself must *always* be *contained* in the present moment. But we can see that the river lies in linear space, while the past, present and future lie in time measured by a clock and not by a yard stick. In this lies the negation of the theory. If this analogy were to be accepted as a proof, we could, in the same way, prove that a clock is a yard-stick—which is preposterous.

A similar effort to confuse time with space and make stock of the fourth dimension as a *physical* possibility, is to be found in Ouspensky's book, *Tertiam Organum.*

I have accused Science of making no protest when illogical theories were advanced to uphold its sacred dogma. As if with evil intent, Science seems to desire to put palpably idiotic ideas into the hands of the layman via the Scientific Attitude—this in order that the layman may make a blind assault on anything threatening the dogma. As proof of my accusation, I quote now from the *Encyclopædia Britannica,* 14th edition, heading, " Psychical Research " ; sub-heading, " Precognition." Note the impression left after a casual reading : the impression that, while not proven, the theory advanced by Dr. Dunn (or that of telepathy) is not entirely condemned by Science as represented in our authoritative publications. I quote :

> " Precognition, if it is a genuine phenomenon, does not fit very easily into any theoretic scheme based on the more generally accepted phenomena, such as telepathy. Some people, however, seem to find modern ideas as to a ' space-time complex ' of assistance in enabling them to accept precognition. Dunn's *An Experiment with Time* is interesting on the theoretical side. . . ."

"CITY OF REFUGE." TEMPLE IN KONA, HAWAII (RESTORED)

Dr. Dunn's method of obtaining precognitive data from dreams, however, is a very valuable one, and we have to thank him for that even if we do not accept his theory of time. He has reported very valuable data, not the least part of which is the following : With practice he became able even to get premonitory information concerning the contents of a book before reading it. Sitting with mind receptive, and a book in his hands, he occasionally got such premonitory information. From this data I am inclined to conclude afresh that there was a premonitory dream going on in his subconscious mind, which was sent up to his conscious mind.

We have from Dr. Dunn the first description of a mechanical way of getting premonitions almost at will. The mechanism seems to be that of an expectant attitude or held both by the conscious and subconscious minds, at one and the same time—either while asleep or awake.

Let me present data taken from experiments which I made to check on the practicability of Dr. Dunn's method.

CASE 29

GETTING PREMONITIONS THROUGH DREAMS BY USING DR. DUNN'S METHOD

Preliminary Notes :

The method advised by Dr. Dunn is this : One determines to awake from sleep as often as possible and write down his dreams so that they will not be forgotten. These written records are saved and are checked from time to time to see if any of the dreams were premonitory. A warning is given that one should not read the records with an expectant attitude of mind, hoping that some dream is pointing to a future event. It is explained that this attitude of mind may prevent the experimenter from recognizing the event when it comes. The attitude of mind to hold is given as one in which all recorded dreams are to be looked upon as dreams relating to something which has happened in the past.

In my own experiments I did not find this warning of any great importance. Very soon I developed the ability to know at the moment I was dreaming the dream, whether it belonged to premonition or not. I feel that the premonitory dream is usually more vivid and perfectly pictured, although I cannot tell in words just what there is about one that makes it possible to distinguish it from an exceptionally vivid dream which is not premonitory.

It is a part of Dr. Dunn's theory that, while awake, we focus our attention on the present moment of physical actuality; and that, while asleep, we spread our attention over past, present and future—thereby seeing some of the events *in*, or a mixture of events *from*, all three departments of time. This mixture is frequent—as I can attest.

The Case:

I read *An Experiment with Time* on a Sunday afternoon in Honolulu in 1926. That night I took pencil and paper to bed with me, determined to write down all my dreams in order that I might watch for those relating, not to the past or present, but to the future. It was a restless night and I arose in the morning with several dreams and one sketch on my pad of paper. They ran like this :

Dream : Strange, big, fattish man. Came to me and asked if I would help him on an invention—something of an optical nature. Dream : Was at my desk. Had before me a piece of a machine. The piece was two feet by six inches by four inches. Black electrical cord and white one running from rear of the black enamelled lid which was before me. In a side of this lid, or cap, was a square hole about four inches by four inches. On the top of the lid was an hour-glass-shaped set-screw of blued steel. (I made a rough sketch.) Dream : I was in a latticed, low kitchen. Fat man there. Stranger there. He was tall, slim, light, and about forty. Small Hawaiian woman there. On a bench before me was the lid, but in the opening was a small machine upon which I had been working. The thin man asked if I was " ready." I said I was. He turned out the white light, leaving only a red one. I took sensitive paper from a box and placed it in a small opening in the machine. The thin man touched a switch. A light flashed. I took out the paper and developed it in one of three strange little white photo trays. The developed image was a scale, and a pointer which indicated a large number. I looked at the men. We laughed. I said: " Well, it works."

That was Sunday night. On the following Thursday afternoon the dreams started to come true. The man I had first seen in my dreams came to call on me. He wanted help in splitting a ray of light to get an image of a weight-scale on both a ground glass frame and a piece of recording photo paper. The top mechanism of the scale was described to me. I agreed to help him.

The next dream was partly wrong. The lid was as I had seen and sketched it, but it was never brought to my desk. Later I was taken to the kitchen with the latticed wall, to work on the machine. The thin man was the mechanic of the experiment and the small Hawaiian woman his wife. The machine was one for weighing sugar syrup in sugar refineries.

When the problem had been solved and the mechanic had made changes in the machine at my direction, I went with sensitized paper to help make the test. As it happened, I had acquired the strange little photo trays the day before— in a trade.

The results were exactly as I had dreamed them.

I also dreamed two weeks into the future and saw other things that were yet to come, but not things as strange to me as the work with a machine I had not known to exist. In each case I showed the papers with my recorded dreams to my friends before the dreams came true. Everything was down in black and white, and being watched by several interested persons from dream to following event.

Comment :

With the success I had attained so easily by the use of Dr. Dunn's method, I accepted without reservations his statement that all dreams were made up of about equal parts of the past, present and future. However, my ability to see into the future by the simple process of awakening and writing down my dreams was short-lived. I lost it before the month was out ; but from the experiment I learned one thing, the importance of which I *cannot overestimate.*

I learned that when a complex is formed in the subconscious mind it *can no longer be forced* by the conscious mind to give up any memory of a premonitory dream or any message which it may have received from *outside ;* this, when such memory or message is *contrary* to a complexed belief or idea.

I must try to make this point very clear. I will illustrate. When I awoke to write down my dreams, it was the dual consciousness of the former dream experiment which caused my awakening. My conscious mind had all but lost (by my giving up the former practice) the ability fully to retain the dual consciousness state in sleep ; however, it remained able to cause me to awaken frequently and write down the dreams. Now the complex which developed in my subconscious was caused primarily by my conscious dislike for the torture of sudden light and the equally irksome necessity of awakening and forcing myself to write. My conscious mind sent complaining thoughts to the subconscious to hold as memories of the unpleasant experiences. The *physical effects on the body* impressed these complaints on my subconscious *much more rapidly* than any thinking process *alone* could have done. In less than a month the complex had become fully developed. I consciously desired to keep on indefinitely with the experiment, but the now complexed subconscious had contrary desires. It reacted with overpowering force on my conscious mind while in sleep : it gave the conscious a *dream of awakening* with which to replace the *actual awakening* and writing.

I did battle with this odd turn of subconscious activity—this revolt. I charged my conscious mind to maintain the dual consciousness state and so remain able to observe the subconscious and circumvent it when it endeavoured to trick me with a *dream* of awakening and writing.

In former experiments I had controlled the subconscious in every way and caused it to dream for me to order. Now a complex had developed and given my subconscious a power greater than my conscious possessed.

Night after night I made war on the subconscious in an endeavour to keep it from tricking me. But in an ever-lengthening dream series, the conscious mind was tricked by such a performance as this : The conscious mind would accept a dream of awakening for a reality. It would feel the pain of sudden light in the eyes and the struggle to arouse the body and make the arm write. Just as the writing was finished, the conscious mind would *suspect the trick* and make a great effort *really* to awaken and write. Again, it would be tricked into accepting a dream in which it triumphed—only to become again aware that it had been tricked, etc., etc., over and over, until the conscious at last became convinced that the *last* dream forced upon it had been an *actual* awakening and writing. Always the paper remained blank— the subconscious, armed with its new complex, was entirely the victor.

In addition to my subconscious mind's success in keeping me from waking, it achieved another signal victory, thanks to the complex which had given it the upper hand. It refused entirely either to register premonitory dreams or to send them up to me as a memory upon my awakening—I do not know which. At any rate, my complexed subconscious accomplished its purpose, and I can only say that for years after that I never became aware of a dream of the future. I had fondly hoped to dream into the future and see myself with the secret of secrets of the kahunas in my hands—as I expected some day to have it. I hoped in this way to shorten the long search which seemed to lie ahead, and so to become aware of the very heart of hearts or primary clue to the secret. Nine years were to pass before that hope was to be fully realized, and then only through patient and stumbling study and research.

.   .   .   .   .

We have now come far enough in collecting data and conclusions to make our second important contact with the kahunas and their system of psychology and practice. Up to this time I could not begin, even in a simple way, to try to describe what I shall now describe with confidence.

We have concluded that there are ghosts and spirits who exhibit various degrees of visibility, of power, of ability and of intelligence. Also we have our " X." Members of the Round Table will, since they no longer have to stop to fumble with data, be able to follow me when I say that in the kahuna psychology, the subconscious and the conscious are considered separate things or separate conscious entities. In life they work together in the physical body, but they may be separated by means of what we call hypnotic force and the kahunas call *mana*. After death the two entities make two separate ghosts who wander either *alone* or *together*. These ghosts—even as in life in the physical— have at uncertain intervals a contact with the " X."

The subconscious is called the *unihipili*, pronounced oo-nee-hee-pee-lee. This name holds for any living or ghostly subconscious entity. The conscious has for its name *uhane*, pronounced oo-ha-nay, both in physical and ghost life.

In séances the *unihipili* is the spirit with the.perfect memory, but which lacks ability to reason. The *uhane* is the spirit which has to guess at its own past because it cannot remember, but which is very logical and can reason. If the two come as a pair they resemble the human being who has a normal use of both the conscious and the subconscious.

The kahunas also are very familiar with entities lower than the human plane—the poltergeist type.

Now we come to the place in our study where we must compare the data to be had in the West with the idea held by the kahunas that the conscious entity can come and go, in and out, of living bodies in sleep or at other times—that even the subconscious can come and go on rare occasions although it usually does not leave the body until death.

In the West we have all the data on cases of " multiple personality " to assemble and examine. Psychologists agree that consciousness, or " personality," cannot and does not leave the body. The kahuna differs radically upon this point.

Let us now see what actually is indicated by the data when examined without the hindrance of the dogma of Science.

MULTIPLE PERSONALITY

Preliminary Notes :

Source books : *Outline of Abnormal Psychology*, by William McDougall (Scribner's, 1926) ; *Encyclopædia Britannica :* article on Multiple Personality.

The word personality as used here is one not too well defined by Psychology. Jung, who has followed Freud in his investigations of the complex, describes the word and takes us back to its Latin origin : *persona*, the mask worn by actors when they change from one character to another in a play. This describes the thing changed in cases of multiple personality. It is the individuality, or traits, which distinguish one human being from another.

In describing the changes of personality in a body, little distinction is made between the subconscious and conscious —these being considered by most investigators to be component parts of personality. Jung, however, leads the way in his work by making the distinction of *anima* (Latin for breath or soul, and corrupted in French to *animal*) for the subconscious, and *persona* for the conscious.

The correct descriptive of the phenomenon we are now to investigate should be " multiple *anima* and *persona* " instead of " multiple personality."

There are three points which we must watch in the following cases : (1) The appearance or disappearance of either the conscious or subconscious alone, with corresponding changes in personality ; (2) The appearance or disappearance of both units combined as a pair ; (3) The memories retained by the personalities as they come and go.

If our theory is correct—that the subconscious alone can remember—then by watching memory we should be able to tell which unit goes or remains.

Webster's International Dictionary speaks of this phenomenon as an abnormal condition of " mind." I prefer to think of it as an abnormal condition of body in which minds come and go, rather than of the various minds involved. Each mind observed is found perfectly normal while in possession of the body—unless lack of memory of its state when out of the body or asleep within it may be considered abnormalities.

The terms used in describing the elements of consciousness involved and the states of consciousness are : A personality cut off from control of the body and brain is said to be " dissociated " ; the original personality in a body is the " primary " one, and those that come in to replace it are " secondary " ; the personality in temporary control of the body and brain is said to be " dominant," while those who have once appeared and have gone, or who have not yet appeared, are said to be " latent."

In cases of " alternating personalities " two personalities only are involved in the change. If there is " reciprocal amnesia," neither personality remembers anything the other did while in possession of the body. If there is not reciprocal amnesia, one or both may be able to remember what was done in the body during its absence. Under the influence of hypnosis, one or more of these personalities can usually be brought from the latent state and made to answer the questions of the operator. The answers are none too logical as a rule, but they tell such things as could be remembered by any subconscious mind if such memories were stored in it.

This phenomenon is not a new one. Down the ages men have changed personalities or become " possessed." This usually refers to conditions of insanity, but not always. Our attention is now to be fixed on cases where insane personalities were not observed.

The Case :

I will condense a few typical cases which McDougall discusses in the source book mentioned.

Rev. W. S. Plumer first described the following case in *Harper's Magazine* in 1860 : Mary Reynolds, a normal girl of eighteen, was subject to fits for a year. Then, while reading in a meadow one day, she became unconscious. She awoke blind and deaf. This affliction passed in three months. One morning she could not be awakened. Some hours later she awoke of her own accord—to all seeming a new-born baby. She could, however, repeat a few words. Learning with great rapidity, the "baby" began to grow mentally and use the adult brain. In a few weeks the primary personality came back and the secondary one disappeared. This alternation continued for years, the "baby" personality growing up in the process. Neither personality, when dominant, had any knowledge or memory of what the other had done while in possession of body and brain.

Professor Janet describes a case in which one of the alternating personalities knew the memories of the other : Félida began changing personalities at the age of thirteen. She was an hysterical child, but the secondary personality was very different. The secondary personality could remember all the memories of the primary, but the primary none of the memories of the secondary.

Dr. Morton Prince's most famous study was the "Beauchamp Case." At eighteen years of age a young lady began changing personalities. This changing continued for years, five personalities being identified in all—each considering itself a separate individual, and the mutual memories being a tangle.

The childhood of the girl, B, was one marked by emotional stresses and nervousness. Matured, she became a nurse, and received an emotional shock in the course of a love affair. Suddenly "all her peculiarities became exaggerated" and she became ultra-religious. The memory remained unimpaired, but there was a distinct change in characteristics. This change lasted some six years, during which time another personality named "Sally" came and showed her presence only during sleep. At night this Sally talked through the body and took it on sleep-walking excursions.

At the end of the six-year period there came another emotional shock, and a personality called B4 became dominant. This B4 could remember all the events of the life of the original B, but not those of the life of B1.

In the following year B1 and B4 alternated with reciprocal amnesia. Both remembered all that B had done, but knew nothing of the doings of each other. B1 was sickly and mild.

B4 was more healthy and far more aggressive. Both were very emotional.

Dr. Prince used hypnosis on the patient. Under hypnotic influence another personality was brought to light. It conversed freely. However, this very interesting personality puzzled the investigator. He was inclined to think she was the original B restored to normal condition and much improved. She resembled both B1 and B4 to some extent, seeming to be a mixture of them and of herself. She is described as "A person of even temperament, frank and open in address—one who seemed to be natural and simple in her mode of thought and manner." She had all the memories. B, B1 and B4 continued to alternate—B now commanding the memories of B1 and B4. During this time B1 and B4 seemed at times to partake of the "emotional characteristics" of each other—a trading back and forth.

After some years the original B became dominant and grew healthy and normal.

Sally was interesting. She could be contacted in hypnosis and questioned, although she would alternate with one of the other personalities and often upset the procedure initiated during hypnotic investigation. She considered herself a separate and distinct personality and remembered all the things she had done through or with the body at night. She said she had learned what the other personalities (except B4) were doing by reading their minds when she found their thoughts interesting. When they were reading a book which she disliked, she stopped reading their minds and amused herself with her own thoughts. She disliked B1 and often forced upon her visual hallucinations and certain motor automatisms. At times she took control of B1's voice ; often she forced B1 to do things she did not wish to do—things such as telling lies.

When Sally took over the body she could not open her eyes. One of the automatic actions she forced on the others .was the rubbing of the eyes. In this way she eventually got her own eyes open and so was able to see, and to dominate the whole organism. Her first success in this came at a moment when the then dominant B1 was drowsily resting.

Thereafter, Sally was able at will to displace B1 in normal as well as in hypnotized states.   At such times, B1 returned with no memory of what Sally had been doing with the body. In struggles of will, Sally seemed to be able to " paralyse " the will of B1 who, although seemingly dominant, was forced to obey orders much like a hypnotized subject, which resulted in Sally's being able to play practical jokes on B1. Unravelling the knitting was a favourite joke.   Neither B1 nor B4 had any memory of Sally or her periods of dominance. Sally could not read the thoughts of B4, and could not often force automatisms on her ; this, she said, was because B4 had heard of her and fought against any control.   At certain times when Sally became dominant she could not get the eyes of the body open ; and the skin, deep tissues, and " muscular sense " were all in a condition resembling that of the body when in sleep.

Comment :

Dr. Prince holds that all the various personalities using one body are " split off " parts of the one real personality. His method of treatment was that of blending two or more personalities to get a dominant third.   In this he was none too successful.

Professor McDougall, in his study (our source book), decides that each personality is a separate " monad " or entity in itself.

None of the psychologists are willing to admit that these personalities can come and go in and out of the body, and that the subconscious mind can be used by one or more personalities or changed in the body.

My own study of multiple personality data resulted in my accepting the kahuna system of psychology as one better explaining complicated changes which take place.

In some cases which have been reported, a "baby" personality arrives and becomes dominant ; in others, an adult personality comes and brings with it a complete change in health—even a paralysed limb—and a definite memory of a past life in another body.

As psychologists and kahunas disagree, let us go on to

see what proof we can find that a " personality " actually can leave a body and return to it.

CASE 31

DID THE CONSCIOUS AND SUBCONSCIOUS MINDS OF GENERAL LEE'S MOTHER LEAVE THE BODY AND RETURN ?

Preliminary Notes :

This case was reported in the *Hollywood Citizen*, December 14, 1934, in the *Strange As It May Seem* daily feature. I take it that it can be authenticated by the originator of the feature. In any event, there are many more similar cases which are perfectly authenticated.

The Case :

Fourteen months before the famous Confederate soldier, General Robert E. Lee, was born, his mother seemingly died. The doctors found that her heart had stopped beating and that she had turned cold and stiff. Thinking she was dead, funeral services were held and her body placed in the family vault. Fortunately in those parts, at that time, bodies were not embalmed.

A week later the keeper of the cemetery went into the vault to remove withered floral offerings, and was startled to hear a moan from inside the casket. Hurriedly he opened the coffin. Inside it he found Mrs. Lee—again back in her body, alive. Apparently she had but then returned, for she had not smothered. She recovered and lived to give birth to the son who was later to become so famous.

Comment :

In this and many similar cases we have proof of the cessation of all activities of the conscious mind in the body. Those of the subconscious all but ceased. To account for the absence of decay in the body we are forced to conclude that there was a slight connection—perhaps by an ectoplasmic thread—between the body and the subconscious which must have been partly removed because of the death-like state of the body.

In this connection it is well to remember the yogis of India. These " holy men " use some form of autosuggestion to throw their body into a death-like state while the conscious mind goes away for long periods of time and the subconscious becomes dormant.

In the two cases we have just examined there is data which will later be of value, but in the next two we will come upon the data which finally showed me the significance of all data —pointed me to the secret of secrets of the kahunas.

CASE 32

THE STRANGEST PERSONALITY OF ALL APPEARS

Preliminary Notes :

One of the early members of the Society for Psychic Research, and one who has taken part in many investigations, is a resident of Honolulu. He is Dr. Leapsley, a brilliantly educated man who is as trustworthy as he is wise. He makes frequent journeys away from Honolulu, on this quest and that. Often he lectures to a group of friends to give them the findings of his latest investigation. I give this case and its data from notes taken at one of those lectures.

The Case :

Dr. Leapsley (Ph.D. and a biologist), in company with two medical doctors, was called in as a ranking expert in matters of multiple personality—the case to be investigated and treated being that of a young lady twenty-eight years old, the daughter of a prominent California attorney.

From the age of four, this young lady had alternated personalities regularly every four years. Only two personalities were involved and there was complete reciprocal amnesia.

The change of personalities which came with such regularity would be made in a moment of deep sleep. The secondary personality had been a " baby " when it first arrived, but had learned very rapidly and soon equalled the mental growth of the primary personality.

Through the years, each of the two personalities had continued its growth and education in its times of dominance, and each was able to learn with amazing rapidity anything the other had learned before her. Neither had the slightest memory of the experiences of the other. Upon returning to the body, neither personality could remember what it had done or where it had been while away. There was always surprise and momentary bewilderment at the time of returning to a body grown four years older and unfamiliarly dressed.

The primary personality was quiet and studious. It loved to sew and was shy and retiring. The secondary personality was an aggressive and unabashed tomboy. Their tastes and recreations were different.

One of the changes took place one afternoon while the mother was reading to her twelve-year-old daughter. They were in the sitting-room and the primary personality, whom we may call Miss First, was then dominant. The child was listening quietly and happily to the reading when she suddenly fell asleep. It was little Miss Second who awakened in the body a moment later.

Four years passed. Miss Second, now sixteen, was in the same room with the mother. The mother was reading another book, but this time not aloud, as Miss Second did not care for books. The body fell asleep, as it happened, in the same big chair in which it had sat four years before and on much the same kind of sunny afternoon.

Suddenly the eyes opened and Miss First looked wonderingly out. " Why did you stop reading, Mother ? " she asked. She was unaware that four years had passed. She thought she had dropped off to sleep and that the reading of four years before had suddenly stopped. When told what had happened, she knew by remembering similar experiences what must have occurred. Also she could see that her body was larger and that it wore a dress much too colourful to suit her quiet taste.

So, every four years the girls changed places in the body. At the age of twenty-eight, or nearing it, each girl had lived fourteen years in the body. With each change, the wardrobe had to be made over to suit the personality which took over the body. Amusements were instantly changed, as well as diet, habits and occupational hobbies.

At last the parents decided to call in experts to see if there was not some way in which the secondary personality could be forced to leave the body to the primary. In this the parents were much perturbed as they had come to love both personalities as they would two different daughters, as indeed the girl seemed to have become to them.

The investigators took the young lady and explained to her that they were going to hypnotize her and endeavour either to cause both personalities to blend into one, or to get Miss Second to leave the body entirely to Miss First who now had possession, but feared the approach of the usual time for the change. Most eagerly she submitted to the treatment.

Under hypnosis the usual thing occurred. Both personalities appeared in turn and could be questioned. Each personality showed a complete memory of its own periods of life in the body, and each said that it knew all about the activities of the other—not by sharing those experiences but by " reading " what was in the memory of the other. They were not sure whether they stayed in the body or not, when latent, and they showed the usual lack of reasoning power. When the subconscious of Miss Second was told that she must go away and leave the body, the reply was vague and unsatisfactory. The order seemed to be accepted, but the doctors were convinced that nothing would come of such a command. So convinced were they that they also gave the usual hypnotic suggestion aimed at forcing a blending of the two personalities. (Note : As the subconscious alone can be hypnotized and made to act upon given suggestions, the blending must be between subconscious entities. Such a blend would give the dominant conscious entity a double set of memories and so imitate a completely blended pair of personalities. It would seem quite impossible—if the kahunas are right in their postulations—that two conscious entities could blend without becoming instantly aware of their duality.)

After the first treatment it was found that no blending of personalities had resulted. The treatments were continued daily until the usual time of the change drew near.

It was hoped that with Miss First well aware of the fact that they desired her to stay in the body and blend consciously and subconsciously with Miss Second, something would be accomplished. However, when the change occurred, Miss First was not blended with Miss Second.

Hypnosis was applied again, after the new arrival had heard what was being done. Again the subconscious minds were questioned. Miss First remembered the instructions given her to try to blend with Miss Second, but said she seemed unable to do anything about it. When asked where she was, she answered only, " Here."

Suggestion was next tried in an attempt to drive Miss Second out of the body. Then a startling thing happened. The body became as if dead. No response from either subconscious could be obtained. The doctors and parents became much alarmed. It was their desire to be rid of the invading personality, but now it seemed that they had driven it out but could not recall Miss First. While suggestion was being laboriously continued, a still more startling thing happened. The lips opened and an entirely unfamiliar personality spoke to them with such wisdom and authority that they were confounded.

This new personality spoke with a resounding voice which had in it an evasive but undeniable masculine quality. It was much like the gentle but very firm voice of some old man. The group about the girl's body listened in amazement. Immediately the doctors realized that they were hearing still another personality addressing them. To add to their confusion, they realized that this new personality did not think as they thought. It seemed not to be logical, but superlogical. (It did not reason—it *realized*.)

This new personality, with the undeniable male quality in its quiet voice, neither argued nor seemed to use reason. It seemed to know definitely and to the smallest detail what had gone before and what was being attempted. It asked no questions but began at once giving one statement after another concerning the girls and their lives. Each statement was precise and covered ground with which parents and doctors were familiar. As soon as the new personality had summed up the condition, it became silent.

The doctors asked who the speaker might be. The answer was another statement, and it was to the effect that this personality was one which had the two girls and the one body under its care and guardianship. In answer to more questions, more facts were stated—always without arguments such as a conscious mind might use, and always without explaining reasons. The group was told that the two girls were using the one body for the purposes of living.

The doctors then contrived their best arguments. They told in full the way in which the change of personalities was ruining the life of the girl. She could not marry and could not live a normal life. To this the new personality answered with statements, the logic of which was apparent without argument or reasoning. Statement followed statement, each giving some definite purpose of living—the various purposes of growth and experience.

The learned doctors were helpless. Each statement was so profound and perfectly reasonable that they could find no logical argument to advance against it. They were like children before age-old wisdom. The type of thinking with which they were confronted was not human. The doctors would have been able to produce arguments in favour of the statements which were given them seemingly as eternal verities, but they could not have given arguments against them.

In a very short time they lapsed into silence. The personality which addressed them had left them helpless.

In desperation one of the doctors cried out that if Miss First was not allowed to have the body, they would keep it hypnotized indefinitely. To this the answer was another statement to the effect that no one would do anything to injure the body. Still another statement was then given—a final one which closed the interview for ever. This statement was simple and to the point: " If you interfere with my work, I shall withdraw the girls and leave you the corpse."

There was a long silence. Not one in the group doubted for an instant that the wise old personality would fulfil its threat. There had been a conviction of truth and serene power in every word. At last someone ventured to ask another question . . . but no answer came. More time passed. Suggestion was made to release the body from hypnosis. Miss Second opened her eyes and smiled. Doctors and parents gave up. They had been confronted as if by God Himself. They realized the futility of their efforts.

Comment :

In the old man personality we find something quite different from either subconscious or conscious. The difference lies in the manner of thinking. I have put my own words into my account of Dr. Leapsley's lecture in order to say that the old man personality seemed to "realize" rather than use memory or reason. While the lecturer did not use this word, it was very plain that what he described fitted exactly into what I am next to offer the Round Table for consideration—"Realization."

CASE 33

REALIZATION—A WAY OF BECOMING AWARE OF
SUPERPHYSICAL REALITY

Preliminary Notes :

We have no word in English to describe what is called *samadhi* by the Hindus, or what is still more accurately indicated by *ko* in Hawaiian. Our word "realization" comes from the Latin root, *res* or *rei :* a "thing." To the French we owe the present word "real." Realization has come to mean a mental awareness of a "thing." Unfortunately, a "thing" calls to mind at once a physical object.

In attempting to get the idea across into English, the translation of the teachings of Sri Ramakrishna[1] calls the state of Realization, "God-consciousness." He explains that from the conscious state one passes to a superconscious

[1] Bhagavan Sri Rama Krishna Paramahamsa was a Hindu born in Bengal in 1834. He came from a Brahmin family and entered the service of the goddess Kali, eventually becoming a priest of the order. He attained Realization and taught many disciples, among them being Vivekananda. His teachings were set down by his disciples and now form the *Gospel of Sri Ramakrishna.*

state in which the pattern verities of creation are contacted by the ego. As that state deepens, one leaves behind the pattern world of colour, form, sound and so forth, and comes into the patterns of emotion—love being the inclusive pattern from which earthly ambition, desire and liking are cut as poor imitations—(the absence of these giving us the negative emotions of hate, revulsion and so forth). The process of becoming consciously aware of these superphysical pattern-idea realities is one of blending with the pattern-ideas—the blending with Love being the blending with God in His highest phase, creative or externalized—although *all* is God that is touched in Realization. In the blending, the realizing individual loses sense of self and finds that he is one with the patterns and so with God and all creation. To describe this state the phrase is used: "Thou and I are one." It is the idea of God-the-Father and God-the-Son— ONE in eternal reality but individual in the physical. This is a paradox. All attempts to describe this "Oneness that is Separateness" have been paradoxical in all scriptures, be they Vedic, Islamic or Christian. The state of Realization is necessarily of the same paradoxical nature. One drops all memory, individuality and reason—drops all selfness—as he enters the state by *becoming* an integral part of the thing to be realized. None of the five senses are used in this realizing, but only the mysterious ability to be aware of what one *is* when an entity stripped to nothingness and made a part of an *idea*—this idea becoming more real to the inner sense of the ego than any physical reality. I illustrate: With the physical senses one learns all he can of the air about him. He breathes it, smells it, tastes it and sees its transparency; he feels it on his skin as it moves. His skin feels its temperature and humidity. This is physical reality —the sum total of our earthly sensing of air. Now one goes into Realization. He *becomes* air. He knows air from the inside. He knows how air feels as a conscious thing apart from everything else in the created universe. He knows how air can "feel" its own being, without any sensation similar to those produced by the five senses.

Sri Ramakrishna, in struggling to describe the state of

Realization, could use only word-symbols to make vague comparisons between the inner feeling of *being* the thing contacted, and the outer feeling of touching it with the five senses. He said : " When I become one with God I have to transcend all thought, all time, all space." He calls the plane of Eternal Verities, or Patterns, " the plane of the Ideal World." He describes the state as one of " Divine Ecstasy." Others have called it " Bliss," or " the Joy of the Lord," or " Nirvana." In Realization, what things would be utter nothingness to the physical senses become " I " as well as All Things or the One Reality contacted by a superphysical sense.

Before going on, I must try to give the members of the Round Table a more definite and personal feeling of what forms the material of this case. Happily, this is not impossible. There is a mechanism in the brain or mind which enables us to make a preliminary approach to super-consciousness at the very beginning of that practice which eventuates in full Realization.

As this mechanism is seldom used, most of us are unaware that it exists. In the top of the skull—the outer layers of brain matter—there is a place called the " door of Brahma " by the Hindus. It is " the Place of the Most High " in the Bible. It is not for nothing that the human family has always felt instinctively that God was above them, or " up."

The centre of consciousness—or its location—is usually just behind the eyes. If the Round Table members will examine themselves and try to locate the centre of their conscious being, they will find this statement correct. Close the eyes and think the word " I "—see where your consciousness collects or focuses itself in the mind and brain.

Now this centre can be moved from one location to another. Try fixing the eyes intently on some external object. Do you not find that the centre of consciousness seems to move out of you and to that object for the moment ?—an elementary effort at becoming a part of it and " realizing " its nature ?

Now fasten the attention on a toe. Wiggle the toe. Feel the skin-touch that it feels. Does not the centre of consciousness move just as well into the toe as into the object outside the body?

Next, move the centre of consciousness from behind the eyes to the very top of the skull. This can be done by an effort of the will and an accompanying tensing of eye muscles —this latter being a part of the effort at first, but having little to do with the moving.

If you have succeeded in moving the conscious centre far up to the top of the brain, you will have, by now, experienced the primary step in Realization. You will have found that you suddenly were in a partial blankness of mind—the subconscious cut off with all its memories and the conscious, with its thinking and reasoning, left behind. (Silence is a help in this experiment, as a noise pulls the centre down.) In the new and high location. the consciousness will at first seem to be no consciousness at all, but a blankness. With the continuation of this practice the blankness fills itself with a new form of consciousness, in which—without memory, reason or thought—one realizes himself to be something else. This something else is a superior entity or YOU. Gradually it will identify itself as the real you—the old you becoming a lesser and more unreal entity, hardly an entity at all. In due time the new YOU will begin to give impressions of the states it contacts—becomes a part of, at will—and, strangely and paradoxically enough, the memory of that state can be brought back by the conscious mind and given to the subconscious to hold for life. The real YOU is not forced to depend upon the subconscious or conscious physical organisms for memory and reason: it has ALL forms of consciousness combined in its one form of sensing. It knows directly. It has no need to reason or hold memories. What it desires to know, it knows *completely* by becoming instantly a part· of it.

After this necessarily long explanation we are now ready for the case proper and the data to be derived from it.

The Case :

When I endeavoured to see for myself what truth there might be behind the statement that there was such a thing as Realization, I was fortunate enough to find a good teacher. This was a white man—Bishop Kirby of the Zen (Japanese) sect of Buddhism. He had taken his own training in a monastery in Japan and had come to live in Honolulu. He was ready and willing to do all he could to assist me.

The Zen system of training is very simple. It was described to me thus : The pupil goes to his "master" and is given what is called a *ko-an*—this being something like a riddle except that it has no answer that can be given in words. My first *ko-an* was : "This is the sound of two hands (the hands being clapped together) ; now show me the sound of one hand."

The pupil then leaves the master and dwells almost constantly on the *ko-an*. Knowing that he is to feel a new state of consciousness, he aspires to God in any way he may feel is best suited to his particular temperament. In time he may suddenly enter the state—or he may never enter it. If it is once entered, there is no difficulty in giving the answer to the master without words. A few vague gestures will suffice to carry meaning to one who knows what is being described.

I pressed Bishop Kirby for a description of the state before deciding that I must take time to experience it for myself. He strove patiently to give me an idea of what I might expect, but the more he strove the more puzzled I became. All that I could gather was that when one was stripped of memory and of reason, then left without any of the five senses, one was supposed to know by a process of "realizing as a fact" the entirety of something which could not be seen, touched, smelled, heard or tasted. It seemed to me that when I reached my goal I could expect nothing better than to find myself unconscious in a black nothingness, but Bishop Kirby assured me this would not be so. Unfortunately for me, I did not know then of the method of raising the centre of consciousness to the "Upper Room."

Off and on for months I kept my *ko-an* of the "one hand" in my mind and endeavoured to win through to Realization. After some months had passed, Bishop Kirby found it necessary to return to the Orient, and so turned me over to a very kindly Japanese priest living in San Francisco. This new " master " wrote me a letter in which he gave the information that it was not necessary for the master to project the experience of Realization, as by thought transference, to the pupil. As the letter is a brave effort to describe the indescribable, I will give parts of it here :

" If you really want to devote your leisure space of mind for Zen-meditation, you cannot afford to wait for a Master coming to you. You had better start it by yourself bravely. Realization is all around and inside you. You do not need a Master to send it to you. You can touch it for yourself.

" Just carry your problem (the ko-an of the hands), and fill up the space of your mind with this question of the Master Hakuin. There is no explanation. No imagination allowed here. Just try to tell the Master what you have heard. You have to get out of your logical circle of thinking to meet this problem. If you sit in a quiet room and just carry this problem for an hour or so every day, then you will get a habit to concentrate your thought upon this problem, even when you are walking or talking. Your everyday life will be nothing, but the sound of one hand. . . . You will see then (when Realization is attained) the sound with your eyes, and hear the colour with your ears. You can taste the fragrance of the flowers with your tongue, and you can smell the music with your nose. Your body will not be your body. It will be the body of the whole universe. Your mind will not be your mind. It will be a moving wave of infinite ocean. . . . Never stop to think that you have entered into realization. Just keep on asking by yourself ' the sound of one hand.'

" You are always welcome to ask me any question about the Ko-an, but you have to fight your own battle to actualize it. I can only encourage your work, advising you to step on the right road."

Encouraged by the letter, I continued to practise. Then at last came my first Realization, and to my great delight I recognized the state as one I had known and occasionally experienced from early childhood.

As a boy of seven I had considered the state a most amazing and delightful dream. So delightful had it been that I mentioned it frequently in my prayers and asked that I be allowed to dream it over once more. My prayers had been answered twice, but with dreams of states as different as they were thrillingly blissful.

I can give an idea of Realization by telling of those dreams. My first dream was one in which I wandered afar and came into a field of virgin snow of incredible whiteness. As I gazed at snow which could be so very white, I suddenly became a living part of the whiteness of the snow. In that state I was part of a whiteness, the utter perfection of which made the other snow of my dream muddy and impure—at least it seemed so to me ever afterward when I compared the visual sensation with the sensation of being whiteness itself. During the time of being whiteness, I lost all memory of the small boy in the bed.

When I awoke I attempted to describe my dream. In this I failed and fell into confusion. No one seemed to understand so simple a matter as that I had not seen the whiteness or felt it with my hands or with any other part of me. I explained over and over that I " turned into whiteness "— which was exactly the sensation I remembered. While I was that whiteness I was not aware of feeling any size. I was not in a place. I had no feeling of time, and so could not say how long the wonderful dream had lasted. I was very sure that I had not become snow for the simple reason that I had felt neither hot nor cold, softness nor wetness. My last sorrowful words usually were, as I remember them : " No, it was not like any of that. I just turned into all the loveliest and whitest whiteness there is."

My second dream came and went, leaving me thrilled and amazed. I had formed the opinion that nothing could be utterly pure and perfect but whiteness. I brought back with me a memory of having been tumbled into a fantastic world where all the trees and flowers were made of a wonderfully beautiful pearly grey material which was translucent.

As my snow had faded, so this fantastic world had faded—leaving me a part of the translucent greyness. From this state of being such a greyness I had returned to my own self and my own world, bearing the breath-taking information that greyness could be as utterly beautiful and perfect as whiteness.

In my third dream I fell upward into a roseate sunset and became what I called "pinkness" for want of a more descriptive word. After that I knew the utter perfection of pinkness, as well as the fact that it was as gracious an experience to be a part of it as it had been to be a part of whiteness or greyness.

My fourth "dream" came years later in Hawaii. I was awake and seated in meditation on a straw mat. I had been pondering many occult problems for some minutes and my mind had wearily become blank. Suddenly the thrill of the remembered experience of my childhood was mine again. All memory was lost. Max Long ceased to be, and in his stead was a living consciousness which was a rock. Upon becoming Max Long again, I was very certain that I had been a rock, but, had I been pressed for a reason for that sureness, I could only have answered that I knew beyond question because I was certain that a rock felt just that way and no other. It had been a grand and comforting thing to become a rock. The sensation had been one of being firm and firm and firm—nothing more. From that experience I returned with the happy knowledge that it was as glorious to be a rock as to be a man—perhaps more glorious. Everything dropped away and was replaced by a perfect firmness, a sensation of being solidness. Centuries could have passed and I should not have been irked. To be a perfect something is an end in itself regardless of time or place—regardless of anything.

A month after this fourth experience of Realization I came across an account in Will Levington Comfort's *Child and Country* of a fellow-human who had shared the experience which I had thought peculiar to myself. A young man had come to Mr. Comfort and described an odd experience which he had just had. He had found himself a microscopic organism living in water. While " being " that tiny creature, his entire content of consciousness had been a sense of individuality plus a greed to eat and a fear of being eaten. I was delighted with the account. It told me that I was not alone in my experience, although I had been a rock instead of a tiny water creature.

Under, my Japanese friend's guidance I came upon what was, to me, only a continuation of earlier experiences. I must have dozed off after an early awakening in the morning, for I dreamed that I was sitting beside a friend who was dying. Beside the bed stood a strange dark man whom I seemed to know very well indeed. I asked him if I might go with my dying friend and share his experience in death. The brown man smiled his benignant smile and instructed me to clasp both of the hands which were growing cold. I did this, and at once felt the sensation of flying through a vastness of space which was filled with amber light. Then the familiar thing happened. I ceased to be a man and became that amber light. It was the old story of perfection and of thrilling bliss unmarred by time, place, memories, thought or physical sensation.

Upon my return to the normal state of consciousness in the body, I knew for the first time that Realization was nothing strange to me.

There followed at irregular intervals and unpredictable times, a number of Realizations. My realization of whiteness came back twice, being always a joy to experience, but now coming with no preliminary dream of snow—coming as a direct step from consciousness on the physical into being the consciousness of whiteness as a living and vital thing. I did not go back to pinkness or greyness, but went on to become uncoloured light in which I was the potential of all the colours known on earth, but was none of them. I was shimmering, glowing, flashing, colourless light—a thing which can only be suggested in words.

My later Realizations brought me more directly into the ideal pattern world—for want of a better name for it. I became in turn the ideals from which all the crude earthly counterparts have been formed which we think of as straightness, motion-speed-quiet, sharpness-pointedness-edgedness, curvedness, fluidity, extension-nonextension-space-nonspace, duration-nonduration-time, and sound that is not sound at all, but quite something else—a variation of what I call "silent-harmony" but which was neither silence nor harmony.

I can only give a vague and paradoxical description of what I sensed in Realization. The state has to be experienced to be understood. I cannot say that I remained an individual entity and still was not an entity at all, but the entirety of something not myself; however, that is exactly what I did.

In all this experience of Realization I found no practical application which I could make in the physical, of the facts I had perceived in the superphysical. I brought back ideals of perfection, but I could in no way force physical material to conform to those ideals. If I had kept on until I had Realized the perfect Love (the final "seeing God" of the Hindus), I might have found something more practical; but before such a time I again turned my attention to the kahunas.

Comment :

For our data : (1) We have a state in which memory and reason—the identifications of the subconscious and the conscious—play no part. (2) We have a state of consciousness indexed " X," in which the superphysical can be sensed so clearly as to leave an unshakable conviction that the superphysical is the perfect reality. (3) The " I " becomes a part of the super-real and loses its identity with the physical self, at the same time becoming one with all and everything contacted in Realization. (4) In the state of Realization, one needs no five senses, no physical objects to sense, no reason or memory to tell them what is near. One knows by the process of becoming, the thing they desire to know. (5) In the " old man " personality of Case 32 we have an entity of seemingly human type which has superior knowledge and uses a process of realizing what it wished to know. This process is superior to that used by the conscious or the subconscious. It would seem logical to guess that a similar entity is attached to each one of us and that it is the source of all superphysical knowing in monition and premonition—also, that this knowledge is transmitted to us through the subconscious.

.   .   .   .   .

As the state of Realization is so little known in the West, and as Round Table members may not have hitherto associated such a thing with Religion, I will now go back to that great religious teacher who tried to convey the truth of Realization to those about him—Sri Ramakrishna. I select him because he is fairly modern, having lived from 1834 until 1886. I have already mentioned his " Gospels." For a full account of his life, I suggest Dhan Gopal Mukerji's absorbing book *The Face of Silence*.

In trying to explain God to a doctor, Sri Ramakrishna once said :

" The conviction that God is in all objects—that there is Unity in variety—is called Knowledge of Oneness. Knowing Him intimately is Realization. . . . The Absolute is beyond Knowledge and Ignorance, beyond sin and virtue—good works and bad works, cleanliness and uncleanliness—as understood by the limited faculties of man. . . . But how can I make it clear to you ? Suppose someone asks you what is the taste of clarified butter. Is it possible to make the matter perfectly clear to him ? The utmost that one may say in reply to such a question is, the taste of butter is precisely like the taste of butter ! . . . But there has been as yet in this world no created being who has been able to express by word of mouth the nature of the Absolute. . . . There is unspeakable joy in the company of the Lord. Words of the mouth cannot describe it. He alone knows, who has felt it. . . ."

Here is a prayer used by Sri Ramakrishna :

" From the unreal lead us into the Real. From darkness lead us into light. From death lead us into immortality. Reach us through and through our self. And—Oh, Thou Terrible !—evermore protect us from ignorance, by Thy sweet compassionate Face."

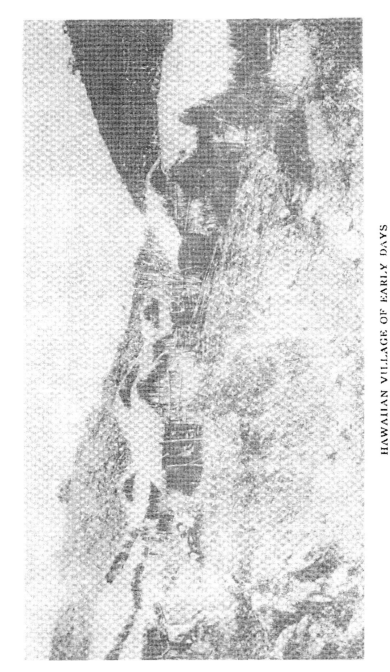

HAWAIIAN VILLAGE OF EARLY DAYS

Here is another :

"Om! Brahman, The Truth, the Knowledge, the Infinite. He is Bliss and Immortality. He shines. He is Peace. He is Good. He is One."

We are reminded strongly of how Jesus taught that " The Father and I are one," and " The Father is in all men and all men in the Father."

In all the teachings originating in the Orient, as did those of both Jesus and Sri Ramakrishna, we come upon unmistakable evidence that the teachers had seen something in Realization which they found more than difficult to put into words—a something which was often active in a paradoxical way when viewed in the light of physical experience. Listen to this effort of Sri Ramakrishna to explain a fact which he considered very simple in Realization, but which refused to be described in terms of any reason or memory related to the physical plane of consciousness :

" . . . I really don't know what to say ! There is, however, one consolation for me. I look upon all human beings—in fact, all creatures—as incarnations of the Deity. I see God evolving into all things, God manifest in everything—in Man and Nature. I see God himself has taken these multifarious forms that appear before our eyes in this universe."

In searching through the ancient religious teachings of India which were acceptable to this modern sage and which might show how the kahunas had originally looked upon the conscious, the subconscious and the superconscious, I came upon what I wanted in a discussion of various topics, which being on page 93 of Vol. 1, Fourth Edition of the *Gospel of Sri Ramakrishna*, I will condense as I pick out and quote the significant parts suited to our data (the parentheses will be mine) :

. . . God the Absolute (as contrasted with God made manifest in creations), is the one Substance to be realized —not described or known. The sign of True Knowledge or Realization is cessation of doubt and therefore of all philosophical discussion . . . the master stops talking as soon as the disciple has been illuminated (attained Realization).

The result of the foregoing position is that the Higher Self alone knows the Higher Self. He, Knowledge Absolute, is capable of being realized by Himself, the Knowledge Absolute alone.

The differentiated Soul . . . cannot, as such, realize God the Absolute. The Undifferentiated alone realizes the Undifferentiated. This is the true meaning of the expression, "God is unknown and unknowable."

All facts of the universe—every object, every phenomenon—that comes under creation, preservation and destruction—under *Body, Mind and Soul* . . . all come under the Maya (the world-system considered as unreal because God is the only true basic reality as seen in Realization). . . .

It is absurd to say " the world is unreal " so long as we remain convinced that we ourselves are real ! A person who has not realized the Absolute cannot realize that the world is unreal.

The sage goes on to explain that while in Realization one knows utterly that he is contacting the only Reality ; but upon return to the " differentiated ego "—the conscious and subconscious ego—the physical takes on all the semblance of reality again.

Translating the italicized words in the third paragraph above into the terms of our study, we have then the evidence from this source that in India there has been an ancient teaching that there exists a " *Body, Mind* and *Soul* "—a body (a subconscious), a mind (conscious) and a soul (super-conscious). The kahuna names for these are *unihipili*, *uhane* and *aumakua*. To be certain that we are right we have but to go to the ancient scriptures which Sri Rama-krishna studied and accepted in part, to find there the division of the human consciousness into the " lower self, the self and the Higher Self." (See the *Bhagavad Gita*, Judge Translation. Also *Katha-Upanishad*.)

Many have experienced and taught Realization from the time of Christ to that of Sri Ramakrishna. If members of the Round Table will consult their *Encyclopædia Britannica* under the headings of "Mysteries" and of "Mysticism" they will be able to read the history of Realization—such history as we have in the West. The best known of the Greek Mysteries in which Realization was taught were: the Eleusinian, the Samothracian (with a confessional), the Mithraic (borrowed from Persia ; Mithra was the Sun-God or personification of God as Light), and the Orphic (a later adaptation of the god Dionysus-Iaccus mysteries).

In all the Greek Mysteries may be found the same Father-Son idea of Oneness or separate-unity that is found in Christianity. Often the Mother-Daughter idea is used as an alternative, and some of the Mysteries were celebrated by women under this idea. Frequently the Father-Mother idea is found.

In India there is a very ancient tradition which tells how man's three conscious entities evolve from one grade to the next, the subconscious to the conscious and the conscious to the superconscious—to put it into our words. The conscious entities of one man and one woman join together to become one dual-sexed (not sexless) entity: the superconscious. This idea is also found in ancient symbolic carvings and garments in Polynesia. The symbolic higher union is the mystery behind phallic worship. It is the origin or the "soul-mate" idea which has of late been degraded to a mating on the physical plane by some misguided occultists in the West. It is a conception which is vague but tenacious, and which clings obscurely to much of magic and religion. In the Mysteries we find the god Hermes, who is the goddess Aphrodite in his female aspect. He is the Divine Hermaphrodite—Hermes-Aphrodite—from whom comes our English word for an individual who is of both sexes. He was "the messenger of the gods" who had winged feet and other miraculous equipment. He fits neatly into our idea of the superconscious which gives premonitions and which is our inductor into the state of Realization. He is—of all symbols —most rational and complete. In him we find the answer

to the great mystery of there being two sexes. In him we
have the answer to why the Realizers or " mystics " of the
middle centuries found that when they touched God in
Realization they found in him the man which the female
mystic (such as St. Catherine) could adore and find complet-
ing her lack, and the woman which the male mystic had
failed to find on earth, but whom he had always held as an
ideal possibility—an ideal of all that was womanly and all
that man needs to fill a great spiritual longing for com-
pletion. The nuns' " bride of Christ " idea was far better
suited to innate human and spiritual needs of womankind
than the monks' " brother of Christ " idea was to the needs
of men. In the Hermes-Aphrodite or the double-sexed
aumakua of the kahuna, or in Sri Ramakrishna's Divine
Mother, *Kali*, we find traces of a lost tradition which may
possibly explain the passage in the New Testament (Matthew
xxii 30) " For in the resurrection they neither marry nor are
given in marriage, but are as the angels of God in heaven."
If this " resurrection " refers to the graduation of a mated
male-and-female consciousness to the next higher plane,
that of the superconscious, it solves an ancient mystery. In
any event, there is no greater beauty of romance in all Magic
or Religion than this ideal of a perfect and inseparable
reunion of the two sundered parts of a being who can only
become One when they become each other and at the same
time become a part of God in his outer or creative manifesta-
tion. The tradition dims at this point, but still one may
trace the definite logic which assigns to this bi-polar *aumakua*
the superlative creative ability of an androgynous god—
makes it able to create things and events on the physical
plane by a process of " realizing " them into existence
through the use of the *mana* of the third or highest grade.

To get back to those who have attained Realization : In
the scholarly article in the source book of the moment, we
find all efforts have been made to learn just what was the
very heart of the Mysteries. Here we have our secret of
secrets again, or something which was never divulged because
it could not be put into words. All possible sources of
information are traced for us and the findings faithfully

reported. We can read that the password or formula of certain rites (Phyrgia ?) was : "I have eaten from the timbrel, I have drunk from the cymbal, I have carried the sacred vessel, I have crept under the bribal-chamber." The creeping under the bridal-chamber seems especially significant in the sense that the initiate may have seen beyond the earthly meaning of human mating. The other parts of the formula are supposed to refer to some sacred "communion" similar to the breaking of bread and the sharing of wine.

I will quote a few significant lines taken here and there from the article in the *Encyclopædia Britannica* in which the search is made for the secret of secrets—they relate mostly to lines salvaged from early writings on the subject of the Mysteries :

". . . the late rhetorician, Sopatros, who supposes the strange case of a man being initiated by a goddess in a dream ; they admit him to their full communion merely by telling him something and showing him something." (Realization ?)

"We gather also from Proclus and Hippolytus that in the Eleusinian rites they gazed up to heaven and cried aloud 'rain' and gazed down at the earth and cried 'conceive.' The ritual charm—we cannot call it a prayer. . . ." etc.

In the above bit of information we find an exact duplication of the ending of the invocational or incantational "prayers" used by the kahunas. This ending is, almost invariably, "*Amama, ua noa. Lele wale akua la.*" The first word is an invocation or call to the *aumakua ;* the second and third translate, literally, "rain," and "release or let go." The last part of the ending translates, literally, "The sacred silence—create ! " In the prayer of a kahuna by the named Hewahewa (see page 276) we will see that he used the customary symbol "rain" with the meaning "rain of blessings." And as this ending is found in all "prayers" of the high Magic of the kahunas, it would seem that the Mysteries of the Greeks and other races had this formula ending as a part of the secrets.

From our second source article in the *Encyclopædia Britannica* we learn that the word "mysticism" comes from

Greek words translating, "to shut the eyes" and "one initiated into the mysteries." The author says :

"Mysticism . . . a phase of thought, or rather perhaps of feeling, which from its very nature is hardly susceptible to exact definition. It appears in connection with the endeavour of the human mind to grasp the divine essence or the ultimate reality of things, and to enjoy the blessedness of actual communion with the Highest. . . .":

"Beyond the virtues which purify from sin, lies the further stage of complete identification with God. To reach the ultimate goal, thought itself must be left behind. . . . 'I myself,' says Plotinus simply, 'have realized it but three times as yet, and Porphyry hitherto not once.'"

" . . . The appeal is still to the individual who, if not by reason then by some higher faculty, claims to realize absolute truth and to taste its absolute blessedness."

The author of the article stresses the point that those mystics who have had a mystical experience tend always to revolt against the dogmas of religion. This is a fact that is important for us to remember. Later on we will see that an adherence to dogma makes contact with the Higher Self all but impossible.

· · · · ·

With Realization I have completed the listing of the non-kahuna sources from which I gathered data during my study in Hawaii.

My next step after gathering this data was to begin comparing it for the final time with the recovery of Magic in the West. Let us now go to that phase of our search for the mechanisms of kahuna Magic. I say "mechanisms" because we have now identified the source—the *aumakua*—of man's supernatural powers. It remains but to discover how that source may be contacted and persuaded to assist man in his life on the physical plane.

AS I have said, the recovery of Magic in the West began with experiments in the use of animal magnetism and the discovery of hypnosis. Next came the Rochester Rappings and the sudden spread of Spiritualism. Mysticism had never died out ; it was represented in Europe by various sects of Christianity, and in America by the Quakers.

The ingredients of Magic, therefore, were present in the West but not assembled and put to use. The plight of Christianity was never more desperate than at about 1830. It was stripped of Magic and groaning under its dogmas. Puritanical doctrine was especially oppressive in America although the Church of Rome still retained its saner and more tolerant attitude toward human frailties.

In 1847 Magic was given a second birth in the West—in America. Its father was a diminutive New Englander with piercing black eyes and a mind as investigative as it was deep and inquiring. This man was Pheneas Parkhurst Quimby. The foster-mother of Magic was Mrs. Patterson, who later became Mrs. Eddy. Its later godparents were the Swarts, Dressers, Dr. Towne, Prentice Mulford, Rev. Evans, Ralph Waldo Trine and others.

Our source books here are *The Quimby Manuscripts* (1921), edited and commented upon by Horatio W. Dresser of the second generation of godparents, and *Mary Baker Eddy* by Powell (1930). I give what seems to me to approximate the true story.

P. P. Quimby became an hypnotic expert in about the year 1840 and gave public demonstrations until about 1847. In his work he ran into occasional monitory, premonitory, mind-reading and healing abilities on the part of his favourite subject, Lucius Burkman. Puzzled and interested, Quimby made a long and experimental investigation to discover the source of these superphysical abilities. His search took him through Spiritualism—in which he found nothing useful—and finally led him to develop his own powers. This done, he was able to duplicate the puzzling abilities which were exhibited at infrequent intervals by his subject. Inevitably Quimby had come into Realization.

As do all mystics when they have had a glimpse behind the physical scene, this man threw aside religious dogmas, keeping the one central truth of the Father-Son.

In Chapter IX of the first-mentioned source book are to be found a number of his letters to his patients. In them we see one who has won through to Realization and who is attempting to expound his doctrine in parable and para-doxical explanation in order to heal his patients. His healing practice and his title of " Doctor " are coincident with the year 1847 and his practice lasted until his death in 1865.

His method of healing included the basic practices of the full Magic, but his understanding of its mechanisms was incomplete. He would sit beside a patient and make a psychic examination, using what he called the " Wisdom " within and what we would call the superconscious ability of monition—a monition without memory or reason, but which contacted and so realized disease origins and states. He did not attempt to cure all ills, often refusing to treat blindness and similar disabilities, but treated general health in the hope that the more fixed infirmities might respond.

His next step was to explain to the patient just what his intuitive examination had revealed. Repeatedly he states in his letters that his explanation—once accepted by the patient—was the cure. He would explain that the disease had been caused by the acceptance of suggestions applied by doctors or friends, or resulting from autosuggestion. His method of healing was primarily one of correcting these suggestions—we call it draining off complexes. But as this method worked no miracles—did not make cures beyond the ability of the suggestible conscious entity to make (the modern terms are mine)—he used the power he had contacted in Realization.

His method of using this power was simple. He had developed his monitory ability to the point of being able to use it at will. He watched his patient from a distance in his " absent treatment " and used a force higher than hypnotic force to send healing. He was usually able to predict the changes in health which would follow his treatments, and was therefore able to tell the patient how symptoms would react under treatment given mentally and from a distance— treatment which embodied the superconscious power to make changes in the body. His healing work was very successful.

He had discovered the kahunas' high *mana* and called it " Power." He found that it could make changes in the physical bodies of men, once they could be rid of the suggestions of disease and the faith in its actuality. Knowing that any force must have an intelligence to control and manipulate it, he here approximated the kahunas' *aumakua* and spoke of it as " Wisdom." Both the Power and the Wisdom were things he had touched and found to give him superphysical abilities. He taught that all men should be able to touch them. In this, his practice was of a philosophical as well as of a healing nature. The healing could be done by the lesser magic of changing mental attitudes, but it was more successful and greater in scope if the full Magic could be attained through an inner development of the patient— a development leading to personal contact with the Power and the Wisdom behind it.

The two main obstacles to health were considered to be medical and religious dogmas. Both of these he fought with all his might. His system was a science of verities and not a religion. He used no prayers to God, and classed sin and disease as things made potent by the " error " thoughts of men. So far as I can learn, he did not treat poverty conditions except by way of eliminating fears of poverty.

Mrs. Patterson (later Eddy) was brought to him as a last resort when she had been an invalid for years and was thought to be dying. Her illness was partly due to spinal trouble. In a week she was able to leave her bed and climb a long flight of steps. She became a fast friend of Dr.

Quimby and studied all his methods and philosophies. Upon her return home she undertook to heal, using his methods. He gave her every encouragement, and when at times she became ill or the old spinal affliction came back, he came to her rescue at once with his " absent treatment."

After his death this favourite disciple had a bad fall and the spinal trouble came back in full force. With Dr. Quimby dead, she was forced to make full contact with the super-conscious for herself. This she set about doing, and success eventually came. Undoubtedly she reached Realization before this final healing.

Now fully equipped and having her own source of Power and Wisdom to draw upon and guide her, she went rapidly ahead with the full healing and with teachings which she continued to expand and augment through the years. As her temperament differed from that of Dr. Quimby, she added to his rather non-religious philosophies the basic tenets of Christianity—trying to avoid hampering dogmas at all times.

Quimby's philosophy was of such a nature that he considered injurious thoughts " shadowy " or unreal, and in his teachings the paradox of the real-unreal physical plane constantly occurred. His idea of the physical, however, was not that of unreality on its own plane.

Mrs. Eddy's philosophy tended to give less reality to the physical and point always to the greater reality of the higher plane of consciousness.

Both of these pioneers of Magic in the West came in their turn to touch the state of Realization for themselves. Too much credit cannot be given either of them. When the difficult nature of all explanations in physical terms of the superphysical is understood, as it must now be understood by all Round Table members, a more intelligent approach can be made to the teachings of these torch-bearers in the West. That there was a slight misunderstanding about authorship and discoveries is a matter unworthy of remembrance on the part of those who look beyond the physical and glimpse the unified human being who has recovered his heritage of full contact with his own third entity of consciousness—the entity that is one with God-Externalized, and so, one with the higher entities of all men.

.   .   .   .   .

I have said that the lesser mechanics of the Magic recovered in the West were not fully rediscovered and put to use. Now, in Part Three, I come to the kahunas and the mechanics of their practices. We of the West have still many important " tricks of the trade " to learn. It is one thing to be able to accept abstract truths on faith and put them to work, and another thing to have at hand a concrete system grounded in data and acceptable to logic.

PART THREE

CHAPTER I

THERE were three main schools of Magic which survived in less civilized lands while Magic was being lost in the West. Let us examine them one by one.

THE VOODOO SCHOOL:

In Africa, centuries ago, there arose two great groups of magicians who were long unknown to each other. One group lived in the Congo and the other in Guinea. How any school came by its knowledge of Magic we can only guess. It may be that mediumistic savages saw "spirits" and from that seeing evolved their magic. It is evident that the approach was not always the same.

The Congo type of Magic in Voodoo rites includes much blood sacrifice. The Guinea rites include little. The former is largely concerned with propitiating devils, while the latter occupies itself with efforts to gain help from more friendly "gods."

That Voodoo magic is effective there seems little doubt, now that investigators like William Seabrook (see his *Magic Island*) have begun to describe it. In Africa investigators have done little, owing to the uncivilized state of native magicians and to language differences and other difficulties. In Haiti, where Congo and Guinea rites are combined, and where there is less savagery, we have a group much easier to study.

However, in Haiti Magic has been in contact with civilization for several centuries. This contact has resulted in such an alteration and contamination of the genuine or *workable* forms that the system is now about one-half garbled Christian dogma, three-eighths empty ritual or superstition

191

and one-eighth pure magic. To get to the one-eighth is like hunting for a needle in a haystack.

An observer in Haiti can see many "charms" or *ouangas* made and used—some seemingly with good results—but aside from the *zombies* or corpses raised and half-restored to life so that they may be enslaved, there is little reported which is satisfying or informative to the student.

The lack of a cult of secrecy in Voodooism makes it possible for a Caucasian to be initiated into the rites, once the confidence and friendship of the natives has been gained. But that very lack of a cult of secrecy has made contamination of the rites inevitable.

When we come to Kahunaism we will see a secrecy which raises great barriers, but which has served a marvellous purpose.

THE YOGA SCHOOL OF MAGIC IN INDIA :

This ancient school may or may not antedate Voodooism. In many respects the two are similar, especially if we consider only the Magic of Guinea. However, time has made great changes in yoga. In India, Religion seems to have risen almost as a thing apart from Magic. Religious dogmas gave artificial standards of right and wrong and imposed those standards on the magician and his pupils. Where right and wrong were lesser matters at first, they later came to be all-important. Brahmanism seems to have been foremost in demanding that men adopt its dogmas, and such an adoption being made, the magician found himself all but helpless.

Consider trying to be a magician in the India of to-day where you have a complexed religious belief which insists : 1. That the sole purpose of life and many incarnations is to help man to *escape* from life and be swallowed up in God and Brahma—to lose all individuality. 2. That to escape life and self, one must kill out *all* desire for earthly life, possessions or honour. 3. That to use magic for any other purpose than to promote "final absorption" is a sign that the devotee is not killing out desire, but is wickedly striving to gain some earthly thing or glory. 4. That magic must be used only in so far as it helps one to become " selfless " and so a step nearer assimilation with Brahma.

The " mahatmas " of Buddhist sects are a little less restrained by dogma ; but their use of magic is also a thing permitted only for spiritual purposes. It is true that Madam Blavatsky, founder of Theosophy, was taught simple magic by the mahatmas and was allowed to use it ; but it is necessary under most forms of Buddhism that one practise magic only under a " master " and after having given up most of one's earthly ambitions.

Under this hampering system of religious taboos, works of magic in India are now confined almost entirely to the practice of throwing oneself into the semi-dead state of trance in order that the spirit may leave the body and pass into Realization.   As to healing sickness in either self or friend : *it is not done*.   The dogma of " karma " prevents. Karma embodies the idea of eternal justice in India.   For past sins, in this or any other incarnation, there is no vicarious atonement as in Christianity.   One must suffer all ills of body or circumstances and so pay off the " karmic debt." For this reason, the magic found in modern India is forbidden to all but the " holy men." Thus Magic, in India, has been replaced by ANTI-SOCIAL RELIGIOUS DOGMAS.

The Theosophical Society has given Europe and America many of the best ideas of India ; but after the death of Madam Blavatsky, Theosophy slowly became more Brahman than Buddhist. At the present time, although it describes· possible methods of practising magic, its literature is crowded with warnings that such practices must be attempted only under the direction of a " master "—than which nothing is harder to find.

Many Americans have sought such a " master " ; but, so far, I have not known of a single instance in which the search has been successful. As Theosophy stands to-day, it is valuable to us as a comparing source for the mechanics of the human composite—man. But as for assistance in recovering Magic for *practical* and *social* use in daily living, it offers little or nothing.

THE KAHUNA SCHOOL OF MAGIC:

So far as I have been able to ascertain, the Polynesians are the only people possessing a workable and socially helpful magic such as the ordinary run of white laymen might be able to use. Most of my investigation has been made in Hawaii, but there are other and closely related schools, all identical in principle, in other Pacific islands. Hawaii, however, has been longest isolated—its magic, therefore, is less contaminated.

Students of Polynesia are now generally agreed that the homelands furnished the basic elements of custom and religion, also that changes came very gradually. It is my opinion that the basic principles underlying the original practices of magic have survived intact. Unquestionably there were classes of kahunas who had touched Realization and were so able to use the full Magic. Equally without question is the fact that the lesser kahunas had never touched Realization and so were able to use only a form of magic comparable to that which we have so far recovered in the West.

Generally speaking, there were three groups of kahunas. First there were the various kinds of mediums, few of which ever accomplished results of value. Next the group used a lesser magic based on a psychology superior to that of the West to-day. Last came the group able to use the powers of the plane of Realization and so perform seeming miracles.

I will sketch briefly the history of Polynesia and of Hawaii. Johannes C. Andersen's *Myths and Legends of the Polynesians* is our present source book. To supplement it we will use Thomas Thrum's *Hawaiian Folk Tales* and his *More Hawaiian Folk Tales*. My outline is based on these comprehensive works.

At about the time of Christ we find the several Polynesian tribes living in a land bordering on India and lying in the direction of Arabia. At that time came a steady invasion of peoples of Aryan affinities, and the tribes were forced, one by one, to migrate to the South Seas. These migrations covered a period of about five hundred years.

The several tribes can be recognized in the following

related groups: The Hawaiians and some of the New
Zealanders belonged to one group. The Samoans, Tongans,
Futuans and some of the Solomon Islanders and natives
of the New Hebrides belong to another. The Rarotongans,
Tahitians, Taumotuans (Paumoutans), Marquesans, Manga-
revans and most of the Maoris of New Zealand belong to still
another group.

The customs and religions of each group can be traced
back to the same source as those of India. The language
comes from Indian roots. Here, however, we run across a
most important difference. In the matter of Magic the
Polynesians seem to have brought with them a complete
and original system of which India was never fully aware—
or if aware of this system, the knowledge of it was partly
lost at a very early date. Particularly was the knowledge
of the methods of applying that knowledge lost. The seven
" bodies " of man are better known in India than in Polynesia
at the moment, but the use of that knowledge is entirely
lacking. It would seem that the " complex " was never
known in India, while in Polynesia the kahunas work with it
constantly and expertly. Even the correct mechanical
methods of attaining to Realization seem never to be found
in the Vedas, to say nothing of being found in the many
religions of India of which Realization is the very heart.
Furthermore, no practical use of the forces of the plane of
Realization has been seen in any age in India.

This original lack, or later loss, may have been due to
an accretion of religious dogma, although there are a few
evidences of an extremely early knowledge—if not practice—
of Magic. To-day the use of Magic seems confined to the
rite of fire-walking in some cults, and to the attainment of a
deep trance condition by the yogis.

The religion brought from the land near India contained
the idea of God as a Trinity of gods—the names of the
individual gods differing with the group. In Hawaii the
names were *Ku-Kaua-Kahi*, or, later, Ku, Kane and Lono,
represen'ing Sunlight, Substance and Sound. This trinity
was God the Absolute, the Akua; but God Externalized in
creation and in man was the *Aumakua*.

The above treatment of the *Aumakua* is not to be found in our source books, but is a part of the system as I have found it.

Aside from the Trinity and the *Aumakua* there were hosts of "gods" who formed a class of superphysical entities presiding over nature. These were the ones largely worshipped in the forms of idols. Below man ranged subhuman entities or "godlings."

The Father-Mother idea of God was always present, as it was in India, the Sky and Earth being the usual symbols of duality—and this duality extending down to the *Aumakua* and to man and woman on the physical plane.

The Hawaiians arrived in Hawaii about the year A.D. 500. They were entirely isolated from outside contact until about A.D. 1100 when a few Samoans came in. They were again isolated until the year 1778 when Captain Cook came and the white invasion was begun.

From early records may be learned much of the social condition of the Hawaiians at the time of the first influx of whites. The outstanding feature was the generosity and kindliness of the natives. The chiefs and kahunas were of about equal power in the land, one governing in matters of war, the other in matters of morals and dogmatic rites. The common people belonged to the chiefs and seemed to live happily although under many taboos.

Unquestionably there had evolved much useless dogma which had hindered the use of Magic and made life less free than it had been at an earlier period. Also there had come to be much imposition on the part of the lesser kahunas. The lives of the people were made difficult by forced observance of ritual in almost every act, and fear of the kahunas was great.

This condition was remedied in part by Kamehameha after he had finished conquering and uniting the islands. He outlawed all the lesser kahunas and gathered the really powerful ones from all the eight islands to act as his helpers. However, history seems to be at fault just here, as it is known that when the missionaries came some years later they found that only then had the temples and idols been destroyed and the old taboos lifted.

RESTORED HAWAIIAN TEMPLE AT NAPOOPOO, HAWAII, WHERE CAPTAIN COOK WAS WORSHIPPED
AND WHERE HE TORE DOWN THE FENCE FOR FIREWOOD

He was later killed on the shores of this bay. The foundations to the left once upheld the grass houses in which the kahunas lived and in which the gods were stored in bad weather. The platform at the right was the altar. On its top is a small phallic stone. Out of sight at the left is a monument to Henry "Obookiah" who was responsible for the influx of Missionaries.

This final outlawing of the kahunas and giving up of old dogmas did not come from Kamehameha, but from one of his queens and the young prince who came into power after the death of the conqueror. At the root of the change was the white man and his influence.

With the passing of the kahunas from power came the breaking down of an excellent moral policing which had been backed by punishment sent by Magic. This was not a condition that continued long, however, as the kahunas were soon at work again in secret. Meantime, the natives revelled in their freedom from all moral restraint and enjoyed themselves to the full with wine, women and revenge, until the missionaries took over.

With the coming of the missionaries the natives were bribed with instruction in reading and writing their own language, and coerced with threats of hell fire. The latter seems to have been very effective. At any rate, Christianity soon became supreme in the externals of life, and Kahunaism in the internals. One went to church to avoid hell and gain heaven, but one went to a kahuna when the practical things of health and prosperity were lacking. This condition of affairs still maintains to-day to some extent.

As a matter of fact, Christianity, when stripped of dogma, is identical with basic kahuna beliefs. A person can be a good kahuna of the highest class and still a genuine Christian. Many are both. The combination leads to a very social and beneficial order of things.

Nearly all of the Hawaiian Histories of to-day are derived largely from the writings of the missionaries, and, as might be expected, the reading of such histories gives the impression that the kahunas were wicked men who had no Magic and who battened on the superstitions of their fellows. It took fire-magic to help me get past the beliefs inculcated by such reading.

Between Christianity and Science they left nothing of a truly informative nature to be found in standard literature in so far as Magic is concerned. Denial and misrepresentation went hand in hand. Even the Hawaiian historian, David Malo, was unable to tell what he knew to be the facts of

Kahunaism. His book was edited by the missionaries and printed by them—enough said.

In recent years an endeavour has been made to present the kahuna in his true light, but even in this the Scientific Attitude has stood in the way. For those of the Round Table who may wish to check my report by the little material available, I can only offer a most scant list of sources : *The Twenty-Sixth Annual Report of the Hawaiian Historical Society*, 1918, by J. S. Emerson (who learned to perform weather magic without knowing how he did it), is perhaps the most authoritative and complete. In it are contained several of the old kahuna "prayers," but the translations given fail to get the secret meaning of the old words, and so leave the impression of utter ignorance and childishness. The files of the *Honolulu Star-Bulletin* for the Sunday issues of November, 1923, contain some good material in article form, the authors being a reporter, Howard Case, and an Hawaiian, John D. Wise. The December issue of the *Paradise of the Pacific* magazine for 1931 contains an excellent article by Johanna N. Wilcox.

In the above sources the classification of the kahunas do not agree, nor do the descriptions of methods of practice ; however, such agreement is more than could be expected at this late day. The only dependable information may be outlined as follows :

1. Kahunaism had degenerated until the kahunas were a privileged class in which few real magicians were to be found. The very name " kahuna " had come to mean " anyone skilled in some art," whether it be the art of farming, building or fishing. Over nearly every activity of life there was some kahuna to preside and to demand his fee. Before a house or a canoe could be built, the particular kahuna of that art had to be consulted. Many were, of course, expert in their line and able to give valuable advice, but the thing had been carried too far.

2. Doctoring with herbs, keeping the oral history, temple rites and the treating of lesser ills, were in the hands of a slightly higher grade of kahunas.

3. Prophecy and killing were in the hands of the most

powerful and highest grades of kahunas. Their ability to foretell the future was often demonstrated, and their killing could not be accounted for entirely by the use of poison or threats which caused the victims to die of pure fright.

4. A ritual of cleansing or forgiving sin was used, and invocational prayers were used.

While magicians of the finest still practise in other parts of the Pacific, in Hawaii they are disappearing very rapidly. The dogmas of Science and Religion have been taught in the schools, and the members of the younger generation are unfitted to learn the ancient practices, even if they desired to do so, which they do not.

In recent times it has been all but impossible for a white person to find a kahuna, to say nothing of contacting him to any purpose, although tales of their exploits are constantly to be heard on every side.

.   .   .   .   .

With this brief explanation I will go now to comparisons in which we will set kahuna beliefs and practices beside the data and conclusions we have so far accumulated.

In these comparisons may be seen either the true conditions and verities of the spirit world as seen by individuals trained in the possibilities of Realization, or we may see groundless superstitions. In either case, we shall see the mechanics of a workable magic becoming more and more clear as we progress.

CHAPTER II

IN the West our belief in brownies, fairies and the like has passed into the hands of the children. In Polynesia, however, the brownie, in the form of the *menehune* still persists.

Where we have given up our belief in mermaids and other semi-human beings, the Hawaiians have not. To the Polynesian the universal consciousness extends from God to minerals. They even refuse to sweep dust from the house after dark for fear the conscious dust will feel injured because it is cast out into the darkness.

CASE 34

BROWNIES IN THE WEST, BUT *MENEHUNES* IN HAWAII

Preliminary Notes :

Polynesian legends are filled with the tales of the activities of the " little people " or brownie-like *menehunes*. They are accredited in some legends with miraculous powers and even with being the ancestors of mankind.

In the several islands of the Hawaiian group there are numerous ancient fishponds beautifully and lastingly made with stone walls which extend over tidal plains. The origin of these is unknown, as is also that of stone irrigation canals on the island of Kauai. The Hawaiians say they were built for them by the *menehunes* in the good days when each race lovingly served the other. For verification of the following account see back numbers of *Thrum's Hawaiian Annual.*

The Case :

There are two well-authenticated instances of the appearance of *menehunes* in very recent times. Both were delightedly discussed at length by Honolulu newspapers and recorded by Thrum in his review of the year.

In one case a *menehune* was observed by an entire family of Hawaiians. In the other, one was seen by a large group of school children. This last instance will serve our purpose.

During the noon hour the children were playing as usual in the school yard. Suddenly some of them began to shout and point. The other children looked, and there, walking sedately along one side of the yard, was a little brown man about two feet tall, dressed in a *malo* or loin-cloth of *tapa* such as was worn by the Hawaiians of yesterday. He was bare-headed and slightly bearded. His face was wrinkled and old. As he walked along he cracked peanuts and tossed aside the shells.

The astounded children remained silent a moment then raised cries of excited delight. " *Menehune! Menehune!* " In a moment all the children in the school yard were there.

The little old man surveyed them indifferently for a moment, then, when they began to close in on him, took to his heels. This was, very naturally, an invitation for pursuit. " Catch him ! Catch him ! "

But the little man was as swift as he was clever. He fled to a teacher's cottage which was built low on the ground, pulled aside a loose strip, and dived to safety under the floor.

The children swarmed to the loose strip and peered under the house. Another strip was pried off and some of the bolder boys crawled in to continue the search. It was some time before anyone thought of the precaution of surrounding the cottage to cut off escape into neighbouring cane-fields.

The teachers heard the shouts and came out of the building to investigate. They heard the story and saw the great excitement of Hawaiian, Japanese, Chinese and Filipino children, most of whom had arrived in time to see the *menehune*. All their accounts were the same. Also, the fresh peanut shells were found where they had been tossed aside.

Time came for classes to be called and the bell was rung despite the tearful pleas of the children that they might be allowed to continue their search for the droll little man.

Comment :

In both cases the *menehune* had been seen in broad daylight and by more than one person. Both *menehunes* had run for cover and disappeared. There seems to be little doubt that actual *menehunes* exist, as tales of their appearance are not infrequent.

·   ·   ·   ·   ·

Of the "gods" ranking between the *Akua* and the *Aumakua* there is one who runs through countless legends and who is more frequently reported seen than the *menehunes*. This is Pele, the goddess of volcanoes and, conversely, goddess of the enemy of volcanic fires, the waters. The fire and water relation are a little obscure, but her aspect as water goddess is invoked in fire-walking over hot lava.

I have met several Hawaiians who have sworn that they have seen this goddess face to face when she had taken the form of an old woman. Tradition has it that she appears at isolated houses as an old Hawaiian woman, and begs food or tobacco. Usually her coming predicts a volcanic outburst.

Another of the lesser gods is the "Shark Goddess." As there is more definite data concerning her, I will give it in a case.

CASE 35

SHARK GODDESS

Preliminary Notes :

In the lore of India as presented in Theosophical teachings the existence of varieties of superhuman and subhuman spirit entities is affirmed. There are sylphs, undines, nature spirits and so on, but nothing resembling Pele or the Shark Goddess very closely. In the West we have nothing at all of this nature.

Polynesian legend is replete with tales of the pacts made

between men and the Shark Goddess. In Hawaii it is said that an ancient pact still holds and that, for that reason, sharks do not molest humans in the water surrounding the eight islands. Oddly enough, this is a fact. I have yet to hear of a living person being eaten by a shark, although the remains of a drowned soldier were found in the stomach of one. Sharks of many kinds abound in the region, and in many similar Pacific localities the danger is one long recognized.

Fishermen gcing to the island of Lysan, which lies in similar waters, have been attacked even in very shallow water by sharks, and have had to fight their way through knee-deep surf with flailing oars.

If we are to believe Hawaiian history, the chiefs were in the habit of feeding the victims of battle to the sharks and also of fishing for the sharks with great hooks. A certain class of kahunas had the duty of feeding special sharks who came for food at stated times, and also the duty of observing the ancient rites of worship accorded the Shark Goddess.

What the true relation may have been between man and shark, I am unable to learn.

The Case :

Shortly after Hawaii was annexed by the United States, the naval base at Pearl Harbour was established. The entrance to this beautiful harbour was dredged and work begun on a great dry-dock of reinforced concrete and steel.

Experienced builders had the contract and the plans were such as were ordinarily drawn up for that type of structure. As the work progressed it was checked at every step by Government engineers and inspectors.

Almost as soon as the ground was being prepared, an old Hawaiian came to the engineer in charge. Excitedly he explained that the dry-dock could not be built in that exact location. Under the shore lay a great submerged cave which was the home of the Shark Goddess at such rare times as she returned from her many travels. If she found the way into her cave blocked she would use her supernatural powers to clear it. Certain disaster was predicted.

The old man was very insistent, but his warning was laughed at. He came again and again, however, and his story spread abroad. Many of the Hawaiians on the job quit.

From a diver engaged in setting the great foundation blocks, I have the story of what happened. He had been on the shift which had just come off the job and was present when the nearly completed dry-dock began to break up as if repeatedly dynamited. It was as if a great earthquake confined to the surface of the land just under the structure was sending in wave after wave in the earth itself. The shore trembled, but the dry-dock was shattered, this in spite of the steel reinforcements and its great thickness. Several men were killed.

Naturally the old man's warning was recalled, but still the white engineers were slow to believe that the Shark Goddess had actually done the damage. However, no possible explanation could be given for such a complete breaking up of the structure. Earthquake and tidal wave were out of the question.

The men who had bonded the contractors paid in to the Government because it could not be proved that a super-natural agency had undone the work. New bids were called for, but none was made. The builders did not believe in the Shark Goddess, but they were unanimously agreed that something was very wrong and that the job was one to be avoided.

After some time the Government called in the famous builder, Drydock Smith. This gentleman came. He looked over the ground and listened to all that was said either by white or by Hawaiian. In the end he agreed to undertake to build another dry-dock, but specified that the site be moved a good half-mile toward the sea. His request was granted and the second dry-dock is in use to-day.

The mystery has never been solved and no other solution has been offered other than the one of the angry Shark Goddess opening the entrance to her home. I have heard several stories of how the Goddess has been seen in Pearl Harbour from year to year, but have been unable to get a description of her appearance except that she is a marvellously large shark.

Comment :

From our data we have nothing to compare with this semiphysical entity unless it might be a gigantic poltergeist—which brings us to absurdities and little else.

· · · · ·

For the next case I turn to Polynesian activities in Samoa which were reported by Mr. George W. Hutchinson, Secretary of the National Geographic Society, in the *Geographic News Bulletin*, issue of December 10, 1934.

CASE 36

SAMOAN CHILDREN WORKING MAGIC BY THE USE OF INCANTATIONAL RITUALS

Preliminary Notes :

This story is told by Mr. Hutchinson as an eye-witness, and so should be authoritative enough for our purpose as the gentleman is an official of an organization which for years, either by accident or by intention, has refrained from publishing pictures of fire-walking—pictures which might raise questions not sanctioned by the Scientific Attitude of our times. I take it that this story is a good omen and that the *National Geographic Society* may soon see fit to get and publish data on fire-walking, even if no explanation of the phenomena is attempted.

The Case :

(I condense.) Mr. Hutchinson heard of the strange ritual of the " Calling of the Shark and Turtle " in Samoa. Through the aid of white officials he was able to investigate.

At the village of Vai Togi—" Hurled Waters "—the natives gathered and the children were sent alone to a point jutting over the sea. There is an old legend telling how a prince and princess had been sacrificed to a god in times of trouble. They had jumped from the promontory into the raging water at the base of the cliff where the waves broke and had been drowned. As a reward for their courage and patriotism the gods had turned them into a shark and turtle respectively. As such, they still are called to appear by chanting children.

Standing overlooking the sea and being drenched with spray, the children went through the first part of the ritual invocation with its accompanying beckonings. "In about four minutes" a small shark, some four or five feet long, appeared in the clear water beyond the breaking waves. It remained in sight "a minute or more," then swam away.

The chant and ritual changed slightly for the second part, and soon a turtle appeared and swam here and there, departing as the shark had done after "a short visit."

Comment :

Mr. Hutchinson seems to have no doubt in his mind but that the ritual of magic actually resulted in the appearance of both turtle and shark. Certainly those who perform this magic, as their ancestors had performed it before them through the years, could have no doubts.

In several printed accounts of South Sea travel I have run across mention of similar relations with sharks and turtles. One account told of a shark who came into shallow water to be fed and admired daily by the natives. It was shot one day by a white man who did not know that it was a "sacred shark," and much trouble followed.

As we find little useful data here, we may simply note the fact that the "X" power was used and the sharks fed down the years and worshipped by certain kahunas set aside for that purpose. To this worship was added the very personal relation of numerous families who were blood relatives of the shark spirits—if they may be believed when they tell of the strange relation.

In the West we have the dim tradition of vampires and werewolves, but nothing like the shark-human, unless it be the mermaid.

CASE 37

SHARK-BABIES

Preliminary Notes :

In the West, as in Hawaii, a woman occasionally gives birth to a bag of water instead of a baby. An instance of this is said to have occurred in the Russian Royal Family not many years ago.

In Hawaii it is almost universally believed that this " water birth " is connected with the shark relations set up by the kahunas in olden days. I am not certain that this belief is grounded on facts, but I feel sure that there is still much to be investigated and brought to light concerning it. Dr. Brigham told me that he had investigated several such cases and had even been in the same house when such a " water baby " had been born. After much questioning he had learned that the Hawaiians firmly believed that a spirit was born with the bag of water—always a spirit of human kind, but intended to inhabit the body of a shark. He was told that the baby could use its magical powers to bring its shark body up out of the sea if the home of the parents was not too far from the shore, and that food set out on nights when the " moon was right " was " eaten " by the visiting shark-baby.

The Case :

Wishing to test this assertion, Dr. Brigham waited with a family one night to see the visitation. Between the hours of ten and eleven there was heard a fishy flopping outside the house. Everyone remained quiet for fear of frightening the " baby " away, but Dr. Brigham was posted at the door to watch.

It was an overcast night and the moonlight was faint as it fell on the sandy beach and the narrow strip of grass which separated it from the house. After watching for over an hour, he suddenly saw what seemed to be the softly glittering body of a young shark flopping steadily toward the house. It passed noisily within ten feet of the watcher and entered the room in which *poi* and other choice viands, including raw fish, had been set out on a platter.

For several minutes the " baby " made much commotion in the room, pushing the platter and pounding its tail enthusiastically on the floor.   In due time it took its flopping departure by the same route over which it had come.

Much intrigued, Dr. Brigham had lighted a lantern and gone to investigate.   The platter had been upset and the food scattered about the room, but nothing had been eaten. Across the sand, the trail was clearly visible.

Dr. Brigham's comment on the matter was characteristic of many similar comments made to me after telling of one of his " kahuna experiences."   He smiled and spread his hands helplessly as he said, " I am forced to tell you exactly what I saw and heard, even if I cannot explain it.   This shark-baby business has puzzled me greatly for years.   I never could come to have any real belief in them until after I had seen so many weird things that I could see no reason for singling out the shark-baby phenomena to deny."

Comment :

Among my Hawaiian friends I have one, an old man, who solemnly and repeatedly has assured me that his family is connected closely with the sharks.   His fathers had made offerings to them, and in his own family a " water baby " had been born and watched both in shark form and in childish spirit form.   As a child, the baby played around the house for hours, overturning things, crying when hurt and always being more or less clearly seen and heard by the mother.   At times it could also be seen and heard by the old man—the father.

The child grew up to be a fine man in the spirit world, and often came to give his parents valuable advice.   In its shark body it was often seen at sea coming to swim for hours beside any canoe in which the father might be sitting.

On one occasion the old man was caught by a storm at sea. His small canoe was swamped and he was in danger of drowning.   He called wildly for his shark-son and a moment later felt the great shark rise under him and bear him up.

Clinging as best he could with his legs, he rested until he had recovered his strength, then, with the assistance of the powerful " son," managed to right the canoe. With the water bailed out, the shark set out before him and acted as guide through the gathering darkness through the reefs. When near the shore it playfully splashed water on the father with its tail, then swam rapidly away.

I once talked to a brown mother who claimed to have given birth to a " water baby " of this kind, one who grew to maturity as a spirit living partly at home and partly in the body of a blue shark.

If a multitude of legendary tales are to be believed—even if the testimony of some of the Hawaiians is to be taken at all seriously—the possibility of getting a human body for the water-spirit is not too remote, always providing the proper kahuna can be found.

All traditions agree that the kahuna follows the example of the god Kane (one of the Hawaiian Trinity) when he made the first man. Red clay is obtained and a body moulded from it. White clay is moulded into a head. When all is ready the kahuna calls the baby spirit to him, uses high magic to change the clay into a body, and installs the baby spirit.

Such a proceeding shocks the Scientific Attitude complex unbearably, but I am forced to call attention to the materialization of small living animals in the séances of the West, also to the Voodoo magicians who raise the dead to make " zombies " of them, if reports are to be believed. But let the matter rest. I doubt if there will be an epidemic of water babies in the West which will demand attention even when the full Magic is recovered.

CHAPTER III

NOW we come to more familiar ground. We are ready to compare the spiritualistic phenomena of the West and of Polynesia.

In the earlier cases which we have examined we have come upon spirits showing high and low forms of intelligence, also we have seen visible ectoplasm and the thing we have, for the time, called "invisible ectoplasm," but which is something very different.

For the purpose of comparison, let us first take the poltergeist. It is, as we recall, an invisible ghost which makes its presence known by racketing about with the furniture and by making weird noises.

In all the less civilized parts of the world the poltergeist is well known. In Malay lands he is greatly feared and is considered a "devil." A Jesuit priest writing in 1934 reported on his investigation of these "devils" and told how he had found them throwing stones through the windows of native houses—the stones following the dodging victim about the room and striking him.

In kahuna lands the people fear these "devils" less. The kahunas are impatient with maurauding poltergeists—the *lapu* in Hawaii—and chastise them promptly when they become too bold.

Through language differences the word "kahuna" has changed in different parts of Polynesia. It is *tufunga* in Tonga and Samoa, *tuhuna* in the Marquesas, *tahua* in Tahiti, *taunga* in the Cook Islands, and *tohunga* in the Maori land of New Zealand. But under any name the kahuna, when of the most expert classes, handles the poltergeist in a way that puts our mediums of the West to shame. They could even give valuable pointers to such a proficient ghost layer as Bishop James of London.

I know of but one case in which a poltergeist made a nuisance of itself, and even then it was not a genuine poltergeist coming under the definition of being subhuman. It was one of our " less intelligent " human ghosts which we have identified by its lack of power to reason.

CASE 38

A POLTERGEIST IN HAWAII

Preliminary Notes :

I have this story from a friend who knew the man involved and who assures me that it is true. I will give it for what it may be worth, as I lack another case of this type.

The Case :

A young Hawaiian was repeatedly struck in the back by something which he could not see or hear. He could not find who was striking him. Guessing the nature of the attack, although such attacks are rare indeed in Hawaii, he went to a kahuna.

The kahuna listened to the details of the attacks, then requested one of his intelligent spirit friends to find and bring in the poltergeist. In due time the culprit was found and brought to the kahuna. He was one of the reasonless spirits, but had a fine memory. He had belonged to a class of lesser kahunas whose work was to charge throwing-sticks with *mana* and use them in battle to kill on contact with an enemy.

Now this spirit had discovered a great resemblance between the young Hawaiian and a hated enemy of other days. Lacking power to reason, he mistook the Hawaiian for the enemy and began throwing a ghostly stick at him. He complained that his *mana* seemed surprisingly weak and that he could no longer kill.

The kahuna explained the mistake to the spirit and then

used his "medium *mana*" (hypnotic) to impress his order to let living humans strictly alone. He also used his power to strip the spirit of its ability to gather more "low *mana*" (animal magnetism) with which to charge his ghostly stick.

Thereafter the young Hawaiian was no longer troubled.

Comment :

Legends tell of the *mana*-charged throwing-stick, and the older Hawaiians claim that its use was efficient in battle. For the sake of other comparisons with aboriginal magic we have but to go to Brinton's account of the American Indians and their magicians. These not only knew fire-magic, but they were expert at collecting forms of *mana* which they grouped under the name *orenda* in some tribes and under other names in other tribes.

Both *mana* and *orenda* check with our animal magnetism and hypnotic force, each, we may say, has a different voltage and works on a different plane.

Brinton saw medicine-men demonstrate their *orenda* in a startling way. They approached a man and knocked him unconscious by touching him on the chest with one finger. This feat was also observed by Carver and Fletcher while studying the Menominee and Sioux tribes in 1850.

The kahunas have three grades of *mana* in their system of Magic. The third and highest is the next above the hypnotic *mana* and is used in performing the full Magic.

These *manas* correspond with three grades of consciousness long recognized by the kahunas as separate ENTITIES which make up man and which use his physical body. These entities correspond exactly with our subconscious, conscious and superconscious. These entities bear the same name whether in the physical body during life or outside of it as in death or trance. The names are, *unihipili, uhane* and *aumakua*. The ghosts bear the same names and usually are composed of but one entity, although frequently the subconscious and conscious entities (*unihipili* and *uhane*) keep together after death and become the reasoning and remembering ghost or *kinowailua* (ghost of two waters—water being the symbol of life). The *lapu* is any *unihipili* or subhuman entity who makes himself ridiculous—the name *lapuwale* being applied to any living human who is ridiculous.

The *aumakua* or superconscious entity does not live in the body, but is attached to it in a psychic way. It corresponds to the " Wisdom " which P. P. Quimby identified, while the high *mana* corresponds to the " Power ",—it being the force used by the superconscious entity to make actual physical changes on the earth plane and mental changes on the mental plane.

I make these statements at this time without giving the proper proof that the high *mana* and the *aumakua* of the kahunas are what I represent them to be, but the proofs will come in due time. Just now I am involved in the task of trying to report on many things which anticipate the present stage of our comparisons, therefore I mention these matters.

We will next examine cases in which the spiritualistic phenomena of the West is partly duplicated but largely augmented by the use of hypnotic *mana* to control subconscious entities, or *unihipili* spirits.

CASE 39
THE KAHUNA AND THE ILLOGICAL GHOST

Preliminary Notes :

I am passing over the mediums of Hawaii who are some- times called " kahunas," but who use no potent force to perform a magic different in any way from that of the séance-room in.the West.

In demonstrations of monition, premonition and material- ization we have contact with the *aumakua* as a " spirit," and there the real Magic begins. I am, therefore, passing over the mediums who do not contact the *aumakua* except at uncertain intervals.

The genuine kahuna is an individual who has established contact with his *aumakua*. The degree and ease of contact together with the completeness of contact—up to full identification—is the measure of a kahuna's power and class. Most kahunas have but an uncertain degree of contact and so of power, but even these can perform the lesser magic with the use of hypnotic and animal magnetism *manas* alone. In this they resemble the bulk of our practitioners of lesser magic in the West.

The difference between a medium and a magician may be clearly defined. The former is used by the spirits, while the latter USES THE SPIRITS. In this use the subconscious or *unihipili* spirit is the only one which may be so used and commanded. The *uhane* is able to reason and, also, is not to be controlled with the hypnotic *mana*, as that is the *mana* of its own plane. Only the next lower plane of existence can be controlled by the one above it. By this I mean that there are two things to be considered: The " Wisdom " and the " Power " of the superconscious plane and their duplicates on the mental plane. Wisdom is thought and it controls by controlling the thoughts of the entity next lower. Power is *mana* or force, and it makes changes in the lower *manas*. As the electron is the unit of force of which all physical material is composed, those changes are changes in the force of the electron.

With this very brief and unevidenced warning of the trend my report is to take, I will now go back to the case of the moment. We are about to consider one of the lesser kahunas whose work is primarily with the two lower *manas* and with the two lower entities of consciousness. In the use of these two elements we will find valuable data as well as proof of the correctness of the kahuna system of psychology.

As I am giving but one case of this type—one in which the magician controls the subconscious ghost and accomplishes feats of magic thereby, I must now give the details of the procedure and the philosophy behind it.

The kahuna knows the fact that three separate entities of consciousness exist both during physical life and after physical death. The reason he knows this is because he can use these entities as tools. For low magic the *unihipili* is the tool and the *uhane* of the kahuna the user of the tool.

Ghostly *unihipilis* are either inherited from another kahuna or are captured by the use of hypnotic force. The *unihipili* is a subconscious entity and hypnotic force will control it. It has memory, but not reason. Without reason it cannot learn of its condition as a slave of the kahuna, nor can it learn that there is any course to follow except the one outlined by the kahuna for it.

In order to keep the *unihipilis* " strong " and able to work, they are fed on animal magnetism which is generated in the body of the kahuna and transferred to food and drink. It is also possible that, under hypnotic influence, these spirits can absorb alcohol and food vapours and use them as foods. In any event, the " feeding " of the *unihipili* spirits is the daily chore of this grade of kahuna. At times when work is to be done, an extra feeding with " low *mana* " is given— the foods being laid out in what is called a *papa*—" the forbidden." Around the food are laid small stones, bits of wood and other objects, the purpose of which seems to be to store the animal magnetism which is to be discharged into the *unihipilis* to give them power to act against the *unihipili* of a living person whose subconscious or physical body is less highly charged.

As we are not to see the kahuna at work in this case, I will describe his usual procedure—one which is well known in Hawaii even though the underlying purpose is not understood.

The spirits are called, fed and charged. They are then given orders which have the power of suggestion enforced by hypnotism. As the *unihipilis* cannot reason, the orders are most detailed and explicit unless the spirits have long been trained to act in a certain way when the order is given in a ritual " prayer " such as the one following :

> " O Lono,
> Listen to my voice.
> This is the plan :
> Rush upon and enter ;
> Enter and curl up ;
> Curl up and straighten out."

In this translation the name of the third god of the Hawaiian Trinity is a mistake. No kahuna would use it in such a way.

The process is one of sending one or more *unihipilis* to force themselves into the body of the victim and paralyse the body in the "straighten out" part of the work. In multiple personality cases we have seen entities come and go, so we can understand what happens.

With the orders given by the prayer or in thrice-repeated and detailed form, the *unihipilis* are now ready to go to the victim. In order to be able to reach him without a mistake being made, a mechanical aid is used in a way which suggests nothing so much as setting a dog on the scent. A part of the victim's body has been procured and is now called to the attention of the *unihipilis*. It may be a hair, some spittle, a finger-nail, or even some perspiration-soaked garment. It is called the *maunu*, or "bait." After the presentation of the "bait" the spirits go at once to the original owner of the *maunu* and carry out their orders—this taking from one to three days to bring death.

The progress of the work is followed by the kahuna with his monitory ability, and he can use his *mana* to recall the *unihipilis* or to keep them at their task.

Later on we will take up a case in which another kahuna takes a hand and interferes with the killing.

The only two grades of kahunas who kill are the "death prayer" of *anaana* and the *kuni* or burning. Killing is a very small part of their work and they are usually engaged in more pleasant occupations. Never do they kill when a less drastic treatment will suffice, and never does a guiltless individual die at their hands.

The Case :

I have selected this case in preference to several others because it proves beyond question that various assertions made concerning the mechanics of the killing are false. No poison was used here or it would have been discovered. The victim was not hypnotized by the kahuna. The victim was not "frightened to death." And last of all, the victim was a white man who did not believe in Kahunaism— a belief supposed to be necessary to one before he can be killed.

During my stay in Honolulu there were three *anaana* deaths a year on the average in one of the large hospitals. For two of those years I had information concerning the deaths from a young interne whose bump of curiosity was almost as large as mine. During those two years all the victims but one were Hawaiians or part-Hawaiians. The cause of death was not discovered in any case unless it was magic. The victims were brought in suffering from a slow paralysis beginning in the lower limbs, or from general collapse. The frantic relatives knew the symptoms, even if the less well-informed of the doctors did not.

A famous hypnotist practised in Honolulu for a part of this period under close observation by my interne friend. This operator used his power successfully in treating nervous disorders and as a substitute for an anæsthetic. He also had the opportunity to see what he could do for three of the kahuna victims, but found that he could not hypnotize them. One case which was thought not to be the result of a " death prayer," but of fright following a threat, was cured.

Now for the case proper : A young Irishman came to Honolulu with the first of the modern taxicabs. He was rough and ready, his hair was red and he was afraid of nothing.

Before he had been long in the city he had contrived to get a fine Hawaiian girl so much in love with him that she broke off her engagement to a Hawaiian boy. The girl's grandmother did her best to break up the new affair, seeing as she did that the Irishman had no good intentions. She even went so far as to make veiled threats that heaven would punish him if he did not leave the girl alone.

Very naturally, the Irishman had no fear of heaven. He was very much of the Scientific Attitude and quite accustomed to the futile threats of angry mothers and grandmothers. It is certain that such threats could not have had the least effect on him.

One day his feet " went to sleep " on him. He did his best to right matters, but the prickling numbness crept slowly upward. In the course of a day he had passed through the hands of two doctors and landed in the hospital.

Every effort was made to discover the cause of the malady, but no cause was found and no treatment availed. In fifty hours the prickling had reached his waist. When several doctors had interested themselves in the case, including my friend, there came head-shakings and grave suspicion. An old doctor who had practised long in the Islands was called in. He recognized the symptoms at once as those of the " death prayer."

Taking the patient in hand he questioned him closely and soon learned the story of the girl. More questioning brought back the memory of the grandmother's threats. Saying nothing, the wise old gentleman set off to visit the grandmother. Later he gave the substance of the conversation he held with her.

" I know that you are not a kahuna and have had nothing to do with this case, Grandma," said the doctor. " But, just as a friend, will you tell me if you think anything could be done to save the man ? "

" Well," said Grandma, " I know nothing about the matter, and I am no kahuna—as you know. But I think that if the man would promise to take the next ship for America and never return or even write back, he might recover."

" I will guarantee that he will do just those things," said the doctor.

" All right," said Grandma.

The situation had to be explained over and over to the unbelieving Irishman, but when the idea finally was driven home to him, he became terrified and was willing to agree to any terms. That was in the early afternoon. That night he was on his feet again and able to catch a Japanese ship for the " Coast."

Comment :

In this case we see the proof of the several statements which I have made concerning the falsity of opinions generally held by the whites in Hawaii. We also see that the *unihipilis* can be recalled.

. . . . .

As I can give no well-authenticated case of the practice of the kahuna of " burning "—this owing to the extreme rapidity with which death comes to the victim—I will simply outline what is known of the method used.   In passing, may I say that the kahuna in the play, the *Bird of Paradise*, was made to use a combination of the *anaana* and *kuni* methods of sending death.

So far as I can learn, the *kuni* kills only to avenge one murdered.   He may or may not use spirits of the *unihipili* order, but I am inclined to think that he does not.   He is said by some investigators to use a " bait," and if he does, he would use *unihipilis* in all probability, but his invocation is made to Pele and offerings are made to both fire and sea— these offerings including the ashes of a burned part of the murdered person's hair or flesh.   The symptoms are a terrible burning sensation.   Death is the only relief.   From prayer to death only a few hours elapse.   No kahuna can undo this form of Magic, if I am rightly informed.

As data and proof are self-evident in the above case, I will now present a case in which a " death prayer " was sent back to the kahuna who sent it.   Again we will get a new light on kahuna beliefs and practices.

CHAPTER IV

CASE 40

DR. BRIGHAM TURNS KAHUNA

Preliminary Notes :

IN the lesser magic—such magic as is practised in the West by our healing sects of Christianity and Psychology —much confusion of method has resulted from the lack of a clear understanding of the nature of man and his three conscious entities. This lack of understanding has largely been caused by scientists refusing to consider the possibility of a superconsciousness, and by the fact that superconscious activities such as monition, premonition and materialization have appeared in connection with the subconscious—at such times as they appeared at all—making such phenomena seem to come from the subconscious.

In the kahuna system of psychology the complex has been known for years. All lesser magic revolves about it and its relation to the activities and possibilities of the conscious and superconscious entities and their forces.

I will explain this more fully a little later, so let me give the application of the kahuna psychology in the case to come : There is no sin before God or Magic, to the kahuna way of thinking ; but what replaces sin is the complexed belief in guilt or unworthiness which may be held by the subconscious or *unihipili*. If such a complex is present it makes a person liable to punishment or death by Magic—this, because the subconscious entity will accept punishment if it has a complexed belief that it is deserved. If no such complex is present, the *unihipili* is quite able to repel any attack made by other *unihipilis*.

Knowing the nature of his own *unihipili*, the kahuna, after sending out a " death prayer "—should he suspect that it might be returned to him—*kalas*, or forgives himself in a certain mechanical way so that his subconscious mind will not be open to the attack of the trained and *mana*-charged *unihipilis* should they be turned against him.

The fact that the *unihipilis* can be sent back to attack their master is well known. The *unihipili* is perfectly understood. It is known to be affected by hypnotic *mana* and to be so lacking in reason or logic that a second kahuna can argue it out of its original intention and make it believe that the first kahuna deserves killing. When it is returned, it is usually given a fresh charge of animal magnetism and backed by strong hypnotic influences which have a dangerous quality inasmuch as they increase the original power of the " death prayer " and make it far more dangerous than before.

The Case :

I will give this case as I transcribed it from my notes shortly after an evening spent with Dr. Brigham. I will use his words as nearly as possible.

" I went to Napoopoo on the Big Island," said Dr. Brigham, " soon after the Museum was built. I wanted to climb Mauna Loa to collect indigenous plants. It was to be a three-weeks' trip with native guides and a pack train.

" At Napoopoo I spent five days getting men and pack animals together, but finally set out with four Hawaiians and eight horses and mules. It was good weather, and aside from the usual difficulties of those days when trails were all but lacking, we got on very well.

" I had reached the barren country above the rain forests and was making for the summit crater of Mauna Loa when one of my boys became ill. He was a strong lad of twenty. I left him behind with a man to care for him and went on to the summit, thinking it was the altitude which was bothering him and that he would soon be all right.

" We spent the day in the crater and got back to the lower camp and the sick boy early in the evening. He was stretched out on a blanket, now too weak to rise. I decided to move him to a lower level the next morning, and was about to sit down to my evening meal when one of the older men came to me.

" ' That boy very sick,' he said. Then, after much beating about the bush, it came out that the Hawaiians had decided that he was being prayed to death. I was slow to believe, but went to the boy and questioned him.

" ' Do you think you are being prayed to death ? ' I asked.

" ' No ! No ! ' He was instantly frightened within an inch of his life. I next asked him if he had any enemies who might want to have him killed. He could think of none, and was more than anxious to have me say that I still thought it was the altitude that was bothering him.

" I made another and more thorough examination, but found nothing significant except the usual symptoms of slow paralysis of the lower limbs and threatening general collapse, all of which symptoms belong to the death prayer. At last I became convinced that the old man was right and that some kahuna was at work. When I admitted this, all the men became frightened. For all they knew the whole party might be killed.

" I went back to my meal and thought things over. Meantime, one of the men kept on questioning the boy. After a while he got some interesting information. The boy's home was on the windward side of Hawaii in a little out-of-the-way village in a narrow valley which ran to the sea. There was little to bring the *haoles* (whites) to the village, and its old kahuna had endeavoured to keep the people isolated and living in the old way. Among other things he had commanded them to have no dealings with the *haoles* under penalty of being prayed to death. The boy had left home and gone to live in Kona several months back. He had all but forgotten the command.

" Up to the time of my arrival at Napoopoo, the boy had lived entirely with his Hawaiian friends and had not come into contact with white men—at least not in a business way. When I was hiring men for my trip up the mountain, he had joined me without a second thought. It had not occurred to him that the command still held outside his own village.

"As I heard about these things I became more and more angry. My temper was no better in those days than it is now when it comes to someone injuring my friends. I sat there wishing I could lay hands on the kahuna, and also facing the fact that my work would have to stop if the boy died and I had to take him down to the coast.

"While I was thinking things over, the old man came to me as spokesman for the others and made a perfectly natural suggestion. He politely called my attention to the fact that all Hawaiians knew that I was a great kahuna and even a fire-walker. To him it seemed simple enough that I should adjust matters by praying the kahuna to death and saving the boy.

"The men waited expectantly, and I could see in their eyes their confidence that I would turn back the death prayer and that all would be well. On my part I was cornered. I had bluffed for years, and now my bluff had been called. I was most uncomfortable. If I refused to do the obvious thing they would be sure that I was afraid of the kahuna and was not the strong fellow I pretended to be.

"Now I've always had a considerable pride, and at the thought of showing what might be mistaken for the white feather before my men, I decided there and then to try my hand at sending the death prayer back to the kahuna. This is perhaps the easiest thing an amateur magician could be called upon to do. The spell had been initiated and the trained spirits sent out. All I had to do was to put up the usual big arguments to talk the brainless things over to my side, and then exert all my will to send them back and make them attack the kahuna. I felt this would be fairly easy as the boy was guilty of no actual sin.

"I was a long way from the *ti* leaves which are usually brushed over the victim as a part of the ceremony to help drive out the spirits, but I had never believed them very necessary. Moreover, I was angry and impatient. I got up and said to the men : 'You all know that I am a very powerful kahuna ? ' They agreed most enthusiastically. 'Then watch me,' I growled. With that, I went over to the boy and set to work.

" The trick of the thing is to put up an argument of such cunning that the spirits will be made to think that their master must be a devil to send them to kill one so pure and innocent. I knew that if I could win them over and get them worked up to a high emotional state and ready to revolt, I would be successful. Of course, I had to chance the kahuna having *kala*-ed (cleansed) himself; but I thought that improbable as he would have no fear that I would send back his death prayer. I doubted if he had ever heard of me over on that side of the island.

" I stood over the boy and began to advance arguments to the spirits. I was smoother than a politician. I praised them and told them what fine fellows they were, how deserving and clever. Little by little I worked around to tell them how sad it was that they had been made slaves by a kahuna instead of being allowed to go on to the beautiful heaven that awaited. I explained just how they had been captured by the kahuna and imposed upon. I told them how pure and innocent and good the boy was and how black and vile the kahuna was. I still consider that argument a masterpiece. The Hawaiians blubbered from time to time as I described the pathetic condition of the spirits.

" Finally I decided that I must have the spirits ready to pull the kahuna limb from limb. I was ready to give them the command to return and visit the kahuna with tén times the punishment he had ordered for the boy. I could bull-roar in those days with the best. I can yet ! (The Doctor threw back his head and gave a roar that shook the house.) Well, I gave my commands in about such a tone. I yelled so loudly that I frightened the pack animals. The men drew back hurriedly and the boy whimpered like a frightened child.

" It -was a supreme effort, mentally, emotionally and physically, with me. I put every particle of will and concentration into that command. When I had repeated it three times, I sat down by the boy, trembling and dripping.

" I continued to keep my mind fastened like a vice on the project in hand, never letting it waver from my willed determination to see that the spirits obeyed my orders. The

KAHUNA OF THE PAST GENERATION

light faded and the stars came out. The boy lay silently
waiting. From a safe distance the men watched me with
faces now expectant and now reflecting horrible fear of the
unseen. At times the air about us seemed to tremble with
the fury of some unearthly conflict of forces.

" The longest hour in history was about gone, when I
suddenly felt an odd sensation. It was as if the tension in
the air had gone in a flash. I drew a deep breath. A few
minutes later there came a whisper from the boy. ' *Wawae
...maikai* ' (' Legs ... good ').

" I could have shouted in my triumph as I set to work to
massage the twitching limbs which seemed to react as if they
had been frozen and were gradually becoming warm again.
Little by little circulation was restored and the toes began to
wiggle. The men crowded around me to offer timid con-
gratulations. It was the high point in my career as a kahuna.
In an hour the boy was up and eating his *poi*.

" But that isn't the end of the story. I had a pleasant
conviction that I had killed something. I wanted to check
on my performance and see what had happened to the
kahuna. I decided to cut my trip short so I could go down
to the boy's village—the collecting had been less successful
than I had hoped, anyway.

" We covered the ground rapidly in the few days we stayed
on the mountain-tops. We camped one night at the lake
on Mauna Kea, and explored the crater of Mauna Loa. We
roasted by day and froze by night. The botanical finds were
nothing to boast of.

" In due time we pulled out for the lower country on the
north side of the mountains. Water was easier to get, but
the country was badly cut up and the forests heavy. At
last, however, we got down to the ocean and struck a trail
which took us along the bluffs and up and down through
valleys and ravines. Always we followed the sea.

" Late one afternoon we came straggling out of the brush
into a clearing in a fair valley. An old woman and a girl
were working in a *taro* patch as we came along. They took
one look at me and the boy, then flew screaming before us.
We followed and soon came to a cluster of grass houses. Not

a person was to be seen. I sat down outside the big hut where the kahuna had lived, and waited while the boy went to see if he could find someone.

" I heard him shouting for a time and then it was quiet for several minutes. Pretty soon he came back with news. On the night I had sent back the death prayer to the kahuna he had been asleep. He had awakened with a scream and rushed around to get *ti* leaves and began to fan himself and tried to fight off his spirits. Between gasps he told the people what had happened. He had neglected to *kala* himself and the white kahuna had taken a low advantage of him. In a very short time he had fallen to the ground and lay there groaning and frothing at the mouth. He was dead by morning.

" The people were certain that I had come back to wipe out the entire village. I told the boy to go back and tell them that I had taken my revenge and that if they behaved themselves I would consider them my friends.

" We waited some time before the head man came back at the head of his flock. He wasn't at all happy, and most of the women were frightened nearly to death. However, I soon reassured them, and in no time we were all great friends. In fact, they seemed to consider me quite a fellow. No one seemed to resent my having killed their kahuna— that was all a part of the game to them.

" Some of the horses were tired out, so we accepted an invitation to stay and be fêted. They gave us a *luau* (feast), which, considering the poverty of the village, was not bad. They had no pigs, but the dog was as tasty as you please— being *poi*-fed meat. I had never taken kindly to dog, but as a full-fledged kahuna, I no longer hesitated. We parted blood brothers.

" The one thing which I could never understand about this matter is this : The old kahuna had found out that I had hired the boy—and by psychic means—but he had not found out that I had turned kahuna and was sending his death prayer back to him. The only way I can account for this is that he must have turned in for the night at dusk and gone at once to sleep.

"Another thing which seems certain is that the kahuna was of a fairly powerful class. Only those well up in their art can see at a distance. Just why he had not seen into the future, I cannot say, unless he was not quite up to that."

Comment :

Monition is less difficult than premonition for the simple reason that a kahuna can send his trained spirits to a distance to learn what is going on, that they may bring back the information. That is undoubtedly what the kahuna did. It is also probable that he had a similar report to tell him the boy was well on his way to death.

In the matter of the varying abilities of magicians, one thing seems very sure. The ability varies with the degree of contact with the plane of Realization. The full Magic is only possible to those who have been able to identify themselves with the superconscious entity. Many attain a sufficient degree of Realization to be able to see some of the greater verities, but the full " Wisdom " does not come without complete identification such as Jesus had with the Christ— His *aumakua.*

Before the end of my report I will try to substantiate the statement I have just made. As this statement is necessary at this time, to throw light on cases now to come, I wish to detail it to some extent.

Going back to the pioneers of the recovery of Magic in the West : I said that both P. P. Quimby and Mrs. Eddy must have attained Realization. What I did not say was that it was equally certain that they did not touch more than the fringe of either " Wisdom " or " Power." Neither of them ever seems to have demonstrated at will the full power of premonition. Neither of them learned the secret of being able to command changes in physical matter and of making those changes take place instantly. Had they attained that power and that identification with their own Higher Selves, they would no longer have had to depend on the lesser magic.

In the lesser magic all changes have to be made by enabling the *unihipili* in man to make the changes for him.

If contact has once been made, however, then the " Wisdom " and " Power " can be called into occasional action through prayer even if contact cannot be had at will. Monition is the first stage of magic. Premonition is perhaps the second. The final stage is Identification at will with the *aumakua* and an ability to use the " Power "—if not the " Wisdom "—at will. When we come to see how this is possible—how the kahunas use this High *Mana*—we will be able to see wherein our recovered magic is lacking in fullness.

.   .   .   .   .

For a case to use in comparing the materializations and levitations of the West with similar practices in Kahunaism, I turn to an account which I have from my friend J. A. K. Coombs of Honolulu. Such phenomena are rare in Hawaii, and the only cases of which I have ever heard have defied my efforts to run them down to their source. Mr. Coombs has lived many years in the Islands, and has been fortunate enough to have had at one time an intimate acquaintance with a most powerful kahuna of the highest class. She was a woman, and she lived to the age of one hundred and twelve years. Unquestionably she attained almost to full Realization, as she claimed to have acquired all her information and power directly from the " gods " : also, as she demonstrated the full Magic almost at will.

CASE 41

MATERIALIZATION AND LEVITATION IN HAWAII

Preliminary Notes :

In our study of cases of this nature in séance-rooms, we came to no definite conclusions concerning the mechanics of the levitation of objects or mediums, nor yet concerning the materialization and dematerialization of objects or of ectoplasmic faces and forms. Now, however, I wish to give an explanation from the kahuna view-point, and this, without stopping as yet to give data and evidences to substantiate statements which I make.

The physical body is the " vehicle " for both conscious and subconscious entities during life and during waking moments. After death each entity draws from the body the vehicle it uses outside the body. The conscious entity can withdraw its " vehicle " during moments of sleep.

The " ectoplasm " is the vehicle of the *unihipili*. That of the *uhane* is never visible. It is made up of far more tenuous matter.

The " invisible ectoplasm " is animal magnetism.

In a séance the animal magnetism or low *mana* can be used by spirits as they take it from the medium or as they are able to generate it for themselves now and again. They can use it to move objects. If a sufficient number of " sitters " are present to furnish the required physical force, the entranced medium can be levitated—this involves the use of the major part of the bodily force of the medium at times and leaves weakness after a séance.

When material is needed by the lesser spirits (not of the *aumakua* grade) to form into objects or shapes, that material is taken from the body of the medium in the form of ectoplasm. This ectoplasm is the vehicle of the *unihipili*— its " astral " body—and the thing seen when ghosts are visible to eye or camera.

In table-tipping the animal magnetism of the sitters enters the table and is used by the spirits as a physical force with which to move the table. The spirits involved are either *unihipilis* or *uhanes*, or a combination of both.

Where objects are moved at a distance from the table the spirits have taken over a charge of force from the table or directly from the medium.

Where trumpet voices speak, there is ectoplasm taken from the medium and used with the borrowed animal magnetism to form and operate vocal organs.

In automatic writing the spirit is invariably a *uhane*. This is necessary because only a conscious mind ghost could take over the *unihipili* in the medium's body and use its trained abilities and bodily force as would the *uhane* of the medium in normal states.

In trance states the *uhane* type of spirit is needed to take over the medium's *unihipili* and force it to control the voice and speak the thoughts that are in the vehicular mind of the *uhane*.

The physical brain is a better vehicle for thinking and remembering than is the vehicle of either a spirit *unihipili* or *uhane*—this, as proved repeatedly by the inferior memory or reason exhibited at séances.

In " precipitated " writing where a blank sheet of paper is sealed in an envelope, ectoplasm is the material used for the ink, in all probability. In ordinary pencil and paper writing inside a closed box, an ectoplasmic hand or animal magnetism alone can be used for the writing.

In the materialization of objects from thin air, the spirit is of the *uhane* type and is in contact to a degree with the *aumakua*. The *aumakua* type of *mana* alone can disrupt physical or electronic forms and rebuild them—a creative activity peculiar to the *aumakua* and its nature. (Already explained as a sex-duality of great creative ability.) A distant object, animal or flower may be dematerialized and brought to the séance-room to be rematerialized. Objects in the room can be taken away and returned in the same manner. Objects can be made of the basic *mana* of the *aumakua* plane, for all matter is force shaped on the *aumakua* plane as it originates and passes into the physical plane.

Direct healings—oddly enough—cannot be made by an *aumakua* spirit at a séance unless there are certain necessary changes made in the *unihipili* of the patient. This change has to do with a variety of things and will later be taken up in careful detail as it is the very centre of the mechanics of both high and low Magic.

The Case :

A kahuna of an unidentified class made quite a name for himself in outlying districts of Oahu by putting a girl into a trance in which she was levitated about the room. He made use of her mediumistic abilities in a strange way. As she floated here and there he ordered her to snap her fingers. Each time she did so a gold coin was materialized.

Comment :

I am of the opinion that the reason the kahunas so seldom use materialization or levitation is that they hesitate to allow spirits of any grade to use either their body or their low or medium *mana*. In Polynesian legends, however, both materialization and levitation are frequently mentioned. Perhaps the modern use of materialization is more general with kahunas than it appears to be.

Next in our comparisons we come to a kahuna activity which has no counterpart in the West.

CASE 42

" VOICE CATCHING "

Preliminary Notes :

The kahunas of some classes use *apo-leo*, or " voice catching," as a punishment at times. Usually it is only the singing part of the voice that is " caught " and removed.

This can be done in two ways : 1. By hypnotic suggestion aimed at the *unihipili* of the victim. 2. By sending a *unihipili* to impress the suggestion, or to injure with a powerful charge of *mana* the part of the *unihipili* vehicle used in singing.

The Case :

(A) A Hawaiian woman became a fine singer and her success turned her head. An old friend was made miserable because she was dropped. In her misery she went to a kahuna. The kahuna considered the case and decided that punishment was merited. He " caught " the singing voice of the woman. Her case is famous in Honolulu.

The friendship was never restored, nor was the voice, although it is thought that had the friendship been renewed, the voice would have been given back.

(B) In Los Angeles in early 1934 a young Hawaiian wife became engaged in a bitter quarrel with her Hawaiian husband. He was a singer.

She had inherited " prayers " from a grandmother and knew the art of voice catching. One day, while her husband was singing at a radio station, she " caught " his singing voice and left him a monotone. He hurried home after the programme and demanded his voice back—suspecting her of having done the mischief.

In the end he agreed to let the wife have her way in certain matters, and she took steps to give him back his voice.

I have ·this story from one of my closest friends who happens to be a close friend of the young couple. There is no doubt about what happened, but the wife refused to tell the inherited secret which had made it possible for her to perform her magic. Just what other things she has been able to do with her heirloom of a trained *unihipili* who will obey " prayer " orders, I cannot say.

Comment :

Going back to the data of multiple personality cases, we remember that in the " Beauchamp Case " the personality " Sally " was afflicted by an inability to open her physical eyes and by a numbness of skin and deep tissues. In several cases mentioned in different records, entities have arrived and been unable to use a certain limb or organ—a leg, eyes, ears, etc.

The vehicle explanation is the only possible one here. If a *unihipili* change of personality, accompanied by that of the *uhane*, occurs, and if the *unihipili* just arrived has lived in a former body which was partly disabled, the disability would be brought to the new body invaded.

One of two things, or both of them, are probable : 1. That in the former body the vehicle had been injured with the limb or organ injury which had occurred. 2. That there was a complexed belief in the invading *unihipili* that it could not use a certain limb or organ in the new body because it had been unable to do so in the old.

It is very probable that all the adult " personalities " arriving have not gone through the usual process of rebirth as infants—wiped clean of memories and past training—but have stepped from a dead body into the living body of another. In doing this they would have brought along their own vehicle with any defect which it might possess. " Sally " must have come from a blind and semi-paralysed body.

If the vehicle theory is not to be accepted, we have then only the silent projection of a hypnotic force to fall back upon—a thing less acceptable than the sending of a *unihipili* spirit armed with a paralysing charge of animal magnetism to destroy a delicate portion of the lower vehicle of the victim.

From the evidence given by various practices, I have been forced to conclude that there is a negative and a positive force in each *mana*—one to tear down, the other to build up.

.   .   .   .   .

In the next case we will find evidences and proofs of the vehicles.

CASE 43

SPIRIT CATCHING

Preliminary Notes :

Some classes of kahunas use *po'i uhane* or " *uhane* catching " as a means of bringing death to one deserving punishment, or as a means of threatening death to gain the end of righting some wrong.

The name of the practice—" *uhane* catching "—tells what is caught, so we can be sure the *unihipili* is not involved and still more sure that no *unihipilis* are involved in the " catching " because a *unihipili* has no ability to affect a *uhane* except in case the *uhane* is the one connected with it in life and is affected because of a subconscious complex.

Here the use of the vehicle of the *uhane* is mandatory. No explanation of the phenomenon is possible without consideration of the part played by the *uhane's* vehicle.

The *unihipili* never leaves the physical body during life except in cases of deep trance, and then it goes only just outside the body and leaves enough of its vehicle in the flesh to keep decay from setting in—although not enough to keep the body more than just alive.

During life the *uhane* takes its vehicle and leaves the body, at times, during sleep or unconsciousness. In doing this it always leaves a " thread " of its vehicle to connect it with the body against the time of recall or return.

An entity of consciousness is not material even in a tenuous way. It could not be caught. The vehicle of the *uhane*, however, is material, even if very tenuous. It being material, it can be acted on by the *mana* of the *aumakua* plane. This mades its capture possible to a powerful kahuna who can use that *mana*.

The vehicles have an elementary consciousness only in so far as they keep in touch with the consciousness which informs them.

Without the vehicle it possesses, neither *unihipili* nor *uhane* can live in the body or out of it. As age takes the physical body, so does it take the vehicles. When they die after physical death is long in the past, they cease to have any form in the physical or tenuous-physical. The consciousness of the entities then blends with that of the superconscious entity as a part of it—to be given freshly created vehicles in due time and sent, without memory of former lives, back into the next physical incarnation. (This last I state as my own conclusion and without hope of advancing definite proofs. I draw my conclusion after considering much data still to be found in India and other places where ancient lore has been retained.)

The Case :

I have the details of this case from the victim himself. He is a white man and I accept his statements. His case is typical of several I have partly investigated.

" Jim " was an accountant on a plantation on the island of Oahu. He had married a Hawaiian girl and had succeeded in alienating her from her family to some extent. He was brought to see matters in a different light after being punished with " spirit catching."

One morning, while working in the plantation office, he became troubled by odd " floating away " feelings which came at short intervals and made it impossible for him to attend to the press of work in hand. At times he became giddy and all but lost consciousness.

Having business to transact with the cashier, he rose and walked to the small wicket window. He called to the man inside, but was overtaken by a moment of near unconsciousness. When he recovered, he found himself clinging to the window. The cashier was rubbing his eyes.

"I heard you call," said the cashier, "but when I came to the window I couldn't see you. Then you suddenly seemed to build up before me out of thin air. My eyes must be failing."

Jim remarked that he felt none too well himself, and they let the matter drop. However, a few minutes later a Portuguese plantation foreman came in and stopped to stare at Jim.

"How did you get here?" he demanded. I rode past you just now down by your house. I even spoke to you!"

In the argument which followed, the fact came out that the apparition had deported itself uncertainly and had disappeared aimlessly into a clump of bushes.

"Spirit catching," said the Portuguese wisely. He shook his head. "You better try to remember what Hawaiian you done something bad to."

With difficulty the white man made his way home. He told his wife what had happened and she at once became terrified. Leaving him alone, she ran for her mother. In due time she came back with the old lady—and accompanied by a kahuna.

Meantime, Jim had lapsed repeatedly into unconsciousness. He felt "only half there." His *morale* was badly shaken.

Smilingly the kahuna set about adjusting family matters and forcing Jim to acknowledge that he had been very inconsiderate. When confessions had been obtained from the white man and all was adjusted, the cure was undertaken.

Orders were given in the unintelligible "god talk" common to powerful kahunas. Jim's giddiness passed and he revived. There followed a ceremonial cleansing, and the cure was complete.

Comment :

The one thing in this report to me by the victim which is unique and which I question is his becoming invisible to the eyes of the cashier. I have included this data as it is a part of what I was told and assured was perfectly true. Some member of the Round Table may have data at hand which will throw light on the matter, even if I am inclined to consider it impossible that the physical body could either have been entirely dematerialized for a moment or rendered invisible.

In our few most reliable sources—mentioned some time before—nothing is said of invisibility of the victim. I will quote :

J. S. Emerson says :

" KA PO'I UHANE, spirit-catching, the art of catching one of the two spirits of a person and shutting it up in a drinking gourd for ransom, or, more generally,. to be crushed in the fist of the kahuna and eaten at once by him and his client. This is usually done in the early part of the night, when sleep releases one of the two spirits of every individual, and it begins to wander at large in dreamland. With the death of this spirit, the death of the other, as well as the body of the victim, may be looked for not long after."

Johanna Wilcox says :

" A slightly different kahuna of the *anaana* branch was the *po'i uhane*—catcher of spirits. It was a common belief among the Hawaiians that every person possessed two spirits. One always had to remain with the body to keep it warm while the other went wandering at large in dreamland. At such times the kahuna *po'i uhane* was given the opportunity to catch the wandering spirit and imprison it in a water gourd or squeezing it to death. . . . If the spirit was imprisoned, the kahuna had the owner of the spirit in his power and could extort large sums of money from him."

John Wise and Howard Case say :

> " Kahuna *po'i uhane :* A priest presumed to be capable
> of destroying a spirit whether good or evil. For example,
> if a person believed himself possessed by an evil spirit, he
> would summon this particular kahuna to drive it out for
> him."

Aside from the lack of any mention of invisibility, it will
be noted that only two of these recognized authorities on the
kahunas agree very closely as to just what was done in the
event of such a kahuna setting to work to practise his art.

These short quotations will also show the ridiculous nature
of these grave writings and make it easy to see why the early
part of my investigation was badly hampered. With such
things as the catching of a spirit and eating it set before
one in print, the natural reaction is that of the Scientific
Attitude's most loyal son.

In this case the apparition is easily explained. In moments
of unconsciousness the *uhane* often takes along the ectoplasmic vehicle of the *unihipili* when it leaves the body.
Other matters have been touched on in the preliminary
notes.

The matter of the cleansing ceremony will be treated by
itself very soon.

CHAPTER V

IN the illustrations in *Vancouver's Voyages* may be seen sketches of the wooden idols which once stood in the crude temples of Hawaii. On the top of the heads of most of these may be seen a tiny figurine which is known as the "angel."

In attempting to get information concerning these figurines I came across some data which may or may not be correct, but which would furnish—providing it is true—one more case of materialization which would bear comparison to ectoplasmic materializations in the West.

CASE 44

THE ANGEL SITS

Preliminary Notes :

Whether or not the "angel" on the tops of the heads of the idols was a representation of the *aumakua* or superconscious, I cannot say, although I suspect it of being so. At any rate, there is also the possibility that a most ancient form of mediumism was represented.

The Case :

I was told by a person who claimed to have seen the kahunas use the "angel sits" method many times, that the client arrives and the kahuna goes into a trance. Soon the "angel" materializes and "sits" on the top of the kahuna's head.

It speaks through the throat of the kahuna and gives advice which sometimes is fairly good. It frequently calls for drink and imbibes so much of it that the medium is left

WOODEN IDOLS—THE DOGMA OF KAHUNAISM—SHOWING THE "ANGEL" ON THE HEADPIECES

From Vancouver's Voyages.

very drunk after the sitting. While entranced, the kahuna's body is called " the bones." As the spirit often injures the body or leaves its " death pains " behind when it goes, the client is usually asked to request the " angel " to take the pains with it, and the " angel " seldom refuses to oblige.

Comment :

Here we see a most peculiar form of miniature materialization of face and form on the part of what must be a *uhane*—if the data is at all correct—because of its ability to give reasonable answers to the client's questions.

. . . . .

Next in line for comparison comes what is perhaps the most important thing, from a practical angle, in kahuna practice : the healing of body or purse by use of the lesser magic.

CASE 45

A KAHUNA PRACTITIONER AT WORK

Preliminary Notes :

The method which will be examined closely in the next few cases is one used by both the lesser and the greater kahunas—measured according to their degree of Realization and " Power."

In the West we have the practitioners of Christian Science and New Thought as well as those of other Magico-Religious groups working blindly toward the same ends, and often accomplishing splendid results. Frequently these practitioners accidentally hit on the full use of Magic while practising—that being, of course, their constant aim, but most of their methods are those of the lesser magic—and are pitifully incomplete.

I will give the case so that we may have it before us in detail, and then explain everything most fully.

The Case :

As one of my friends was involved in this case—a Chinese-Hawaiian gentleman—I was able to observe from the side

lines, from the inception of the trouble to the cure, and to
see that the trouble never returned once in the six years that
followed.

" Henry " was a healthy young man who worked in a salt
factory several miles from Honolulu. One morning, while
driving along the open road to his work, he fainted. His
car was wrecked and he was badly bruised. For over a
period of two months these fainting spells recurred. In one
of them he fell into an open fire. In another he fell on his
bed and his cigarette set the bedding on fire, resulting in a
narrow escape.

After three doctors had been consulted and had failed to
discover the cause of the trouble, the young man's Hawaiian
mother insisted that he should go to a kahuna for help.
Henry did not believe in kahunas, being a modern young
man and well educated, but in desperation he did as his
mother advised.

The kahuna listened to the story with half-closed eyes, and
when it ended closed his eyes entirely. He sat there
quietly for several minutes, then addressed Henry sharply :

" I think you hurt some Hawaiian girl, no ? You hurt
bad and she grumble to spirit friends. They find you got
shame feeling eating you inside, so they find easy for punish
you. Come ! Confess up ! "

Henry was amazed, but he confessed. He had intended to
marry the girl some day, but his Chinese father had another
young lady in mind for his son. In the end Henry had
allowed his father to have his way and had stopped calling
on the Hawaiian girl. He did not know how she had taken
his action.

" It is bad kind hurt," said the kahuna. " Your shamed
feeling is eating you inside, and when something is eating
inside, then spirits can do bad things to you. Now, you got
to go to the girl and make present and *aloha* until she forgive
you. You do that and then come to me some more."

Henry did as he was directed and found the girl not unreasonable when she heard of the father's part in the matter.
In due time she forgave him and accepted his present.

Upon his return to the kahuna, the old man again closed

his eyes and made an examination of the case. He reported that the attacking spirits of " grandmama and old auntie " had gone away content.

" But," said the old man. " Funny kind thing is inside of everyone. That spirit live inside you got no sense. It not very smart. Long time it take to throw away your shame feeling. Even when other spirit in you know you make all right with girl, that spirit what make body grow thinks you still got to be punished. Even when grandmama and auntie spirit go home, it going keep on make for same kind push *uhane* outside body so you fall down and hurt you. You not understand this kind. All you got to do is like I tell to you to do. You think you can believe I know what everything about ? "

Henry nodded. He had been convinced that the old kahuna knew his business.

" Good ! That fine ! All you need is be good in faith in me. Now I tell you something. In me is power from gods to forgive you for hurt girl and for everything bad you ever do. I going forgive you in kahuna way what lots more better than church way. Kahuna way forgive both spirits in you. Now I take this raw egg. I hold it over cup. When I do that, both of us hold breath. I put cleaning *mana* into egg. I break in cup. I give to you, you swallow quick and all at once. Then we breathe again. You understand ? "

Henry understood. He obeyed orders. The egg was poised over the cup. Henry held his breath. He was nearly bursting when the egg was finally broken and handed to him. The moment he had gulped it down, the kahuna seized him and rubbed his stomach violently, at the same time panting out compelling words :

" Egg and *mana* is inside ! It clean away all your sin ! You clean like baby now ! You not need shame for anything ! You all clean now ! No one can punish ! You no can punish yourself ! You never go black and fall down some more ! You all new and clean and happy and well ! "

The kahuna smilingly declared the cure complete and permanent. He collected his modest fee, and Henry went back to his work. Never did the fainting spells return.

Comment :

This case gives us complete data on the kahuna use of the lesser magic in healing. It shows that the kahunas have been, for many centuries, conversant in a most startling way with the conscious and subconscious entities as well as with the complex and all that hinges on it.

The " something eating inside " is the complex caused by thoughts of guilt coming down from the conscious mind. Once formed, it becomes the seed from which a multitude of troubles sprout.

The first trouble is that it makes the *unihipili* either willing to accept punishment from outside spirits or unable to repel attacks, or both. The second trouble is that it makes the *unihipili* accept the idea that punishment is deserved—even after amends have been made—and forces it to continue or to originate punishment in the form of sickness or mental ills. The third trouble is that it does what the kahunas call " blocking the path "—a thing we will discuss later.

The kahunas know that it takes a very long time to drain off a complex by sending down to the *unihipili* thoughts contrary to those held in the complex. They also know a better way of draining off the complex—the way we have just seen in our case. The efficacy of the method is great and the draining off is instant and lasting. Let us see why Western methods are not as efficient.

In former cases we looked into healing by the use of hypnosis and found that cures were not lasting and that the method is little used on that account. In the healing of the Magico-Religious groups we see that healing takes much time, much lecturing on the " error " of sickness, much reading of texts, much faith, and often many repetitions of treatment when the trouble returns.

The entire difficulty must lie in the complex. By using hypnosis the *unihipili* can be forced to take up its normal work of healing and repairing the body ; but the complex is not drained off—the complex of guilt or of unworthiness which was the cause of the trouble. Once the hypnotic influence is removed, the *unihipili* sets to work—under the urge of its complexed belief that punishment is deserved and should be administered—to punish the body or the *uhane*—usually both. The old disease or disorder returns.

In the lesser magic used by the Magico-Religious groups the complex is attacked in the slow way. The conscious mind is first convinced that the illness is an " error " and then comes the slow process of convincing the subconscious and so breaking down the complex. This complex may have been formed in a dozen different ways. It may be the result of failure to live up to the demands of religious dogma, or it may be the direct result of a bad conscience following the hurting of another. It may be the result of the suggestions of doctor or friends.

Too often old hurts to others are not made right and so the complex remains untouched. The attack of angry spirits is vaguely understood, if at all. The very lack in the philosophy behind the system of healing is apparent. The basic tenet is that God is entirely Good and Love, and that, therefore, nothing not good or produced by the love of God can exist. To compensate for the bad in life, ungodly thoughts in the minds of men are postulated. When such thoughts are removed from the mind by an understanding of " Mind is All," and still " bad " comes, another theory is forced into being to meet this discrepancy. This theory is that " Love chastens "—an amazing contradiction of the basic tenet When Love is not punishing man for his sins, something else is advanced as the punisher. This is evil animal magnetism collected and projected to the victim by evil human beings. To combat this there is a ritual of returning the evil magnetism to its sender—a procedure not well in keeping with the basic tenet. P. P. Quimby died of a tumour at the early age of sixty-five years. Mary Baker Eddy lived to be nearly ninety, but even after her most complete Realization she was often forced to treat herself for returns of her old spinal trouble, or was forced to take drastic measures to fight back the " malicious animal magnetism " she felt projected against her by former pupils who had become jealous of her success. Unfortunately, the Realization of these two pioneers of Magic in the West was not full enough to give them a complete and working understanding of attacking spirits and the real mechanics of the complex.

The kahunas have not succeeded in projecting animal magnetism across space. *Unihipili* spirits must be used. Hypnotic *mana* seems also not to be projectible. High *mana*, however, is.

Where the superconscious has been contacted regularly, the power of monition is gained, and with it the ability to collect and project high *mana* in healing—this for instant or slow work. We will come back to the high *mana* later.

Where an illness once healed by the lesser magic returns, it is certain that the complex which caused it had never completely drained off or that it was reformed by the same train of thoughts which formed it in the first place. The kahunas know only too well the danger of the complex being built up again. If there is not a definite case in which a hurt done another can be made right and the *uhane* of the patient, therefore, given no chance of feeling that the guilt is back, the kahuna orders his patient never to think again of the old guilt or trouble. In the New Testament we find in Jesus the master kahuna. Constantly He was ordering His patients not to dwell on their ills or on the cure—" go and tell no man " was His command. He knew that we all discuss our healings and that in doing so the suggestion may go to the subconscious and reform the complex. "Your sins be forgiven you," was a part of His draining-off process. With the blind man He used spittle, clay, anointment, and bathing in a pool. This is exactly the principle employed by the kahunas. They use a PHYSICAL something to impress the *unihipili* when the words of forgiveness are uttered.

To make plain the need of a physical stimulation : The *unihipili* has long been accustomed to having the conscious mind or *uhane* dwelling on a multitude of mental images which have no bearing on actual life. When thoughts of this kind come down to it from the *uhane* it records them in memory but pays no further attention to them. If, however, a thought accompanied by a deed which arouses the emotion of the *unihipili* is received, a complex may either be formed or broken.

To illustrate: A healer tells his patient: "You are cleansed of all guilt." The *unihipili* is not impressed because the conscious mind is not cut off by hypnotic influence—and also because the *unihipili* has a complexed belief that it is guilty. It is as if the *unihipili* had laughed and said to itself: "The foolish man is telling my *uhane* that the guilt is forgiven, and the *uhane* actually seems to believe him. But I know better. I know that evil day when we sinned. I know that we are guilty and that punishment must be continued—I was taught long ago that one must be punished for sins of any kind."

Another illustration: In the classical case of the prisoner who was condemned to death and turned over to the psychologists that they might experiment with him, he was blindfolded, tied, and told that his wrist was to be slashed so that he would bleed to death. The wrist was scratched with a bit of ice and a flow of warm water released on the scratch. The warm water felt like blood as it ran down the hand of the prisoner. It sounded like blood as it dripped into the basin. His *unihipili* had heard—through the *uhane*—the words of the psychologists. The *uhane* may have doubted the truth of those strange words, but as soon as the *uhane* reported to the *unihipili* the sensation and sound accompanying the procedure, a complex of belief was instantly established. The *unihipili*—from long force of habit—accepted any report of physical sensation as a true one. It accepted the truth of the cut and bleeding despite any doubt in the mind of the prisoner. It forced its complexed belief and fears on the prisoner's *uhane* and caused in it unreasonable fear. Both *unihipili* and *uhane* took to their "vehicles" and departed.

In healing with Magic, the conscious mind must have a degree of faith in the healer and a degree of confidence in his statement that guilt is being forgiven or cleansed. Next, there MUST be an UNUSUAL PHYSICAL STIMULATION applied to the body to impress the truth of the cleansing on the *unihipili*. There lies the secret of the healing of body or purse with lesser magic.

The healing of purse—financial ills—must also be accompanied by the exercise of the higher Magic, but the work begins in this way : Any feeling of unworthiness or guilt, either conscious or complexed in the subconscious, must be removed to " clear away blocking in the path "—the thing I have promised to take up in due time.

One more thing remains to be said. If a good force of hypnotic *mana* can accompany the words of forgiveness, the draining off is even more certain. The animal magnetism or low *mana* charge given the egg may have been only a figure of speech intended to have the effect of gaining the confidence of the patient. I doubt that the kahuna actually charged the egg. Such charging is rarely reported.

As to the psychic examination of the patient, that is a thing P. P. Quimby learned to do early in his practice. It is an invaluable ability and one all healers should endeavour to develop. It belongs to the abilities gained through contact with the *aumakua* in Realization, and is an ability not of the conscious or subconscious mind, but of the superconscious— as is monition, which this really is, and premonition. If mind-reading through the aid of the subconscious is used in diagnosis, only the mistaken beliefs of the patient will be brought to light—not the real condition.

.   .   .   .   .

In our next case we will watch a kahuna at work in a situation in which no complex was present to cause trouble.

CASE 46

SPIRITS AND NOT A COMPLEX INVOLVED

Preliminary Notes :

This case is needed to prove definitely that suggestion was not the cause of the patient's illness, also to prove that no complex was present, AND, that SPIRITS WERE ATTACKING.

The Case :

While living in Honolulu I learned of this case and traced it to its source. I had the details from the father of the baby girl. I visited the child and also its mother. I believe that the story of the activities of the kahunas is farly accurate in detail.

The infant daughter of a young Hawaiian couple came to have frequent attacks of shivering, perspiring weakness. They would come every few days and last up to an hour. The child was less than two years old. Doctors failed to diagnose the illness. The child was taken to a hospital for children. When the parents began to fear that she would soon die, they took her at night to the home of three old kahunas, two of whom were women.

The man set to work to make a psychic diagnosis of the trouble. He used a crude gazing crystal in the form of a smooth black stone rounded by the action of the sea. The stone was placed in a calabash and water used to keep its surface bright and glistening. While he was at work the women made a decoction of *ti* leaves and added it to a warm bath. They placed the child in the bath and chanted over her as they laid on their hands. In a few minutes the attack of the moment was relieved and the baby fed and put to sleep.

The old man reported that the grandmother of the child—the father's mother—had been angered and had grumbled to the spirits. The spirits had tried to punish the husband and wife, but, as they had no guilts, they had failed. In the end they had attacked the baby successfully.

The father could not believe that the grandmother could be angry with him for any reason : but consented at once to go to her and bring her back with him.

Not without some difficulty, he succeeded in doing this. The grandmother had been deeply hurt because the young couple had not come to live with her—although she had said nothing to them to show her disappointment. She also fancied that the little granddaughter should have been named for her instead of for the grandmother on the wife's side of the family. She confessed to the kahunas that she had " grumbled just a little, but cried mostly," and she was in tears to think her grumbling had harmed the child instead of bringing her son to her with apologies.

With the kahunas acting as judges, family matters were arranged to the satisfaction of all, and the final process of healing begun. This consisted of a *kala*, or cleansing, of the three adults, but not of the baby. They were asked to bare their shoulders and the words of cleansing of guilt were accompanied by heavy sprinkling or dashing of sea water into the face and on the bared skin. It was explained that this forgiving of sins was to insure a complete cessation of causes which might result in further trouble.

The spirits who had attacked the baby were evidently *uhane-unihipili* combinations as they showed reason in their attack and were thanked for their services and requested to leave the baby alone. Their sins were forgiven them by words accompanied by a sprinkling of water in the air.

The baby was never taken with the attacks again. When I saw her she was fat and fine.

Comment :

It is a kahuna belief that the inexperienced *unihipili* of a baby may be robbed of its low *mana*, or animal magnetism, under proper conditions. It is also their belief that nothing can " eat a baby inside " (complex) until it reaches the age of five or six years. This is something which psychologists have learned through their experiments with hypnosis. A small child cannot be hypnotized.

In this case and in the one before it I have constantly used the word " hurt." I have done so intentionally because it is the word used by the kahunas. A hurt may be a physical injury, or a hurt to the feelings—each being a grave offence as each causes pain.

The practice of grumbling to the spirits is an old one which, unfortunately, has not yet been made use of in the West. By that method many lesser hurts are to be compensated. In Hawaii the presence of such a recourse has made the natives slow indeed to be anything but kind to their neighbours—a very excellent thing. When the full Magic is back in the West, the haughty impositions visited on the weak by the strong—within the law—will become more a thing of a past and barbarous age than a proud symbol of civilization.

In bathing the baby, the *ti* leaf infusion was used as it is supposed to have the power to drive away spirits. Undoubtedly a change of animal magnetism was given the baby to strengthen it.

The sprinkling of the spirits must be only a form, but suggestion given with an ingredient of hypnotic *mana* would be potent.

There is no evidence here of the use of the full Magic.

The old man using the crude gazing crystal was evidently a psychic and not a kahuna. Many such are employed by kahunas who have not the ability to use the full Magic of monition. These are called the " eyes," or *makaula*. As a matter of fact, they are using monitory powers and are more closely in touch with their *aumakua* than many kahunas, if they but had the courage to try to use their powers without the aid of spirits or old invocational forms. With a sufficient practice to learn to collect and use animal magnetism and hypnotic force, they should soon be able to demonstrate the full Magic. The tradition that one must inherit kahuna powers or secrets is at fault in this matter.

It will be noted that in this and the preceding case of healing, no appeal was made to higher powers. The entire work was with the complex or the spirits. No higher power was needed to assist in the healing. No element of Religion was involved. There was no denial of the reality of ills, no necessity of a philosophy of the Divine Mind. The lesser magic is not dependent either on Religion or dogmatic ideas of " sin." To the kahunas, sin has nothing whatever to do with any plane alove that of the *unihipili* and the *uhane*, EXCEPT in that a guilt complex " blocks the path " and so prevents the use of the high *mana* for healing.

In the case in which Dr. Brigham set the " death prayer " *unihipilis* on the kahuna who had sent them out, he succeeded only because there was a guilt in the mind and subconscious of the kahuna caused by his unjust act. Had he been able to justify his act and therefore been able to use a cleansing method to drain off any incipient guilt complex in his *unihipili*, it is doubtful if he could have been injured. The kahuna usually *kalas* himself after each use of magic to heal or punish, this to be sure no *suggestion* has gripped his *unihipili* to form a complex or to transfer the symptoms of illness to his body. This *kala* is done with a physical stimulus accompanied by what we would call expert autosuggestion. If a kahuna is hired to kill by a client, and if he doubts that the killing is either possible or justified, he will *kala* himself by the usual means, but not his client. If the *unihipilis* are sent back, the client then is in trouble, and not the kahuna—thus leaving the kahuna to go to the rescue of the client.

The common belief among the whites in Hawaii is that the kahuna—if able to kill, which is doubted—is a devil, and will kill without provocation. This is far from the fact, although a kahuna may use his premonitory powers and find that a person has his " path blocked beyond clearance " and so will be happier dead than if left to suffer on through life. " Karma " has no place in the kahuna philosophy, and death cancels the sins of each life. After death the spirit suffers not at all if the *unihipili* is *kala*-ed either before or after leaving the body. This may be the original purpose of the " extreme unction " of Catholicism.

In the rites and rituals of the Church of Rome, the forms of the full Magic are still preserved. Were it not for the dogma of sin, the confession followed by the absolution would be far more potent than it can be now ; but where so many things are sins to the dogma-complexed *unihipili* of the communicant, the guilt complex is revived almost immediately after absolution.

Let me say again that to the demonstrators of the full Magic in Polynesia it is impossible to sin against God. Their test of a sin is this : IF AN ACT DOES NOT HURT ANOTHER OR YOUR BODY IT IS NOT A SIN. To hurt your body is to render it unfit for normal use.

In this test lies the future freedom of the West from the age-long oppression of dogma.

CHAPTER VI

THE beliefs of the kahunas are often so delightfully sane in comparison with ours in the West that the contrast is startling. Complexed with religious dogmas from childhood, many of us are constantly suffering from a sense of unworthiness which prevents us from praying with any degree of faith.

To live up to the dogmatic commands added to the teachings of Christ (an *Aumakua*) is an utter impossibility, even as the perfect asceticism of the Hindu aspirant to Realization is an utter impossibility. The absurdity of the " sell all and give to the poor," or the " be ye, therefore, perfect as the Father (mistaken for God the Absolute and not the *aumakua*) is perfect," is at once apparent to the kahuna. It is his idea that men were created exactly as God wanted them and that they were intended to live normal lives and to enjoy all the pleasures of the physical and mental planes. The contrast here is between entirely anti-social and social ideas. To the kahuna the full normal life includes contact with the *aumakua* either in Realization or through an unblocked " path " which will allow the *aumakua* to keep the life of the physical man healthy and prosperous.

This brings us to the extremely sane beliefs of the kahunas concerning death and diseases caused by germs. All things " wear out " and death is as natural as birth. The kahuna wonders at a man who would not exchange life for the pleasures of the spirit world—always granting that the *unihipili* and *uhane* are kept together and old guilts compensated and *kala*-ed before death.

The vehicles grow old and die in the spirit world, and the lesser entities of consciousness are gathered home to the Father-Mother *aumakua* who sent them forth—gathered to the perfect love and oneness with all *aumakuas*, all men, all gods.

Down the centuries the disease caused by germs was distinguished from other diseases. It was known that the human body under the direction of the *unihipili* could throw off any disease if its guilt complexes were removed in time. It was also known that the power of the *aumakua* could make any change in the body to heal it, always providing that the " path " was not blocked by a complex of guilt and the *manas* so kept from flowing down from the *aumakua* into the physical.

The " path " will be examined as an idea soon. It has to do with the mechanism which makes it possible for the *uhane* to set up reactions which will cause the flow of high *mana* with the certainty of a chemical reaction.

For the moment let us take up a case in which a kahuna fought a bone infection and lost.

CASE 47

A KAHUNA FAILS

Preliminary Notes :

The patient in this case came to me and was sent to a kahuna. The details are correct.

The Case :

A young white woman, once an ardent Christian, and married, developed a deep sore on the ankle. The doctors found it to be caused by a tubercular bone. They proposed an operation which would stiffen the joint for life.

The kahuna examined the case and was none too anxious to take it. The girl was almost hopelessly complexed by the dogmas of " sin " absorbed in early life.

The kahuna set to work to *kala* the guilt complexes after preparing the patient by having her fast and do penance that she might be consciously convinced that she no longer deserved punishment at the hands of God. He left the *unihipili* to overcome the infection and heal the sore. This it did in a few weeks.

In the meantime, to keep the complex from being reformed, the kahuna had used a method which is a last resort, but which will have to be used on this generation, perhaps, in the West. The method is this: Where complexes are so deep seated and spring in to action at once because the convictions of the *uhane* cannot be changed, the commission of " sins " under the complex MUST BE AVOIDED. In this case the patient had considered many harmless things either sins of commission or omission. Cards, drink and normal sex life were sins to her way of thinking. The kahuna could not convert her to his saner " test of hurt " philosophy, so he ordered her to give up all things she considered sins.

She obeyed orders. He *kala*-ed her in the name of Jesus Christ—a wise thing to do considering the source of her faith—and so freed her of guilt in *uhane* and *unihipili*. At once the *unihipili* responded and healed the sore, as I have said. But soon after the sore was completely healed, she disobeyed the injunction to cease to do things she considered sinful. Thinking her cure permanent, she again went back to her gay parties and to the few healthy activities which were sins against her dogma-complex which the kahuna could not remove because he could not change the beliefs of her *uhane* or mind by his most reasonable arguments.

Suddenly the sore broke out again as if the *unihipili* had resumed the old punishment for sins or had ceased its protective work. The kahuna refused to renew his treatment. The operation was performed successfully by the doctors, but the ankle left stiff.

Comment :

According to the kahuna way of thinking, the operation on the ankle would impress the *unihipili* that its sins had been fully punished, and without further accidental infection which might—because of lesser guilt complexes—result in fresh affliction, the course of life would be smooth again.

In this case it was not the germs or the guilts that " blocked the path " : it was the mass of complexed beliefs in religious dogma which could not be reached because the *uhane* of the woman could not reason about them—this because of the complexes—and so could not change its own opinion.

May I say here that there is no such thing as " salvation " or " repentance " in Kahunaism, and that the idea of them generally held in the West is not the correct one, even in the light of the Bible. *Soteria* gives us the modern word " salvation." It is a Greek word which translates, " a safe return," not a " being saved " from something. The " return " of the kahunas is to the *aumakua* in life or after death. This is expedited by getting rid of guilt complexes. The word " repent " comes from an ancient root which has the meaning " to change the attitude of mind," or to " come to a new viewpoint." In this case the woman could not do this. Her complexes held her to the old point of view.

Basil King's book *The Conquest of Fear* has much to tell of matters of point of view and of the meaning of these words. I give him as a part of my authority as to roots and meanings.

·   ·   ·   ·   ·

In our next case we will see a kahuna who did not fail.

CASE 48

GERMS AND MAGIC

Preliminary Notes :

I have this case from the man in question. I believe the details of treatment are accurate.

The Case :

" Hopii " was a fairly well educated Hawaiian. He was married. He owned and operated a big " rent " car.

Hopii's wife was jealous, very jealous, and not without cause. He loved another woman and was loved by her in turn. Because of this woman there was much trouble between husband and wife—although Hopii also loved his wife, very dearly—paradoxical as polygamous instincts may seem.

This trouble went on for over a year before it came to a

head for the first time. When the wife made life so unbearable for Hopii that he could no longer stand it, he agreed to give up the other woman if only for the sake of peace.

But like many other men of good intentions, he had not reckoned with his lady love. She had made no agreement, so she insisted on seeing him from time to time. He held out against her for a few weeks, then gave in. He used all precautions lest he be found out a second time.

All went well for a few months, then Hopii came down with the " flu." Influenza is bad for Hawaiians at any time, and for Hopii it proved very bad indeed. A white doctor did all he could for him, but he grew rapidly worse. One night the physician took the wife aside and told her that her husband was dying—would unquestionably be dead before dawn. Hopii was burned out and his resistance gone.

There were in the house by then a sister of the wife and a brother of the sick man. When told of the situation, the brother rushed out to get a kahuna—a thing Hopii had fought against from the first.

The kahuna was old and wrinkled, but very active and alert. He went immediately into the sick-room and stood for a moment with closed eyes beside the bed.

" He is dead ! " cried the brother.

" Not yet," said the kahuna. " I will pour my *mana* in to make him strong. Then I will have time to *kala* big thing that eats him inside."

The kahuna took from his bag four carved wooden " markers." He held them in his hands while he chanted " god-talk." He laid them at the " four corners " of the unconscious man and then placed his hands over his solar plexus and continued to chant.

Some five minutes later, Hopii opened his eyes and began breathing heavily.

" Go way ! " he whispered.

The kahuna turned to the brother. " Go way."

" I mean you ! " said Hopii.

The kahuna hurried the brother through the door and came back to replace his hands on Hopii's stomach.

" Lay still and listen to me ! I am going to tell your wife

you sorry for go back to other woman sometimes. She
going forgive you. Then I *kala* sin out of insides of you and
you get well.''

" No ! " said Hopii wildly. " I rather die first ! "

" No good," said the kahuna gently. " You got stay here
and earn money so she can eat. She forgive and I *kala*, then
you going be all right." He went out and closed the door
after him.

When Hopii revived again he found the hands once more
on his stomach and his wife weeping beside him. Again she
was ready to forgive. Hopii also wept. It was good to be
forgiven. He took fresh courage.

The *kala* was done with firm words and water splashed
generously over the bare body of the sick man. The water
was partly brushed and mopped back into the gourd bowl.

" See ! " commanded the kahuna. " All your *hala* (sin-
guilt) is in water. Water wash out and pick up every bit.
Now watch ! I throw water on ground through window.
There ! All your *hala* gone ! Nothing left to eat you inside.
You all clean again ! Now you get well quick because I can
use high *mana*."

The old man sighed and wiped his hands while the wife
dried and covered Hopii. With eyes uplifted and his face
radiant, the kahuna made a very short invocation.

" You are well," he said quietly after the invocation was
finished. " I have talked to the *aumakuas* and called down
the rain for you. Now sleep and rest. After you sleep little
while you wake up so well you only need eat and lay around
few days to get fat back on bones. No tell anyone and not to
remember. If you tell or remember old eating inside, you
pray please forgive for."

In the morning when the doctor came to sign the death
certificate he found Hopii sitting up in bed eating a huge
breakfast.

" Kahuna ? " asked the doctor after recovering from his
surprise.

Hopii grinned.

" I wish I knew how they do it," was the physician's
sorrowful remark as he took his departure.

Comment :

The sequel to this recital is interesting. The kahuna went with Hopii and the wife to call on the other woman. He smoothed over difficulties and succeeded in making fair friends of the rivals in love. Both of them were *kala*-ed and ordered to love each other lest trouble befall them.

When Hopii told me the story, he finished by making the prayer for forgiveness as had been directed. In doing this he unwittingly was using splendid psychology to keep the *unihipili* in him from mistaking his intentions and reviving the old complex of guilt.

Here we see the use of animal magnetism to strengthen the patient temporarily, but the draining off of the complex was of vital importance. With the " path " opened by the very complete ritual with water and suggestion, the " words of power " of the full Magic were effectively used.

In this case we have very little to compare with the healing practice of the West, but we see much which might be borrowed with ease to improve healing with magic.

.   .   .   .   .

Next I wish to present a case in which pure suggestion of the hypnotic kind was effectively used with accompanying physical stimulation.

CASE 49

THE CASE OF THE WHISKERS

Preliminary Notes :

The data of this case is correct in every detail.

The Case :

A salesman who called on me every week for over a year came to me one day with a bald spot on his cheek the size of a half-dollar.

He had been to a *luau*, or native feast, the week before and had met there a Hawaiian woman who took a fancy to him. He was almost girlishly handsome and had a very clear, perfect skin through which showed the dark shadow of his beard.

The woman had been drinking a little and so had my frien d. They became well acquainted and she took him to one side and made much over his fine skin.   The woman herself " was a very whiskery individual who seemed to worry about the hair on her face."

Soon she said : " You would be so pretty if you didn't have whiskers under skin. How you like me to take away. You got lots of trouble having to shave, no ? "

" Sure," said the young man, much amused. " Lots of trouble ! Take them away and see if I care."

" I do," said the woman solemnly. " You sit here and not think about anything except what I say. Just lean back and stop think about anything."

Stroking his cheeks repeatedly, she said over and over : " First come little place where whisker not grow, it get big and big. After while no more whisker at all." She kissed him and rubbed her rough chin against his right cheek.

He thought nothing about the matter the next day, considering it a huge joke ; but the next day after that he was amazed to discover a place the size of a dime on his cheek where there grew no beard.

When I saw him he was much worried. The spot had grown rapidly and the pink skin was covered with nothing, not even down.

" I'll be a girl sure, if this keeps up," he said angrily. " And heaven knows that I look enough like one as it is."

Taking my advice, he began hunting for the woman. After some time his search was rewarded and he begged her to give him back his manly beauty—by then marred by a hairless spot which had spread nearly to the chin.

Again she stroked his face, but this time she suggested the return and healthy growth of the beard.

Ten days later the cheek was back to normal.

Comment :

The kahuna in this case would have been very much surprised had she been told that she was using hypnosis in the standard way and with improvements in the form of physical stimulation. She would undoubtedly have said that she was using the medium *mana* in the way her forefathers had used it for centuries.

It is interesting to note that this healer could not " heal herself " of hair on the face.

In the data from the West I have run across none concerning the stopping of the growth of a beard by the use of hypnotic suggestion, but I see no reason why it could not be done if attempted. Of course, it may be that a still higher *mana* was used as well as hypnotic *mana* by the kahuna.

In the matter of the slight intoxication : The thing to be eternally remembered by aspiring magicians is the test of hurt. A moderate intoxication from time to time does little harm to the body, therefore it is not a " hurt " under Magic.

Dr. Brigham's fire-walker who had to be sobered up before the start to the lava flow was visited one night some years later by the Doctor. He found him roaring drunk and his wife said :

" He be all right to-morrow. He chase crazy out of a kanaka and get money for drink, but to-morrow he be all right."

The next day the kahuna called to offer his apology.

" No hurt," he said solemnly. " Kahuna can do. But suppose I kind what take drink and some spirit come inside me—that no good. Any fellow like that, no good ever drink even little."

There seem to be many degrees of looseness of the *uhane* in the body. In some people it leaves soon after drinking commences and obsession follows for the period of intoxication.

If a practice injures the body, it is a sin before Magic, and only then, if the kahunas are right—as it seems they must be.

CHAPTER VII

A S I have long delayed presenting certain proofs, I now ask the members of the Round Table to turn aside with me for a time while I speak of the several beliefs of India—ancient as well as modern—which will give us an idea what the original kahuna system must have included before the migration of the Polynesians.

The religious literature of India is vast, but leaders of the various Theosophical Societies have combed it and presented to the West the kernel of all beliefs. Our source just now is the *Encyclopædia Britannica* and its article on Theosophy. While this article may be thought by some to deal a little unkindly with Madam Helene Blavatsky, it may serve to give many professing Theosophists a clearer view of what is contained in the sometimes contradictory writings with which they are familiar.

I will follow our source article, condensing and amending. The parenthetical notes will be mine.

From many sources Theosophy has collected various beliefs and has given us the three main elements in them all.

ELEMENT ONE : *The Man.*

The human being and his mechanisms are described. He is composed of seven " principles " (bodies and vehicles), each made up of its own grade of matter, each with its own characteristics and abilities, each controlled by the laws of the plane on which it functions. These seven " principles " begin with the physical body, or " Rupa." They end with the " Buddhi " or sixth and the " Atma " or seventh " principles." In our source article no attempt has been made to compensate the many contradictory accounts of the bodies between the second and sixth. However, they can easily be seen to conform to the kahuna classification. The " Astral " comes next after the physical body, being com-

posed of the visible ectoplasm which we have met in spiritualistic phenomena.   Then comes a jumble of bodies and
vehicles—mental, emotional, karmic, volitional, etheric, etc.
The kahuna gives these as the *unihipili* who uses the astral
vehicle, the *uhane* who uses a still more tenuous vehicle, and
the *aumakua*[1] which touches the High Gods and is the
" Buddhi " blended or in contact with the " Atma " in the
Father-Son relation—it being one with its own vehicle, and
able to use the lower vehicles when conditions are made right
for such use.

These seven " principles " are to be subjected to a process
of *unification* in order that " enlightenment " may be had
and the final goal of life reached.

The process of unification is symbolized by the " Path "—
this becoming the second element in the system :

THE PATH :

By throwing aside most of the dogmas of Indian religions,
and retaining the practice of " Raja Yoga," the unification
of the " principles " is begun, according to Theosophical
practice.   On the Path new ideas of morals must be learned
and a positive rather than a negative " goodness " main-
tained.   (The mechanics of " unblocking " the " path " are
no longer clearly understood in India, and so we must
turn to the kahunas for the full explanation.)   From
Theosophy we gather the information that the One Reality
is something other than the physical and that the " chela "
must keep this fact in mind if he is to touch that Reality
at the end of the Path.   The great hindrance to holding this
true concept of the One Reality is " Avidya " or the normal
thought-attitude of the unenlightened or lower man toward
life.   The task is to see beyond " Avidya " and to the Real or
" Vidya."   (Realization is the Goal, but not so described for
us in easily recognizable terms by Theosophy.)

Progress along the Path is made by bringing about the
unification of the lower " principles."   In the source article :

" Centres of volition, consciousness and active memory
are systematically shifted upwards from the lower toward
the higher ' principles ' until they have become firmly

[1] I now drop the italics on unihipili, uhane and aumakua.

established in the ' Buddhi ' or sixth ' principle.' As this last stage is approached the ' chela ' becomes less and less dependent on the guidance of traditions and scriptures (dogmas).   The truth becomes revealed to him by the opening of his inner vision, and he learns to see Dharma, the Eternal Law as it were, face to face.''

As the unification progresses, the '' chela '' is said to gain new mental powers or '' siddhi.'' These bring monitions and premonitions, and the knowledge of the forces (*manas*) of the various planes. Theosophy teaches that these '' siddhi '' should never be sought for their own sake, but only in order that they may be used to help one along the Path to Perfection. No use of magic is permitted, and many and grave are the warnings against any attempt to use it. (Later we will investigate this phase of the matter most critically. The kahunas have no such commands laid on them, and, if we are to accept those commands blindly, our efforts to recover Magic will be abortive.)

KARMA :

We have here the third of the basic elements of the system. Karma is the natural law which governs the growth of the spiritual man through many incarnations.   Past deeds result in present conditions, be they good or bad. (Under the Law of Karma there is no vicarious atonement as there is in Christianity. In this element of the system we find a distortion of the original meaning of the philosophy. Religious dogma has done its worst. Magic is condemned because it might be used to heal a bodily disease of a poverty condition—both of which Karma demands be suffered to the bitter end in order that '' Karmic debts '' of the past may be paid in full. It is the Mosaic law of '' an eye for an eye, a tooth for a tooth.'' In the kahuna system, the events and conditions of a man's life are the result of the things the lower man sends to the higher man (aumakua)—the materials which are automatically '' realized '' into physical fact in the course of time. To the kahuna there is no higher reality to '' sins.'' He has an atonement—*kala*—which is very practical, but which is in no way vicarious.)

Coming under the heading of Karma there are the ten
" sanyojanas " or barriers which block the Path. These are
borrowed from Buddhism. They must be overcome by all
" chelas " sooner or later. They are : (1) The delusion
that the physical is the one reality and that the conscious
man is the real and only man. (2) Doubt as to the existence
of God or of the individual's ability to reach Him. (3) The
tendency to rely on ritual rather than to drive forward
directly toward Realization. (4) The sin of allowing any
thought of sex activity to come into mind or act. (5) The
tendency to become angered, or otherwise to hold in the
mind (or show in acts) any emotion less high than that of
love. (6) Worldly ambition for possessions and comforts
which are not absolutely necessary to life. (7) Worldly
ambition of any kind—even egoistic longing for the Goal
and the bliss to be found there. (8) Pride in anything
physical. (9) Pride in anything mental or spiritual, such as
pride in progress made along the Path—self-righteousness.
(10) The very human tendency to tire of thinking of the Path
continually and desire the usual relaxations and pleasures of
life. This is the mental attitude of " Vidya " and is a great
obstacle. It is not overcome until every thought and act is
made to progress the " chela " on the Path. (This idea is
anti-social in the extreme, and forces the " chela " to become
a burden on society and a burden to himself. It also hinders
his progress far more than it helps.)

.   .   .   .   .

In Christianity we come upon many ideas similar to those
just listed. To follow the commands laid down by the
dogmas which have developed in Christianity, a person would
have to conform to Puritanical standards and be as much
hampered as they would be by the " sanyojanas." Fortunately, the kahunas brought the ancient philosophies from
India before such dogmas made them of so little use.

I wish to pause here a moment to speak directly to the
Christians who sit at our Round Table. I am painfully
aware of the fact that in presenting the " hurt " test for
sin I have inevitably run counter to the complexed beliefs

you hold concerning sin. Many of you may already have condemned me for the present. Will you allow me my defence ?

I say that Jesus used a *positive* test of hurt whereas the kahunas use a *negative* test. Jesus gives us one command which is " the greatest of these " and it is LOVE. " Love thy neighbour as thy self." The kahunas say : " Do not hurt another or yourself," which is the same thing stated *negatively*.

Most of our dogmas of sin come from the teachings of the disciples of Jesus, not from Him. Paul, who never saw Jesus in the flesh, is responsible for the commands against normal sex life. Jesus was the friend of prostitute and publican. If He said to them, after healing their ills, " Go and sin no more," could He not have been so wise as to see that time did not allow " reconstructing their viewpoint " entirely ? He could only ask that they do this for themselves —" repent." (Remember the true meaning of the word repent, as I have pointed it out.) Like the kahuna who could not cure the foot of the Christian woman, He was also confronted with deeply complexed beliefs in the dogmas of sin found in the Old Testament. Busy as He was, He could only tell them to stop doing the things they thought were sins. When He said : " I am the Way and the Light and only through me . . .," did He not speak of the Christ and not the man Jesus ? Did He not point to the " safe return " (of salvation) to the Christ He taught was in each man ?—to the aumakua ?

You ask : " How about adultery ? " I answer that in it lies the greatest possibility of hurting another who loves the unfaithful one. Surely this clears my position to some extent.

.   .   .   .   .

We have seen the system as taught in modern India, and by Theosophy in the West. As the kahunas came to Polynesia, bringing so much of the lore of India with them— also lore from other lands which must have flanked them on the opposite side—we can conclude that they did not miss the religious teachings. In the unihipili, uhane and aumakua, and in the three *manas* we find a part of the ancient beliefs.

A VERY ODD PICTURE TAKEN DURING THE MISSION CENTENNIAL

The Hawaiian representing the kahuna has—surprisingly enough—put on an Indian turban and caused his attendant to wear her ornament in a way not prescribed in any book—as the serpent symbol of India, to represent the rising *mana* of the "serpent fires," or *kundalini-shakti*. I failed in an attempt to locate this gentleman, or to find out from whence he got his information of the true signification of the whalebone ornament on the girl's forehead. In the back is a typical grass house of other days.

The kahunas are always speaking of " unblocking the path "
of a patient, so that item checks. The " vehicles," however,
are not named in Polynesia, so far as I can learn. They
may have names in some parts, but the only reliable evidence
of them in the kahuna system is found in symbols. These
I have come across in many places. For a concrete example
let me mention two things which can be checked on either
at the British Museum or by examining illustrations of the
symbolic objects in Andersen's *Myths and Legends of the
Polynesians*. On page 460 is a fine illustration of a British
Museum piece taken from the Hervy Islands. It is a long
sceptre with a carved handle and a very ornamental upper
part. The upper part makes a set of three prongs which are
connected by three carved circles. On the three carved
circles which run up the centre prong are three carved heads.
Here we have the three entities very plainly indicated.
Running up each of the outside prongs are six smaller and
cruder heads which give us the six " body-vehicle " symbols.
The aumakua is represented by a complete figure standing
on the tip of each outside prong—one figure male, the other
female. These are the representations of the very ancient
tradition of the dual-sexed aumakua. The gross body is
represented by the supporting handle of the sceptre.

On page 334 there is a fine illustration of a dress worn by
" the chief mourner at Tahitian burial rites." The original
is also in the British Museum.

In this dress we find heaven and earth represented by
drapes and a stomach piece. Across the chest, however, and
reaching from shoulder to shoulder, is an up-curved, crescent-
shaped plate. In the centre of the plate is a large, flat,
circular object which appears to be a sea shell. It is flanked
on either side by two others—five in all—which extend from
shoulder tip to shoulder tip. Above the crescent—in front
of the throat of the wearer of the dress—are two shells cut
straight on the inner sides and set together to make the
double aumakua symbol. Here we have all our seven
" body-vehicles " most plainly represented—the supporting
crescent being the physical body, the two shoulder plates
being respectively the vehicle for the unihipili and the uhane,

the duality of the aumakua being combined in its double symbol to give the sixth and seventh units.

On the headpiece, however, is the representation of the classical idea of the vehicle of light which is used by the aumakua. It is a halo of feathers slightly resembling the American Indian war bonnet, but fan-shaped like the halo around the heads of the Christian and Buddhist saints. The quills of the feathers are thrust into the headband and the tips stand out in a complete halo. This type of head-dress identifies the highest grades of kahunas in many of the illustrations to be found in the accounts of the voyages of Captain Cook and of Vancouver.

The ancient belief was that after Realization one developed about the head a body of an electrical nature and of the shape of a globe. In this body the aumakua had a vehicle through which it could act as a composite part of the man. The " solar " vehicle so symbolized was thought to be born of a man after it had been fertilized by the love of a woman. It was supposed to grow as in the womb of the brain and gestate for eighteen months before being given birth as a full-grown vehicle.

The dual sex of the aumakua is a paradoxical matter of Realization. The perfect male and the perfect female qualities are united in "the marriage made in heaven," according to the philosophy—a very ancient one—which we touched on in our checking on the Greek Mysteries.

In the photograph of the plate in *Vancouver's Voyages*— the one I was at such pains to identify as of Hawaiian origin, in Case 13—there is shown a central phallic stone with a male figure on one side and a female figure on the other. Flanking these figures are halved palm trunks up which run the zigzag symbolic lines of the lower *manas* rising to reach the aumakua (represented by the two figures). These are a duplication of the " serpent fires " or *kundalini-shakti* of India.

. I will go no deeper into the evidence which shows that the kahunas had the knowledge of the " seven bodies." In Magic proper, the vehicles play but a minor part, while the three entities and the three *manas* are its very substance.

CHAPTER VIII

IN dictionaries of the Hawaiian language the kahuna ("secret") meaning of many terms has been lost. This is largely through missionary misunderstanding or refusal to understand. I will give the standard translations below :

APPARITION : " *He* (the) *lapu ; he uhane, he kinowailua.*" (*Lapu* is, in reality, the subhuman ghost ; *kinowailua* is the name for a pair of ghosts joined to make one individual—a uhane plus a unihipili.)

SOUL : *Uhane.*

SPIRIT : *Uhane.*

GHOST : *Uhane lapu.* (An excellent example of lack of understanding on the part of the white dictionary makers.)

UNIHIPILI : (Thrum's translation) " A class of attendant spirits—not ancestral."

AUMAKUA : (Thrum again—not given in English-Hawaiian dictionaries) " Ancestral deity," or " ancestral shades," or " god."

GOD : (dictionary) *Akua ;* Jehovah.

AKUA : (Thrum) " god ; spirit."

AUM: (Not translated by itself, but as a part of other words).

_ A : (root from *aum*) " of ; to ; at." (Thrum.)

AU : (another possible root of *aum*) " I " (dictionary). Also, " a current or flow as of time or water." (Thrum and other sources.)

M : (root) No separate translation, but when placed before *akua* makes *makua* or " parent " with no sex distinction. It also has the meaning of "creator." *Aumakua,* therefore, could be translated from the roots : " I-parent " or " I-creator," using the roots *au-makua.*

The Hawaiian vocabulary contains very few words and is made up by putting together many roots. Most roots have several possible translations according to their various uses. My friend, Theodore Kelsey, of Honolulu, who spends much time delving into this subject, finds that all the old chants and "prayers" can be translated in several ways to get different meanings—often to get a secret meaning.

The usual ending of all kahuna "prayers" used in the full Magic is, "*Amama ua noa. Lele wale akua la.*"

AMAMA : Will not translate, but with the first "*a*" changed to "*u*" it becomes :

UMAMA : The "breast or bosom." Without the "*a*" or "*u*" it becomes :

MAMA : "Light (airy) ; swift ; free." As roots are repeated to double the strength of their meaning, we have also *ma-ma*.

MA : Used as an adverb with another word it has the meaning of "before" or "prior to." Also we get the translation : "Accompanying ; together ; adhering closely ; entwining like a vine."

The word *akua* (god) can be separated into the roots *a-kua* or *a-ku-a*.

KUA : "Back" or "backing."

KU : "One of the triune gods of the Hawaiian trinity" ; "to stand erect" ; "right" with the sense of "rightness." To get a check on the translation "backing" I take the roots of *kokua*, "to help."

KO : means "realize" (dictionary).

KO-KUA : This translates literally from the two roots, "realize backing" as well as "help."

The word for "supply" or "source of supply" is *lako*. This gives us the roots *la-ko*.

LA : signifies "sacredness," as of a god. *Lako*, therefore, is "a realizing of the sacred thing."

Therefore,

AKUA : I-supporter ; I-behind-I ; I-Ku (the god) -I ; I-helper ; GOD.

AUMAKUA : I-breast (synonym for supply of nourishment); flow-or-current—parent-or-creator ; flow-or-current—light-airy–swift—prior-to-or-source—accompanying–adhering–en-twining-together-or-ONE ; I-god-upholder-helper.

.   .   .   .   .

The word *aum* may be a stranger to modern Hawaii, but as a part of the unchanged language of Magic brought from near India it can be traced back to India proper. There the word is found in its full meaning and use. It is the *Aum* or *Om* used in the Vedas as an invocation of the Higher Self. All Vedic prayers or sacred discourses begin and end with " Aum," or " Om "—the English form.

The word was used in rituals, being intoned for as long as breath lasted, as Au . . . m. This was repeated in what is called the two-and-a-half-times beat or repetition, " aum-aum-a."

This takes us directly back to the kahunas when they invoked the aumakua or " aum-god " with the same ritual two-and-a-half-times beat. As all the kahuna prayers were either overheard and stolen in early days, or as the word may have been shortened in writing it down (never in intoning it), it came to be the " *amama* " of the " prayers." It is plain that it should be written as intoned, " aum-aum-a. . . ." It is also plain to see where the roots came from that give us the " accompanying-swift—flow-source," etc. In the light of what we now know of the triple planes and entities, we may be permitted to guess that the sense of " flow-create—flow-create—flow. . . . " is present.

This sense is certainly found in translating the ending, " *Amama ua noa* " : " Aum-aum-a . . . rain of blessings release."

The last of the ending is equally significant : " *Lele wale akua la.*" Let us look into its roots and meanings. The translation is difficult because the word *lele* may be translated " fly or flight," or it may have a vocal-stress meaning as in accenting a word strongly. *Wale* has a very flexible general meaning of " happen or occur to make to come to pass." *Akua la* gives us the place or objective of the " stressed WORD sent in Flight "—to the god or gods—as the Source of the rain or blessings.

To compare them, let us take up other words which are compounded with *lele* :

FAITH : *paulele*, " the end or finish," plus *lele*—here perhaps referring to the spoken and strongly stressed invocation.

HOLINESS, SACREDNESS, PERFECTION : *hemolele. Hemo* is to loosen so that a regular flow can follow or a free action can come in movement. We may ask what it is that needs to be loosened or released from hindrances in order that a " free flow " may follow. Unquestionably the spoken invocation or " word of power " or the " prayer " sent flying to the gods. And why should this result in perfect holiness ? It does not so result. It is here the basic idea of having the " path " unblocked of complexes so that there can be a free flow of power and thought between high and low, and low and high. To Magic, such a cleared path between man's three entities is in itself the ONE AND ONLY SACRED, PERFECT AND HOLY CONDITION.

.   .   .   .   .

In examining the language used by the kahunas we must look for the three basic things which have been recovered in the West as the elements of practical magic. (1) The god-entity or aumakua—the Higher Self, the Christ Principle, Divine Mind, Wisdom. (2) The wiseness or knowledge or ability of this aumakua to " realize." (3) The aumakua's force or POWER. We have been identifying all three, in part, so far. Let us now look particularly for the " Wisdom " which P. P. Quimby relied upon. In *ko* we have " realize." In *ko-kua,* " realize backing." In *la-ko,* " supply " through realizing, or the ability of the aumakua to realize or create.

Now the word for worldly wisdom is :

IKI : " know or knowledge ; to see." This also is a word used as an adverb to express the idea of " incompleteness." Contrasting this word with *ko* we have the difference between the " knowing " of the uhane and of the aumakua. *Iki* is incomplete because it is a surface sensing instead of a " becoming part of " or " blending with." *Iki* uses what it finds in the physical, but *ko* creates what it wishes to have found in the physical.

Another word used for " worldly knowing " is *hoo-ma-opoia :* literally " to cause a lightening of darkness " (lack of understanding). In the *la* in *la-ko* we have the meaning of sacredness, and also that of destination and day (or time of light). We also find *la* in the word for " halo " or " oval " ;

hua-la-la : " collected or gathered " (*hua* has the collective meaning as gathering life.   It translates tree roots or seed, as well as collect or gather) plus " sacred-light." We find it in the word for preservation : *ma-la-ma*, " light-sacred-light."

The word for " ability " is either *hoo-ko*, to " cause realize," or *he-mana*, " the power."

Now, oddly enough (as it might seem to the uninitiated), the word used for an organ of the body, or to signify the thing which is being " eaten inside," is *lala*. This suggests at once the connection with the process of draining off the complex of guilt in the unihipili. The word for this draining off is *ka-la*, " the " plus " *la* " or " the sacred " process—in this case : the process of " making open," " loosening hindrances," " forgiving," or " cleansing."   The word *ka-la* indicates the magical nature of the draining off process. The " path " being opened by this process is called *a-la-nui* : " path " or " of-sacredness-entire."   The " oil-of-anoint- ment " idea still clings to the word for " oil " : *ai-la*. *Ai* is " food " or " nourishment ";   doubled, it makes *aiai* : " brightness "—giving a possible double meaning of " food and brightness acquired through sanctity or opening to the flow of high *mana*."

The idea of the " perfect entity " is found in the roots of *kina ole* : " flawless "—literally " without the gross or physical."   In this case we see that it is not the physical body, but a " gross " ghostly body—the unihipili—which is to be made " flawless."   Remember the word for the uhane- unihipili combined ghost, *kinowailua* : it translates " being- water-two " or " being composed of two life waters."   The aumakua is considered perfect as compared with the uhane and unihipili who are *iki* or " incomplete " in knowledge.

For the word for heaven we have *la-ni* which offers a significant comparison with the word for " to stand in a line " : *la-la-ni*. From this we can guess that the *la-la*— " internal organs " or unihipili—must be aligned with the uhane and aumakua like an ordered " rank " of soldiers, if heaven is to be contacted via the " opened path."

O-LA : is " life," and it translates from the roots " of- sacredness."   Sacredness is a poor substitute for the real kahuna meaning. A better translation would be " of the unblocked flow of *mana*."

Let us next turn to the words enbodying the idea of " Power " :

MANA : force or energy.

MANA-MANA : stronger energy or force.

MANA LOA : strongest force or energy ; Supreme Power.

IKA-IKA is " force or energy." I suspect that the original root of this word for " physical force " was *iki* instead of *ika*. *Iki-iki* would translate " mind-knowledge," and this would fit in exactly at this point.

MANAO is logic or reason. It is also " thought." The roots translate " power or force " (from *mana*) and " derived from " (from *o*). This suggests that the simple *mana* can be generated from the thought activities of the uhane and also that thought is of a logical rather than a realizing grade.

PATIENCE is *hoo-mana-wa-nui* : " make-power-over a period of time."

A PATIENT is called *la-paa-uia* : " sacred-flawlessness-lacking." He is forgiven, or *ka-la* (ed), by the use of *mana* and physical stimulation.

HOOMANAMANA : " any kahuna invocation." Literally, " to generate great power."

HOOMANA : to adore or worship. Literally, " cause power."

KAHUNA : keeper of the Secret.

HUNA : secret.

KOKO : blood or " realization-creation."

KONO : to command. Literally, " realize " plus " immediate," or " on account of realizing."

MANAOIO : faith or belief—" power-thought " plus " acute."

MANAWA : time. Literally, " power-flow."

HOOKO : " redemption." Literally, " to cause realization."

. . . . .

· Inevitably I have made mistakes in translating from roots after this fashion, but if the average of meanings is taken, there can be no question as to what lies behind the meanings of the terms used by the kahunas.

CHAPTER IX

GOING on to our final cases we now come to the full Magic in which monition and premonition is used at will, and in which the aumakua is contacted at will as a necessary preliminary.

In our earlier cases we found monition and premonition, but never as an ability to command. The contact was uncertain at best, and the mechanism was aumakua-to-unihipili-to-uhane—a roundabout way of transmission. In the full Magic the unihipili is cut out of the circuit and the uhane gets its information direct by momentarily blending itself with the aumakua in Realization.

This blending is only possible, however, when the path has been cleared of blocking by the removal of all guilt complexes. So strong is the unihipili that it can, when complexed unfavourably, force its guilt emotion on the uhane and prevent it from having the complete and unwavering faith that is an adjunct to Realization.

The proof taken from a study of language roots is excellent at any time, but would not stand were it not for the fact that the kahunas demonstrate premonition.

CASE 50

KAHUNAS DEMONSTRATE PREMONITORY POWER

Preliminary Notes :

Many of the lesser kahunas have premonitions now and again just as do mediums in the West or as do crystal gazers. Those of the highest grades can see into the future almost at will.

As we come now for the first time to something which

Science has never tried to explain, but has always been forced to deny, it is imperative that all possible proof be given to show that man can, under proper conditions, actually see events not yet transpired.

Johanna Wilcox writes in one of our source articles :

" All kahunas possessed *mana*—supernatural power ; all kahunas could interpret dreams ; and all kahunas were able to foretell future events.

" There was a branch of kahunas known as the *kilo-kilo* —seers, or diviners—which numbered several varieties including the fortune tellers and mediums.

" The kahuna *kaula*, or prophet, represented the highest type and possessed more power than any other class of kahunas.   He was the moral kahuna always representing purity.   He foretold future events as they were revealed to him."

Case and Wise write :

" *Kahuna-kilokilo :* A priest who foretold the future. He might be said to be the forerunner of the fortune-teller of to-day, although he did not pose as a medium nor did he presume to go into a trance in order to ascertain the nature of events yet to occur." (No mention is made of the *kaula* or " backing-sacred.")

The Case :

Here I will mention several incidents that more proof may accumulate :

1. A kahuna prescribed the exact method of procedure to a merchant who wished to sell his business and had failed in three attempts to sell to the only possible buyer.   The day and hour was set and the prediction made that the sale would be immediate—since the " path had been cleared " and the processes of Magic set in motion.   The prediction was correct to the letter.   This data is correct as I was present to check all angles.

2. A young Hawaiian had lost his job and had applied for it over and over without success.   He went to a kahuna, he was *kala*-ed and the proper invocations made.   He was instructed to go the next morning and apply again for

his old job. He did so and was taken on again without comment.

3. A kahuna was asked to look into the future and see how long it would be before a desired event transpired. I was able to see her prediction fulfilled to the letter some five years later. It took the kahuna some ten minutes to get the desired information.

4. There is a famous case in Hawaiian history which seems entirely authenticated. Kapihe was a noted *kaula* living in Kona, Hawaii, in the days before Kamehameha had risen to be more than a general under Kalaniopu. The kahuna studied Kamehameha one day and gave the following prophecy or *wanana* : " That which is above shall be brought down ; that which is below shall be lifted up ; the islands shall be united ; the walls shall stand upright." His prediction was fulfilled when Kamehameha did something never done before : conquered and united all the eight islands. At the time the *wanana* was given, he could have had no such ambition.

Before the birth of this famous warrior and statesman, three kahunas were consulted by the expectant mother. Without knowing what his fellow kahunas had foreseen, each magician gave a *wanana*. They all agreed that the child would be a boy ; that he would cause great strife and bloodshed ; and that he would become supreme in the Islands. Hearing these prophecies, the father attempted to kill his son at birth, but he was saved.

5. At the time that the old taboos had been broken and the temples destroyed, the chief kahuna of Kamehameha's old kahuna guard, Hewahewa, was troubled by the breaking down of the system of moral policing. He looked into the future and foresaw the arrival of the missionaries. Delighted at the prospect of a civilized religion containing the same necessary ingredients as his own, he sent his servant to proclaim to the chiefs and royalty : " The god will soon land yonder ! " The servant—who was the kahuna's spokesman—pointed to the exact spot on the long beach where the missionaries landed a few days later.

Comment :

The story of Hewahewa throws so much light on the change which came at that time in Hawaii that I must give it. He seemed to have been aware that in God and Jesus and the Christ the kahuna system was duplicated as to its main elements. Undoubtedly he looked to the time when morals and Magic would be restored under the new regime. After the landing of the missionaries Hewahewa was so delighted by what he heard them tell of the new religion that he wrote a beautiful prayer of welcome to the gods who had returned under new names, but who were the *Akua*, the Aumakua, and the Man. From the form of his invocation it is evident that he expected his new prayer to work the usual Magic. I will give the prayer here, partly as I have endeavoured to translate it to get out the old meanings, and partly as it was translated by the missionaries :

HEWAHEWA'S INVOCATION

Arise ! Arise through sacredness, stand sacred.
Fill (yourself), arise to the sacred heaven, stand connected (entities connected and path so opened).
Now the sacred blackness, the sacred night. (Blankness of passing into Realization.)
Cleanse the vitality of the insides (of your body), cleanse of the much that you may stand holy.
The god-self, the god-power. (Touched in Realization.)

This ends the usual kahuna beginning. Next comes the part of the invocation which describes and welcomes the new gods.

Jehovah is the God-place unsullied and uncharted, reaching from heaven to heaven, eternal.
He is a God dwelling in the vast far places.
" At the further end of the wind,
Like a floating cloud over the earth,
A rainbow standing on the ocean.
A cloud resting in the air."
Jesus is our cleanser of house (or body-dwelling).
By the same path as from our ancient home he comes to Hawaii.
" He is from zenith to horizon."
A cleansing rain from the heaven.
Jehovah, That, we welcome.
Chant praises through the heaven to God.

Rejoice through the earth.
"We have received the words "
Of the Sight, the Power, of the Life.
Gather in the presence of Poki (Governor of Hawaii).
Gather in the presence of the Wisdom-Power eternal.
Invoke God perfectly.
He is the Kahuna Power of the Islands.
Like a torch he will bring light to the darkness of our guilts.
That life shall be made fuller.
That Life is Jesus.
Aum-aum-a. . . . (Our " amen," perhaps from the same source in
    Magic.)

It was only after hearing the missionaries preach for some
time that Hewahewa became aware of two facts : (1) That
they had retained the form of Magic in their religion, but had
lost Magic itself—so retaining an empty shell which was all
but useless for practical purposes. (2) That nothing was
known of the test of " hurt " for sin, and that, therefore, the
old taboos from which the Hawaiians had just escaped were
as nothing compared with the new ones which threatened
what he considered all the normal pleasures of life.

Although there is no record to justify such a conjecture, I
fancy that Hewahewa hoped to teach the missionaries the
things he knew but which they did not. We know that he
helped build a church and attended meetings for a time, but
he never became a Christian. History abruptly becomes
silent as to his later life, and it can be guessed that he returned
to his kahuna practice in secret and joined his fellows in
their slow work of using Magic to restore order among the
common people.

An unidentified kahuna, some twenty years later, attacked
a missionary with Magic and prayed to death several of his
converts. I have seen the diary of this missionary and
found it most enlightening, even in the many pages left blank
while he was praying vainly to God and the kahuna was
killing his converts one by one with Magic.

Most converts seem to have been made because of three
things : (1) Fear of hell. (2) The musical and social attraction of the Church. (3) The great desire to learn to read and
write—a thing made possible by the teachings of the
missionaries and by the printing of the New Testament.

The fascinating sequel to this story was told me by the relative having in her possession the missionary's diary. She said that during the days and weeks represented by the blank pages, the missionary (she was a child at the time in his home) lost his faith in the willingness of God to come to his rescue and turned to a rival kahuna for help. He learned the mechanics of a certain death prayer and succeeded in killing the attacking kahuna. Thereafter the natives flocked to his church and the diary is again filled—this time with rejoicing.

At the present day both kahuna and the layman of Hawaii may be found regularly at church, ardent Christians to all intents and purposes. The fact is that they have their religion at church and their Magic on the side—a very excellent arrangement, so far as I have been able to observe.

.   .   .   .   .

As to monition and premonition, there remains little comment to be made. Most of the data is before us. Perhaps, however, it is as well that we should recall at this time that the word from which we derive our " prophesy " is the Greek *propheteia* which translates " speaking for the gods." This is exactly what is done in kahuna practice— or shall we say " speaking with the aumakua ? "

CHAPTER X

W E come now to Magic in its full and ultimate form.
At this time our only proof which can come out of the West for comparison is that which was borrowed from the East—the magical practices of Jesus who became one with the Christ within or above Himself and who attained to Realization at will.

I suggest that the book of John be read in the New Testament. Although it has been added to and changed by translators and by the many hands which had copied original versions, we can still see in the recital a great teacher trying to tell in parable the paradox of Realization and of a Oneness that is Separation.

In the miracles performed by Jesus we can occasionally see him use a physical stimulation as a part of Magic. We can see him identify himself with his Higher Self—Christ—the Aumakua—and so be able to use the Words of Power in healing commands. We see little in His teaching to indicate that His idea of sin was very different than that of the kahunas, although much dogma can be seen in the building in the preaching of the disciples after the death of Jesus— a death that may have been a symbol of Realization as the crucifixion took place at Golgotha—the "Place of the Skull," or probably the blankness of mind which comes when the centre of consciousness is raised to the "Door of Brahma," the top of the brain.

I cite Pryse's book, *The Restored New Testament*, for those who may care to follow out this line of thought.

The use of the Word of Power is rare even in Polynesia, but I can give one case reported by an eye-witness and which seems authentic. Later we will probe fire-magic for further evidence.

CASE 51

A KAHUNA USES THE WORDS OF POWER

Preliminary Notes :

I have this case from a close friend. He is a white man and a close observer who has an intimate knowledge of things Hawaiian. He was present at the time of the happening of which I am about to tell.

The Case :

An old Hawaiian woman, known to be a most powerful kahuna and generally considered more or less a saint, lived in a house built on a sand beach.

One afternoon a car drove up and visitors began to get down. The car stood high on the solid ground beside a hollow filled with soft sand. One of the visitors, a kindly Hawaiian man, missed his footing and fell, breaking a bone in his leg just above the ankle. He was slightly intoxicated at the time—a thing not too unusual on a holiday.

The kahuna was standing by to receive her guests. The man fell and the sound of the breaking bone was plainly heard. Immediately she knelt beside him and took his leg in her strong old hands. The skin was pushed out over the ragged end of the protruding bone and the swelling had commenced.

Forcing the bone back into place, she commanded the man to remain quiet. She closed her eyes for a moment, then opened them and spoke the words of power, " Be healed," in Hawaiian.

The healing was instant. The man rose to his feet and walked with the other guests to the house. No one was more amazed and intrigued than was my friend. He had seen and heard everything and had been convinced that the bone had broken.

Comment :

I have heard of several instances in which the kahunas have used the words of power, but have none quite so well authenticated as the one above, so will allow it to stand as our example.

All that we can be very sure of is that changes can be made instantly and miraculously in physical material under certain conditions. The many miraculous healings at holy shrines are perhaps the best proof we can find that this is a fact.

In fire-magic we have no way of knowing whether or not the words of power are used, but we do know—because of our data—that the change in physical materials such as heat or flesh or flame, is made in no long time after the magician sets to work to accomplish the change.

There are two distinct phases to Magic, which must be considered. In the first, the change is made by a command given by one who seems to be blended for the moment with the aumakua and so is able to use the high *mana* as if it were his own. In the second, the process seems to be one in which there is little or no blending or contact ; but in which the aumakua is made to act in response to a " prayer."

This last method seems to be the one used in Polynesian fire-walking as well as in fire-eating.

During such performances no single set of words of command is used at the moment of the performance. The Polynesians do their chanting ahead of time, and the fire-magician of our early case—the white fire-eater of the carnival—seemed to use neither chant nor audible words of power.

Naturally enough, I questioned the fire-eater about his use of Magic. I also questioned his wife who walked on sharp swords with her bare feet and climbed a ladder of them.

The fire-magician was perfectly willing to try to explain the nature of his Magic : but like all individuals who attempt to describe a part of what is discovered in Realization, he was handicapped by the lack of words to describe the superphysical.

He had been born in India of English parents and left an orphan at an early age. He had fallen into the hands of a Hindu fire-magician who befriended him and taught him his art.

The training was long. For hours the lad was made to sit before the flame of a butter lamp and endeavour to see and feel the " god " behind and in it. One day he became aware of the " god." It had " swallowed " him as his teacher had predicted that it would, and he had become fire itself. With more training he became able to " become fire " at will and so was able to handle fire or fire-heated objects as a part of himself without being burned.

I was especially anxious to learn whether or not this magician had been deep enough in Realization to see past the ascetic dogmas of modern India. I questioned him on that point.

" At first I couldn't do anything but pray and watch my flame," he explained. " Everything was a sin from which I must be purified by passing through fire under the protection of my master. But after I came to know fire and that I was a part of it, I found out that I was a part of everything. That knowledge set me free. There are only two things which I cannot do and continue my work. First I cannot injure anyone in any way, and second, I must never give up my practice for more than a few days at a time."

I asked why he could not injure anyone.

" Because to injure anyone in any way or cause them sorrow makes it impossible for me to become a part of fire. I do not know just why, but it seems that to injure someone automatically makes me afraid. I become afraid of fire and so I cannot become fire or touch it without being burned. Twice I had to go back to my master and get him to put me through the fire to purify me so that I could get away from the vague fear that I could not overcome otherwise."

I asked how he went about his daily work—whether he invoked fire or not.

" There are invocations, but one gets past them in time. I have worked so long that just to come near anything hot changes me to a part of fire. While I talk to my audience I have another part of me that is fire, but which never shows itself. It is in the air around the top of my head. If I get out of practice—like I have done a few times between engagements—I have to use the old invocations for a little while until I get so I can become fire again whenever I wish to."

The little wife of the magician was eager to tell me of her training in Japan under *her* " master." She showed me his picture, and I have never seen a more serene face or one which gave such an impression of wisdom and power.

She had been taught Realization by a peculiar method which she failed to describe very well, but the results of which was an ability to identify herself with " the god in me." She became that " god " as she worked, knowing with serene faith that it would keep her from being cut by the swords.

" At first I was often cut," she related, " but my master called silently to the god in me and it healed me before a drop of blood came. Soon I learned to do my own calling. When I walk on my sharp swords I am not myself : I am my god."

She lived by the same rules of non-injury as did her husband, and for the same reason. In the days of her training, her " sins " had been " forgiven " by her master. He had spoken the formula of forgiveness while she had rolled on splintered glass. When she came to him bleeding, he healed her with a single word.

.   .   .   .   .

In the information given by the fire-eater and his wife can be seen the important matter of draining off complexes of guilt. Their masters used fire and splintered glass as the physical stimulant accompanying the words of forgiveness. The other elements of Magic are enlightening. The " fear " was caused by a complex of guilt in the unihipili—this, without a question.

.   .   .   .   .

For those who have not read Mary Austin's *Earth Horizons*, I mention it as another source book. In it will be found the story of the life of this great woman who attained her first Realization at the age of " half-past. four." She tells how she came to know the " I-Mary " who was her real self and who was always able to guide and assist her. Late in young womanhood she found that she was not alone in her great discovery. She found that the medicine-men of the Paiute Indians knew " I-Mary " and called it *wakanda*. But read her book, if you have not done so. It is the story of one who could have become a great kahuna.

.   .   .   .   .

I now come to something for which I can give no proof other than logical deduction based on the data which we have at hand—after so long a time. I will state my conclusions dogmatically, although I feel that our data will substantiate them.

Ordinarily the *mana* of the aumakua flows downward to the uhane and unihipili providing the path is not blocked by a guilt complex. A reversal of this power, however, can be made—a reversal in which the flow is from below upward.

We have seen that when armed with a complexed belief, the unihipili can inflict its beliefs on the uhane and overpower its reasoning ability. Ordinarily, thoughts and the *mana* of the uhane flow down to the unihipili, but the utter belief of the unihipili in the correctness of its complexed ideas enables it to change the flow and reverse the process of thought exchange—old memories being forced up with great emotional power which arouse deadly opposition to any contrary logic.

In the testimony of several magicians I have run across the statement that when the invocations or prayers are " prayed right," the results obtained are as certain as a chemical reaction.

The one way to account for this is by the application of the *reversal of mana by a complex in the unihipili as a principle*, to the next or higher stage of the reversed flow—from uhane to aumakua. In other words, if the unihipili can reverse the flow and force its will on the uhane, the pair of them together can send the flow still farther—to the aumakua. And, as the aumakua's ability is of such a nature that it creates on the mental and physical planes what it realizes, it can be caused to realize into form the things demanded when the flow is reversed.

Mr. J. S. Emerson, the white authority on kahunas who had learned to perform the weather magic, writes : " This god had no option in the matter. He simply HAD to obey the command of his master, the kahuna."

As the uhane is forced to respond to the force of the complexed unihipili, the aumakua is forced to respond to the invocation of the uhane—always providing that the unihipili has been furnished with the proper Magic complex and is, therefore, a helper instead of a hinderer—a manu-facturer of serene and potent faith.

Hewahewa says in his model invocation, " *Pule pono ia Iehova*," " Pray correctly to Jehovah." The usual transla-tion is " Pray reverently," or " with reverence " ; but if this meaning had been intended instead of that of " correct-ness " or " perfectness," *He manao hoomaikai* (the making of power good) would have been used in proper grammatical and poetical form. *Pono* is " right or correct " and not " reverence."

Mary Austin asked the medicine-men if their prayers were always answered. They replied : " They are if they are prayed right."

In kahuna practice the art of " praying right " depends on the clearing the path of old and hindering guilt complexes and the formation of a complex of full confidence and belief —this last being made possible only when all guilts are removed.

" Praying right " is, therefore, the fire-walker's method rather than that of the kahuna who can identify himself with the aumakua and so use the words of power.

.   .   .   .   .

The control of future events is explained by a theory which matches the rest of the philosophy of Magic and which seems necessary to complete it. Roughly, the theory is this :

When the path is blocked, as it is with most mortals, the premonitory information comes to the uhane now and then through the subconscious. In an analogous way the totality of the thoughts, desires, fears and emotions of the uhane and the complexed unihipili gradually filter up through the subconscious to the aumakua and are automatically "realized" into forming events.

As events are so formed from materials sent up to the aumakua, they can be foreseen—also they can be changed by the use of "right prayer" or the use of words of power. Here we have the paradox of predestination which is actually free will. Another paradox is found in the fact that the aumakua plans the general trend of the life of the human trinity on the physical and mental planes. It is the guide and the rescuer—providing the path is not too badly blocked by guilts or guilt complexes.

The ideal life is lived when the path is clear at all times and the superior wisdom of the aumakua guides directly to the ends of happiness, health, prosperity and evolutionary progress.

The reversal of the *mana* flow is symbolized by the "serpent fires" or *kundalini* in India. They are supposed to reverse themselves and flow upward when final purification is complete. Dire warnings are given not to try to reverse the flow before purification is complete. The power is said to be reversible, even by a wicked individual, but the result is said to be either death or insanity. The living of a retentive and entirely continent life is demanded as a preliminary to reversing the forces. This is proven nothing but a false dogma by the very fact that the kahunas—even those who cannot use the full Magic of the words of power—reverse the flow of *mana* each time they use their invocational magic.

The kahuna ideal of life is the normal one in which man enjoys himself as a normal man should and in which all "hurt" is avoided as a blocking of the path and not as a sin against anyone but man.

.   .   .   .   .

Other than the potent method of *kala*-ing with the aid of a physical stimulation to accompany the forgiving suggestion, there is the method of autosuggestion which may be used effectively. I recommend the " decubitus " method outlined by its inventor, Dr. Pierce, in his book, *Mobilizing the Mid-Brain.*

In this method one lies down and slightly lifts arms and legs one after the other in the following way : limb held away from bed until tired, conscious mental centre moved into it, it is dropped and relaxed. The eyes are fixed on a spot on the wall out of line of direct vision—this to tire the muscles—and when tired, are closed. The body should now be in a relaxed condition. The suggestion of the *kala* should next be given. Practice will develop the needed hypnotic power in a short time and the uhane will be able to open the path by acting directly on the complexes of guilt. Of course, this practice must not be begun until all old hurts to others have been compensated UNLESS the effects of such hurts have died away and so become inactive. Nothing can be suggested successfully to the unihipili which is not believed by the uhane.

· · · · ·

My report to my friends of the Round Table now is finished. I wish to apologize for those times when I have inevitably fallen into the common pit—have made a guess, turned it into a dogma, and promulgated it with missionary zeal. However, I beg to be allowed my pet dogma—or truth if you will—which is :

No MAGIC, NO LIVING AND USEFUL RELIGION : NO MAGIC, NO COMPLETE AND JUSTIFIABLE SCIENCE.

It is my hope that in having shared my findings and conclusions with you, you will in turn share yours with me that I may be corrected and further instructed.

Until such a time as I come again to report to the Round Table.—*Aloha.*

THE END

NOTICE TO ALL KAHUNAS:

Aloha. I apologize for any mistakes I may have made in telling of you or of your long-preserved wisdom. If I have hurt any of you, I ask that I be allowed to make amends rather than that punishment be sent. I have violated no confidence. I have written under permission. I have only love and gratitude for you in my heart. *Aloha nui oe.*

M.F.L.

CPSIA information can be obtained at www.ICGtesting.com
Printed in the USA
BVOW081049121212

308018BV00020B/867/P